Fictions of Integration

This book examines how children's and young adult literature addresses and interrogates the legacies of American school desegregation. Such literature narrates not only the famous battles to implement desegregation in the South, in places like Little Rock, Arkansas, but also more insidious and less visible legacies, such as re-segregation within schools through the mechanism of disability diagnosis. Novelizations of children's experiences with school desegregation comment upon the politics of getting African-American children access to white schools; but more than this, as school stories, they also comment upon how structural racism operates in the classroom and mutates, over the course of decades, through the pedagogical practices depicted in literature for young readers. Lesley combines approaches from critical race theory, disability studies, and educational philosophy in order to investigate how the educational market simultaneously constrains how racism in schools can be presented to young readers and also provides channels for radical critiques of pedagogy and visions of alternative systems. The volume examines a range of titles, from novels that directly engage the *Brown v. Board of Education* decision, such as Sharon Draper's *Fire From the Rock* and Dorothy Sterling's *Mary Jane*, to novels that engage less obvious legacies of desegregation, such as Cynthia Voigt's *Dicey's Song*, Sharon Flake's *Pinned*, Virginia Hamilton's *The Planet of Junior Brown*, and Louis Sachar's *Holes*. This book will be of interest to scholars of American studies, children's literature, and educational philosophy and history.

Naomi Lesley is an Assistant Professor of English at Holyoke Community College, USA.

Children's Literature and Culture
Jack Zipes, *Founding Series Editor*
Philip Nel, *Current Series Editor*

For a full list of titles in this series, please visit www.routledge.com.

Tolerance Discourse and Young Adult Holocaust Literature
Engaging Difference and Identity
Rachel Dean-Ruzicka

Child Autonomy and Child Governance in Children's Literature
Where Children Rule
Edited by Christopher Kelen and Björn Sundmark

Contemporary British Children's Literature and Cosmopolitanism
Fiona McCulloch

Prizing Children's Literature
The Cultural Politics of Children's Book Awards
Edited by Kenneth B. Kidd and Joseph T. Thomas, Jr.

Canon Constitution and Canon Change in Children's Literature
Edited by Bettina Kümmerling-Meibauer and Anja Müller

Fictions of Integration
American Children's Literature and the Legacies of *Brown v. Board of Education*
Naomi Lesley

New Directions in Children's Gothic
Debatable Lands
Edited by Anna Jackson

More Words About Pictures
Current Research on Picture Books and Visual/Verbal Texts for Young People
Edited by Perry Nodelman, Naomi Hamer, and Mavis Reimer

Childhood and Pethood in Literature and Culture
New Perspectives on Childhood Studies and Animal Studies
Edited by Anna Feuerstein and Carmen Nolte-Odhiambo

Fictions of Integration

American Children's Literature and the Legacies of *Brown v. Board of Education*

Naomi Lesley

LONDON AND NEW YORK

First published 2017 by Routledge

2 Park Square, Milton Park, Abingdon, Oxfordshire OX14 4RN
52 Vanderbilt Avenue, New York, NY 10017

Routledge is an imprint of the Taylor & Francis Group, an informa business

First issued in paperback 2019

Library of Congress Cataloging-in-Publication Data
CIP data has been applied for.

ISBN: 978-1-138-20314-3 (hbk)
ISBN: 978-0-367-34630-0 (pbk)

Typeset in Sabon
by codeManta

Contents

Acknowledgments

I could not have completed this book without the help of many people who offered support and encouragement of various kinds. A few deserve special mention.

I owe a great debt to the anonymous reviewers for Routledge, who made careful, specific, and thoughtful suggestions for improving the manuscript. I am especially grateful to Erin Little for her patience in answering my numerous questions and for guiding me through the publication process, and to Elizabeth Levine for her initial aid in setting up the project at Routledge. Philip Nel, the editor of this series, gave clear and helpful suggestions for improvement, and his comments helped me to make difficult decisions about the manuscript.

This project developed out of a dissertation, and my committee at George Washington University, as well as other professors there, helped shape this project from the beginning. Gayle Wald and Ann Romines asked incisive questions, and pointed out threads of argument that I had not consciously known I was making. Robert McRuer shared his knowledge of research on learning disability. David Mitchell and Elizabeth Anker made suggestions about methodology and offered encouragement. James Miller guided my research in productive directions, pulling me into his office as I passed by and handing me books he "just happened" to find on his shelf that he thought might interest me. Jim, I miss your sharp critique and gentle encouragement, as do all of us who were lucky enough to work with you.

Colleagues and scholars generously read segments of the manuscript and offered suggestions for revision, sometimes through multiple versions. Elizabeth White Pittman, Peyton Joyce, Karen Chandler, Fred Cooksey, and my long-suffering spouse, Daniel Lesley, you have pushed me to polish ideas and clarify organization, and have suffered through some fairly terrible paragraphs. Thank you.

Mentors, both official and unofficial, have offered words of encouragement and practical advice for constructing book proposals, negotiating for permissions, and making decisions about publication. Gayle Wald, Ann Romines, Tony Lopez, and Jerry Griswold, I deeply appreciate your emails and phone consultations. June Cummins, Kate Capshaw

Smith, and Michelle Ann Abate, thank you for giving me helpful advice when I cornered you at conferences.

Thank you to authors Cynthia Voigt, Sharon Draper, and Mildred Pitts Walter, for being so willing to respond to queries about your work. I am grateful, in particular, for Mildred Pitts Walter's generous words of support and thoughtful conversation about the contemporary state of education.

Daniel, thank you for continuing to tell me that I needed to complete this project, if only for myself, and for giving me the space to work. Joseph, thank you for existing.

Introduction

Unspeakable Conversations and Desegregated Classrooms

On (Not) Talking About Race in the Classroom

I can remember standing in front of a classroom full of ninth-grade students and consciously choosing not to ask a fraught question about race. I was a young, white, middle-class, female teacher (the demographic most often found in the front of the classroom[1]), and all of the students in the ninth grade English class at the Washington, D.C. charter school where I taught were African-American and Latino. We were having a heated discussion about everyday racism; as I recall, we were in the middle of reading Frederick Douglass's *Narrative* and we were discussing the legacies of slavery and the persistence of institutionalized racism. Students recounted their ire and shame at being followed in stores, or at seeing people in downtown D.C. eye them and cross to the other side of the street, or at riding crowded buses to their neighborhoods while more affluent white neighborhoods had Metro service. As I frantically took down the names of students waiting to speak, I wondered whether anyone would mention the fact that nearly all of their teachers were white, while only three white students attended the school. None did. I didn't bring it up, either.

At the same time, a school-wide reading test (administered because the school was under threat of being sanctioned for under-performance under the 2001 No Child Left Behind Act) had just revealed that most of our students in grades nine through twelve were testing at reading levels of third to sixth grade. While the students knew their test scores, none mentioned them in our discussion. No one expressed anger at the quality of education he or she had received. I wondered if I ought to mention these instances of institutionalized racism that permeated our classroom. Shy of introducing awkwardness into a seemingly open and rolling discussion, I kept my reflections to myself.

Later that day, grading papers after school, I brought up my dilemma with an American history teacher who shared the classroom with me. She taught the same ninth-grade students, and she, like me, was a white middle-class woman who had previously taught in predominantly white schools. She laughed.

"How exactly would you start that up? Do you just say, 'Hey, you guys, have you ever noticed that all of your teachers are white and none of you are?' Do you tell them their scores say they can't read? You should totally try that out tomorrow. Let me know how it goes." Needless to say, I did not "try that out" the next day. The subject was dropped.

The following year, my family was transferred to Arizona, and I left the charter school. One winter break, I returned for a visit. A former student of mine was passing the front desk just as I walked in and greeted me with a hug.

"You should come back, Ms. Lesley," he said. "We miss you. Everything is still the same here. Adrian is still driving all the teachers crazy. Angela is still calling all the teachers racist. When are you coming back?"[2]

"That's funny," I said, "I don't recall Angela telling any of us we were racist when I was here."

"No, not to your faces, she didn't," he replied with a grin.

Desegregation Stories for the Classroom

In the years since, memories of these exchanges, and others like them, have come to summarize for me some of the contradictions that characterize how issues of race are handled in the classroom with students, many of whom identify as racial minorities. On the one hand, racial conflict is an open and approved topic, increasingly prescribed as a subject in multicultural curricula and state standards;[3] my classroom-mate taught the histories of slavery and the colonization of the American Southwest, and students in my class read works by Douglass, James McBride, Sandra Cisneros, and Jamaica Kincaid, among others. Discussions of this literature inevitably raised the issue of racism. On the other hand, racial conflict in the classroom as it directly affects the students and teachers—for example, in continuing racial segregation, in teacher hiring, and in school funding—is a buried subject, relegated to silent undercurrents of anxiety. This remained true even at the charter school where I taught, which explicitly encourages teachers and students to connect curricular learning to everyday public policy concerns. My room-mate and I, talking in the after-hours privacy of the empty classroom, could only wonder whether the students noticed the same facets of institutional racial imbalance we did; in the meantime, the students evidently not only *did* notice, but likely wondered the same about us. More importantly from the students' perspective, the power imbalance between teacher and student (which in our case was reinforced by race), meant that students did not feel safe broaching this aspect of everyday racial inequality—even though classrooms are often optimistically touted as spaces for combating racism.

This book is, at least in part, my attempt to revisit the conversations I was too uncomfortable to open in the classroom years ago. It is also an attempt to imagine how that conversation might find its way back into the classroom. In this book, I examine a body of literature for children that address the legacies of legalized desegregation. In various ways, these novels attempt to take up the conversation I dropped, narrating stories of the struggle to achieve racial justice both within and by means of the classroom. The ways in which such stories are framed, and the aspects of desegregation they pull into focus, can help to draw the attention of both students and teachers to classroom dynamics that deserve open discussion and reflection.

Fictions of Integration builds upon an extensive body of scholarship about the *Brown v. Board of Education* decision to suggest that novels directed toward children should be considered an important part of this archive, chronicling both immediate and longer-term effects of the decision. Immediate reactions to *Brown* are well known. The Supreme Court's 1954 decision to legally desegregate American schools was hailed at home and abroad as proof of progress toward the full integration of the nation's future citizenry. Historian Mary Dudziak offers examples of enthusiastic headlines and extensive news coverage of the decision in Brazil, India, and several West African countries. Even in some Southern newspapers, she says, the decision was praised because it gave "'an effective and resounding reply to the Communist criticism of our treatment of our minority group.'"[4] This perception of the *Brown* decision—as a confirmation of American democratic ideals and as a first step toward sweeping racial reform—continues to the present day. Other, less hopeful, immediate effects of the decision are also well known. As Dudziak, Patricia Hill Collins, and Derrick Bell record, one of the earliest responses to the *Brown* decision was the formation of an organized resistance from Southern whites, who pushed against the implementation of the decision using a variety of tactics from delay to exclusionary bureaucratic rules to open violence. Nevertheless, the narratives generally told about *Brown* emphasize triumph in the face of resistance, so much so that even scholars who critique the darker legacies of *Brown* must begin by acknowledging progress.[5]

Some who discuss the failures of the decision frame their critique within a tale of rise and decline, arguing that the *Brown* decision and the legal battles which followed represented positive movement toward racial justice, and that subsequent legal and legislative actions undid and betrayed that legacy of progress.[6] Many other scholars, however, have in the last several decades increasingly argued that the failures of racial justice following *Brown*, both within education and within the larger nation-state, have not been aberrant betrayals of that decision, but are instead integral to the decision itself. Critical race scholars (like Bell himself, who was an active litigator with the NAACP's Legal Defense Fund) have come to believe that the removal of formal legal segregation now not only stands in for more meaningful racial justice and equality, but worse, that it provides an excuse to avoid working toward racial justice. Bell and other scholars like Sonya Douglass Horsford, Patricia Albjerg Graham, Antonio Viego, and Lani Guinier point to the many harmful effects of *Brown*, including academic tracking by race, the loss of black teachers' jobs and of supportive all-black schools, and the self-fulfilling association of racially marked identity with psychological damage. Bell and Horsford suggest that the implementation of *Brown* actually caused, rather than solved, some of the problems and achievement gaps currently associated with majority minority schools.[7] Many of these scholars, like Guinier, Horsford, and Patricia Hill Collins, contend that integration is a goal distinct from the "body-mixing" approach of legal desegregation, and that full integration would require the teaching of concepts like racial literacy and social justice literacy that might reframe our ideas about school achievement and essential skills for citizenship.[8]

A similar range of perspectives on the limitations of legal desegregation, and also on the distinctions between desegregation and integration, is reflected in children's literature. Some perspectives are explicitly highlighted through historical fiction that narrates the violence of court-ordered desegregation, gestures to the loss of nurturing black schools and teachers, and offers hope for progress toward interracial solidarity. Other children's texts reflect the more cynical view that desegregation has created problems of achievement in schools that are still highly segregated. These darker school stories may not immediately appear to be "about" desegregation, and may not reference the *Brown* decision directly in any way. Nevertheless, in order to fully understand how the legacies of legal desegregation are presented in the classroom—and in order for children and teachers to be able to discuss these legacies—such novels must be considered as responses to the classroom conditions arising in the wake of a long and complex post *Brown* era.

Fictions of Integration considers the mutations of public discourse about *Brown* and the politics of the school publication market in order to explore why some novels in this study may receive more attention than others, and why some address *Brown* more directly than others. The redefinition of public discourse about race especially shapes how children's novels address issues of disability and accountability. Michael Omi and Howard Winant describe a process of "re-articulation" in the decades after the Civil Rights movement, when right-wing groups successfully shaped the parameters of school desegregation through anti-busing campaigns and involvement in textbook editing. In doing so, they also redefined what concepts of racial justice meant in common public discourse.[9] Novels that do not otherwise reference school desegregation, such as Sharon Flake's *Pinned*, can help to illuminate for a child audience how concepts of racial justice come to be rearticulated and diluted—and how child protagonists resist the dilution of

Civil Rights goals. The redefinition of what it means to seek racial justice in education also affects the classroom impact of these novels. Novels like Flake's, or like Virginia Hamilton's *The Planet of Junior Brown*, may not be recommended for specific discussion of the long Civil Rights movement, whereas historical novels like Sharon Draper's *Fire From the Rock* that focus on the more violent, but also more distant Southern white resistance to desegregation are popularly used as teaching texts. The genre of the different novels is a key part of this book's inquiry; as Jodi Melamed points out, some novel genres tend to support official, nationally validated visions of antiracism better than others, and resonate with white readers' sense of progressive national citizenship and racial identity.[10] In the children's literature of *Brown*, the school story genre seems to be most popular, and most conducive to supporting comforting narratives of national progress.

These novels can also contribute to an archive of educational philosophy, specifically within the growing field of utopian thought. The students who sought access to schools in the *Brown v. Board of Education* decision were merely seeking legal access, not utopian education. Several generations of educational critics and policymakers, however, have seen the push to desegregate schools as a call to utopian reform. Antiracist teachers and activists have contended for decades that legal right to access should be only the first step, and that humane pedagogies and more inclusive curricula for all children would go even further toward reinforcing American democratic ideals. Disability rights advocates have drawn inspiration from the *Brown* decision to envision educational methods and inclusive classrooms that would equally enrich students with disabilities and those without diagnoses. Such utopian visions of education infuse many of these novels. Children's novels can reflect how utopian strains of thought filter down to students, and they can also help to provide critiques and new visions. In advertising the benefits of desegregation, and in critiquing its poor implementation, authors also imagine idealized classrooms and pedagogies, portray potential reforms, and suggest modes of resistance that might be directed by the students themselves. The students affected by the *Brown* decision, and by related educational reforms, tend to be discussed as innocent and moldable objects of adult decision making. While many scholars do incorporate student voices into their analyses and critiques, they also frequently present students as being victimized by adult decisions. Books written for child readers, however, tend to emphasize children's agency even within the constraints of the school, addressing students as citizens, actors, and decision makers in their own right.

Other children's literature scholars have made the case that children's literature should be considered part of the historical archive of the Civil Rights movement and the Cold War. This book follows the invaluable work done by Kate Capshaw, whose *Civil Rights Childhood* examines the role of family photobooks in shaping the Civil Rights movement, and by Julia Mickenberg, whose *Learning From the Left* uncovers the influence that Leftist authors and publishers had upon children's literature publications during the Cold War. Sara Schwebel's study, *Child-Sized History*, establishes the effect that the educational publishing market has had in both encouraging and constraining the dissemination of children's books that aim to teach the racial history of the United States, including the history of desegregation.

Setting, Genre, and Educational Philosophy

One central argument of this book is that the school setting operates within children's books much as it does in real life—that is, it both limits what can be said about the racial inequalities and racially inflected pedagogies that take place on its grounds, and also provides material for dissent. Because the *Brown* decision affected the identity of American public schools, the public discourse that constrains critiques of the *Brown* decision also, to a certain extent, constrains critiques of the school system as a central node of racial justice efforts. Derrick Bell asserts the power of public discourse about *Brown* by saying, "*Brown* ... purported to clarify for Americans normatively who they were or should be."[11] In other words, by intervening in the school system, *Brown* also attempted to shape what ideal future citizens were to be like. Bell suggests that this institutional approach was flawed, however, because pursuit of justice through the fundamentally limited court system served only to relegitimize this system as the only one possible for redress. Within children's novels, representations of school arrive at a similar result. In effect, the demands of school define who children should be and tie their success as citizens to their success as students. Furthermore, while schools are frequently represented as unjust, school reform is generally presented so as to suggest that the school will *eventually* be the primary engine of democracy. These novels thus reinforce not only the desirability of the institution, but also the desirability of the nation-state from which it derives its authority.

A second argument of this book is that even critical stories about desegregation are molded by their genres. Part of the reason why stories about the legacies of *Brown* tend to soften or edit out the school system's failure to correct institutional racism is that they are shaped by the narrative conventions governing school stories and historical fiction for children, the genres most often used to tell stories of desegregation. School stories tend to adhere to a fairly strict plot trajectory that requires not just a happy ending for the protagonist, but specifically a happy ending in which the student achieves a sense of belonging in a benevolent school and nation. Alternatively, historical novels that recreate past times and places sometimes do reimagine historical educational practices in ways that not only critique the present but also offer other options. Critics of this genre point out, however, that in many cases, historical novels for children often conform to other kinds of narrative patterns; they tend toward a view of national history that is teleological and progressive and portray the contemporary reader's sensibilities as enlightened and evolved in comparison to a depraved past that has now been collectively overcome.[12]

There is a third genre that shapes children's desegregation literature: young adult realistic fiction, which sometimes overlaps with so-called "problem novels" about contemporary social issues such as divorce, addiction, and sexual abuse. Young adult realism specifically allows for, even encourages, critiques of institutional injustice. Realistic novels are also freed from some expectations of unambiguously happy endings. Roberta Seelinger Trites points out that young adult realism is limited by other narrative conventions, as it encourages adolescent readers to accept the injustice of flawed institutions.[13] Nevertheless, as Sheila Egoff argues, this genre incorporates a significant degree of subjective reflection, emphasizing personal interpretations of reality rather than aiming for the literary equivalent of "representational photography."[14] In other words, Egoff emphasizes the flexibility inherent in the genre of realistic fiction. Indeed, realistic novels can disrupt assumptions about childhood "realities." For example, novelists can establish a plot arc that does not match up with the traditional school year. In novels like Jacqueline Woodson's *Feathers* (which is also an historical novel), or Sharon Flake's *Pinned*, this simple alteration in the framing of children's everyday, institutionally scheduled reality can push readers to recognize a timeframe of growth and learning that does not correspond to the prevailing system of class hours and school years.

In fact, all three genres most often used to tell desegregation stories—school stories, historical fiction, and contemporary realism—are bound by the expectation that they will represent certain "realities" of the school experience after *Brown*, but they can also shape which aspects of this reality are noticed, forgotten, accepted, or problematized. Indeed, while many of the novels discussed in this book are shaped and limited by the constraints of genre, they also break these conventions in ways that open up imagined alternatives to contemporary school practices. Furthermore, even when they adhere to the traditions of school stories and historical fiction, these genres can often invite critiques of contemporary racism in the school system and propose risky solutions that are highly contested in the politicized realm of educational policy and that might not otherwise be introduced to young students.

Even accounting for flexibility within each genre, certain patterns are evident. Novels that adhere most closely to the genre of the school story tend to represent pedagogy and models of achievement that are quite normative in their visions of what the school ought to look like and what it ought to prepare its students to do and to be. Thus, while school stories such as Kristin Levine's *The Lions of Little Rock* and Andrea Davis Pinkney's *With the Might of Angels* often portray the implementation of *Brown* in a critical light, they also tend to divert attention from the ways that the classroom continues to be implicated in racial injustice. In contrast, novels within any genre that explicitly focus on problems of pedagogy tend to critique the legacy of desegregation. Such novels more directly call attention to the injustices of the present moment, as in the case of Cynthia Voigt's Tillerman novels. Novels that push the bounds of realism, such as Virginia Hamilton's *The Planet of Junior Brown*, tend to broaden their critiques even further, calling into question some basic premises of school "reality": first, that the goal of school is to achieve academic success, and second, that academic success will and should produce a useful citizen for the nation.

In tracing how the legacies of *Brown* resurface in children's literature, *Fictions of Integration* pursues a third central argument: children's novels about desegregation rely upon portrayals and critiques of classroom pedagogy and student learning as the central method by which desegregated schools might be the engines of racial justice for the nation. The novels wrestle with how the classroom content and skills students learn ideally ought to support the desired antiracist habits of mind. In some novels, students' academic lives are rescued by idealized antiracist schools. In others, inadequate schools serve the project of antiracist education differently, by giving their students an education in productive discontent, inculcating them with a deep understanding of injustice and also providing them the language and tools to combat it.

This focus on student learning links desegregation novels to broader, utopian educational reform efforts sparked by the *Brown* decision, including movements toward standardized testing and accountability, and movements for inclusive education for students with disabilities. Children's novels about desegregation reflect these utopian visions, but they also suggest that various reform efforts are based on conflicting and often mutually exclusive visions of what successful, racially just, inclusive learning might look like. This is a common problem in utopian educational philosophy. Ruth Levitas suggests that education is a central problem for all utopian projects, as citizens must be brought to desire the utopia they are offered—and not merely desire it, but act to bring it into being. Such education famously misfires, producing both conflicting political desires and conflicting timelines for political action.[15] Certainly, in the post-Civil Rights era, as the definition of racial justice is continually rearticulated, students and citizens encounter a constantly changing and fractured vision of what successful school integration and national racial justice means. A comparison of these novelists' visions of desegregation can offer insights into wider questions of how children are invited to think about the efficacy and worthiness of educational reform movements, and how they are invited to connect the reform movements that buffet their classrooms to competing utopian goals for the nation and its citizens.

Reform movements do pressure American school systems more or less continually, and David Tyack and Larry Cuban identify a central, contradictory approach to American school reform. They assert that, on the one hand, United States citizens believe passionately that utopian change can be effected through educational reform, and on the other, school systems resist change so that reforms are implemented by "tinkering" rather by making wholesale changes. Furthermore, both the qualities of "tinkering" and of "utopianism" attract praise and criticism; "tinkering" is practical, but slow and potentially reactionary, while "utopia" is inspiring, but potentially dangerous or impractical.[16] Utopian educational theorists tend to argue on one side of the divide or the other, privileging "tinkering" over bold utopian moves or vice versa. So, too, children's novelists tend to suggest their sympathy for seizing slow antiracist transformations in reach, or for bold, risky resistance and radical dreams. In the process, they also demonstrate differing approaches to how failing students, and students who carry learning disabilities, should be incorporated into reformed, antiracist schools.

One common critique of utopian philosophy is that totalizing visions can exclude some citizens as bad, failed, or unfit to participate in the brave new world.[17] Similarly, many visions of reformed schools are predicated on new categories of exclusion; some desegregated schools in fiction help to filter out those students who are not yet "fit" to help realize the American dream of democracy because they are unable or unwilling to demonstrate the success of the reformed school. Other stories highlight the injustice or immorality of failures at school, and thereby suggest new ways to think about not only effective pedagogy, but effective democratic citizenship. Protagonists in these novels sometimes learn to desire a different utopia from the American democracy they are offered; and so, in order to construct alternate utopian models, they also investigate new methods for antiracist education. Indeed, some of these novels explore fantasies of exiting from the school system altogether and creating radically alternate spaces for learning and structures of citizenship. Nevertheless, the construction of these utopian alternatives does not negate the force and importance of the school in these novels, or of the nation-state the school is meant to serve.[18] Rather, they ask readers to consider why a reformed school is not the ideal site of these alternatives.

All of these novels about desegregation are limited in the ways they invite young readers to think about the continuing struggles of racial justice in their classrooms. Many of them are also limited in the kinds of solutions they imagine. To say they are "limited" implies that they are somehow failed, unworthy, or insufficient. While I may, in some cases, argue that they are, their failures and insufficiencies do not render them valueless as utopian visions. The project of education is also generally limited, and usually involves some failures on the part of students and teachers alike, but I continue to believe that teaching and learning are meaningful pursuits. Thus, while I do find limitations in each of the novels I discuss, I also contend that each of these partial, incomplete versions of utopia may be visionary or useful for thinking about the implementation of desegregation in the school.

Publishing Markets and the Shaping of Desegregation Pedagogy

A central aspect of this project is to ask what kinds of characters and classrooms seem to be too threatening to envision being included in a desegregated school. Some such exclusions occur as a result of the publication and marketing process for children's trade books for the classroom. Adult desires and fears for implied child readers impact every step of getting a book into a child's hand: the writing and editing, the selection for publication, the marketing strategies, the purchasing decisions by libraries, teachers, and bookstores, and finally the ways that classroom and library reading is framed and guided through adult-authored prompts. The school, as an institution, tends to protect its authority; given its status and influence within the market for children's books, this means that what school personnel and teachers perceive as "appropriate" shapes what books get written, published, and disseminated. Books that safely contain critiques of the school system—by placing conflict in the past, for example, or by elevating it as a source of hope despite its problems—tend more often to win major awards like the Newbery and Coretta Scott King and to be found on state curriculum booklists. When more radically critical novels are published and made available in classrooms and libraries—and they are—it can only be through the partnership of committed adults who have alternate ideas about what children should be able to learn about the schools they attend.

The first crucial aspect of how the school market shapes publishing is before the book goes to press, when it is rejected or accepted and edited for publication. Laura Atkins, Joel Taxel, and Zetta Elliott all testify to pressures at this stage, from different perspectives: Atkins as a publisher, Taxel as a scholar interested in the political economy of the publishing industry, and Elliott as a children's writer and activist scholar. Atkins states bluntly that publishing houses try to avoid making school purchasers queasy:

> What I found particularly striking was the degree to which *perceived* market requirements shaped the books that were acquired and developed. The publishers where I worked sold primarily to the institutional markets—to teachers and librarians. In my experience,

> there was concern about what teachers or librarians would accept, with a frequent "lowest common denominator" consideration of what the majority of those in the educational and library systems would tolerate.[19]

As a result, she says, editors (who were mainly white women) pressured writers to pitch their "multicultural" books toward a "universal" audience, editing out culturally specific elements or dark moments that might make middle-class teachers uncomfortable. Similarly, Taxel notes that "multicultural" books written by and for people in a particular cultural community (what he terms "parallel cultural literature") are seen as limited niche books.[20] Multicultural books that are meant to give white audiences a taste of difference, however, are seen as more widely marketable and able to satisfy the demand for immediately high turnover; thus, much of what is selected and packaged as "multicultural literature" is what white people think of as universal and acceptable multiculturalism. Elliott, similarly, testifies to experiencing great difficulty getting her work published. She notes, for example, that her chapter book about a girl whose father is incarcerated was rejected because the white female editor said she felt uncomfortable with the black protagonist's anger.[21] In the meantime, she says, publishers "continue to promote their endless books about Harriet Tubman and Dr. Martin Luther King, Jr., knowing that educators and librarians across the country need *something* to display when Black History Month rolls around."[22] Atkins, Taxel, and Elliott all comment that, while publishers actively market toward white children and their parents, they perceive little demand among Black and Latino families for books and assume that the market for these *children* is actually a market for their *teachers*. Despite increasing activism from grassroots organizations such as We Need Diverse Books, Scholastic's catalog still features primarily books with white protagonists, with a very narrow, and often stereotypical, range of "diverse" books, to such an extent that they were targeted by a Tumblr campaign (#StepupScholastic) in 2016. In such a marketing environment, it is likely that representations of school desegregation and its legacies (including continued racism in the classroom) will be heavily policed and limited in range.

Once a book has gone to press, its sales are heavily influenced by whether it is recognized by the Newbery Award committee (and, more recently, by the Coretta Scott King Award committee) and whether it is taken up for recommendation by widely referenced school-based programs such as the Common Core Curriculum, the Accelerated Reader Program, and published state curricula like those previously used in Massachusetts and California.[23] Kenneth Kidd, in his study of the Newbery Prize, notes that in a book culture of fast turnover and shrinking backlists, Newbery Award winning books remain perpetually in print. Furthermore, as Sara Schwebel observes, they remain in classrooms and recommended curricula, even when they have been repeatedly and publicly critiqued as racist, as in the case of *Sounder.* The Massachusetts State Department of Education, in their published curricula from 2001 and 2011, lists a number of recommended authors by name for each grade level and then recommends *any* book for the classroom that has been approved by the Newbery committee.[24] Significantly, although the Coretta Scott King Award for children's books published by African-American authors has recognized an alternate canon since 1970, Coretta Scott King award winners were not listed by Massachusetts as worthy of teacher attention until the 2011 revision of the curriculum.

Thus, recognition by the Newbery committee confers a special status and influence upon a book. Kidd demonstrates that the committee continues to be conservative about issues of race, honoring few books about race set later than the Depression. As books set no later than the Depression are unlikely to address legal desegregation, this means that the books about racism teachers are encouraged to use are ones that elide the issues they and their students face in the classroom.[25]

This pattern illuminates some obstacles to getting novels that evoke legacies of desegregation into the classroom. One example that does not involve Newbery Award winners is Ann Cameron's series about young black protagonists Julian, Huey, and Gloria. *Stories Julian Tells* is a relatively innocuous book about an imaginative black boy who gets in trouble for eating too much lemon pudding and for fighting with his brother; it is described by Nina Mikkelsen as the kind of pluralist, "universal," "transcendent" book designed to "provide ... cathartic, 'feel-good' experiences for white readers."[26] It is specifically recommended by the Common Core standards, California, New York, and Massachusetts (which normally recommended only authors, but in the case of Cameron specified the Julian books). Cameron's novel *Gloria Rising*, another in the same series, portrays Gloria's struggles with a racist white teacher who holds low expectations of her nonwhite students. That novel is not recommended by any published curriculum.

Classroom teaching is the final step that might shape how children read this literature of desegregation. There is a robust pedagogical debate over books as "mirrors" and "windows," where "mirror" books are considered to reflect a child's own experiences and "window" books are those that provide her with a view of a world outside her own. Critics and educators are divided over whether children ought to be reading "mirror" books or "window" books, and over how various aspects of children's identities ought to be sensitively and accurately mirrored (or windowed) to them.[27] These critics sometimes discuss books as though they provided mirrors or windows in the absence of classroom pedagogy or other adult direction. Yet, as Sara Schwebel and Katherine Simon point out, children often read books in the context of the classroom, and such reading experiences are not unmediated encounters between the text and the student's mind. Teachers (and often, state administrators and curriculum planners before them) get to decide which aspects of a text students will be held accountable for knowing. Through discussion questions, homework assignments, and assessments, they can direct students' attention toward some aspects of a text and away from others. They can, furthermore, incentivize choices to think about literary elements such as metaphor and plot structure in preference to questions about racial stereotyping or biased historical representations. Thus, it is possible for a book that is chosen in part for its "mirror" qualities to be taught in a way that sidelines these elements.

For example, a teacher's guide to Virginia Hamilton's *The Planet of Junior Brown* "universalizes" the text by making no mention of race in the introductory summary. Even more astonishing is the treatment given a key scene, in which Junior expresses his resistance against intra-racial prejudice by painting a picture of himself participating in all the facets of black culture his mother wishes him to repudiate. This important scene, which leads to Junior's running away, is made the subject of a multiple choice reading comprehension question that asks students what art tool Junior uses to paint the Red Man, which is unlikely to prompt critical reflection about the socially conscious content of the painting.[28] In a guide to Cynthia Voigt's *Come a Stranger*, a novel that deals directly with racism in education, discussion questions do ask students to consider whether Mina is dismissed from dance camp because of racism and to describe the ways she is pressured to "act white" in order to succeed. Still, the potential threat to white teachers is addressed in a section of the guide entitled "Social Sensitivity," which proclaims, "Mina develops friendships from both races and behaves in an exemplary way by looking beyond color. Voigt, however, fails to balance her presentation as those people who behave in a prejudiced way are white."[29] Katherine Simon, in a series of classroom observations, records how teachers often shut down discussion of ambiguous issues by providing the "right" reading, as the *Come a Stranger* study guide does, or else move these discussions "off-line" by focusing students' attention on the completion of reading comprehension questions like those in the *Planet of Junior Brown* guide. Simon notes that children continue to ask and to be engaged with sticky questions; however, reading is often structured so that "consideration of moral questions [is] relegated largely to the private realm ... a kind of special interest," rather than the subject of "collaborative, public thinking."[30] Given the ways that politically volatile representations of school can be edited out before books even go to press, *Fictions of Integration* makes the case that an examination of desegregation stories must involve looking for absence, for what might be there but is not.

Text Selection

I focus on middle-grade and young adult American novels that highlight the challenges of desegregated schooling. This focus excludes attention to a number of very important and influential genres in children's media. The study centers on trade books, because they are more widely used objects of study in the Language Arts classroom than are films or television episodes, although film representations of desegregation such as *Remember the Titans* have been influential. Nonfiction texts and picture books about the early desegregation battles are plentiful, and at times, I reference these other genres to provide context for the novels that form the points of focus in each chapter. Nevertheless, nonfiction texts and picture books about the present-day iterations of school battles for racial justice—racial disparities in disability diagnosis, resegregation, and achievement gaps in testing—are much harder to find. Novelists, however, find roundabout ways to represent these issues. For greater ease of comparison, therefore, the primary texts for focus are novels.

For a similar reason, I omit discussion of the wide range of children's literature on other aspects of the Civil Rights movement and on other aspects of racial conflict, both historical and contemporary. Aside from a staggering number of children's books about Martin Luther King and Rosa Parks, there are books touching on children's participation in protests, neighborhood gentrification, and interracial dating, many of which address topics crucial to the issue of school desegregation.[31] My narrowed focus admittedly cuts out some of the interesting ways that novelists represent other continuing Civil Rights issues for young readers. Focusing specifically on one piece of the Civil Rights agenda—school integration—allows me to trace how this issue is represented over several decades as a continuing challenge rather than as a contained historical event.

Furthermore, I limit my project to novels that portray the desegregation of black students and white students after *Brown v. Board of Education*. This, I realize, is a problematic choice that de-emphasizes the struggles of Latino, Asian, and Native American students to be meaningfully integrated into United States schools. Novels like Sherman Alexie's *Diary of a Part-Time Indian*, Gene Yang's *American Born Chinese*, Thanhha Lai's *Inside Out and Back Again*, Francisco Jimenez's trilogy *The Circuit*, *Breaking Through*, and *Reaching Out*, and Juan Felipe Herrera's *Downtown Boy* complicate narratives of integration and bring in questions about how the history of United States imperialism impacts the school system as an engine of democracy. Each of these novels opens up an area of historical contention—about the position of reservations within the American state, about school as a homogenizing force for immigrant students, about language inclusion and exclusion—that is crucial to how the United States conceives of its schools as integrated and democratic. Nevertheless, to give each of these issues the attention it deserves is outside the scope of this project. By focusing specifically on the nominal desegregation of black and white students, I am able to examine in more depth the ways that the potentially explosive and unspeakable history of school racism that followed *Brown* has been represented in roundabout ways and made "appropriate" for child consumption.

Authorship is a highly political issue in books that deal with cross-racial topics. Many novels published for children about racial conflict are written by white authors, and these novels are immensely popular with classroom teachers even when they are critiqued by antiracist groups. Because this kind of cross-racial writing is so prevalent in the books children see, I have included some examples among the novels I discuss. It is also crucial to my project to examine not only what children are given to read, but also what they are not given; thus, I have selected some novels that have gone out of print and placed them in conversation with books that are actively circulating.

Organization

In reading these novels, I did not always find clear correspondences between the books' publication dates and the effects of school desegregation they engaged. Nor were there clear clusters of time settings or genre, with all the historical fiction being set within a single decade, or all of the contemporary realistic fiction centering around a specific phase of implementation. The implementation of *Brown* lasted for decades, and publicly debated ideas about the meaning, and the desired form, of desegregation, were changing even as earlier phases of desegregation were being grudgingly implemented. In recent decades, the Civil Rights movement, including the *Brown* decision, has become a popular subject for children's historical fiction and nonfiction. Nevertheless, conflicting interpretations of historical memory and opinions about the progress made toward desegregation exist now, just as conflicting visions of the Civil Rights movement existed at the time. And while the Civil Rights era is now a sufficiently distanced, sanitized subject to portray in children's literature, more recent phases of implementation, such as re-segregation through disability diagnosis, are much more rarely depicted. Thus, rather than organizing the chapters chronologically by publication date or by setting, I have organized them according to the specific legacy, or effect, of desegregation they seem to engage. This creates a methodological problem of how to discuss, and historicize, novels that may both be written at different times and also be concerned with different slices of national history. The advantage of this organization is that juxtaposing novels in ways that set up potentially long, confusing, and coexisting timelines reflects the way in which school desegregation was implemented unevenly, interacting with various other changes in racial politics along the way.

In Chapter 1, "Scripting History: The Genre of Desegregation Stories," I review the body of novels chronicling the entry of the first black students into mostly white schools, focusing specifically on Dorothy Sterling's *Mary Jane* (1959), Andrea Pinkney's *With the Might of Angels* (2011), and Kristin Levine's *The Lions of Little Rock* (2012). Despite the many years between dates of publication, these novels offer a fairly consistent dominant narrative of the Civil Rights era. Chapter 2, "Counternarratives and the Persistence of White Privilege," includes novels that reflect some of the backlash and critique of *Brown* from within the black community, concerns that were suppressed during the immediate aftermath of the *Brown* decision but that resurfaced later. These novels offer critiques of the *Brown* decision from different vantage points in time; Mildred Pitts Walter's novel *Because We Are* (1983) is a critique of the author's contemporary post-Civil Rights school system, Sharon Draper's *Fire From the Rock* (2007) looks back to excavate an alternate narrative of the Civil Rights era, and Jacqueline Woodson's *Feathers* (2007) looks back to the 1970s, to a school system still segregated years after the *Brown* decision. The novels in Chapter 3, "Pedagogies of Desegregation: Narratives of Disability and Giftedness," obliquely address an insidious effect of the *Brown* decision: an increase in tracking and disability diagnosis as a way of re-segregating students within nominally desegregated schools. Virginia Hamilton's *The Planet of Junior Brown* and Cynthia Voigt's Tillerman novels tell different kinds of stories about desegregation, ones less focused on the decision of whether or not the protagonists should attend a desegregated school and more attentive to the details of everyday school life and policy after the initial shock of contact subsided. Chapter 4, "Desegregating Literacy, Enriching the State," pursues a legacy of *Brown* that is much discussed in the news, but less often in children's literature: concern about the so-called achievement gap between black and white students, which has replaced concern about actual contact and physical desegregation. As with the novels in Chapter 3, the novels in Chapter 4 address this most recent iteration of desegregation only obliquely. Louis Sachar's *Holes* (1998), M.T. Anderson's *The Astonishing Life of Octavian Nothing, Traitor to His Nation* (2006, 2011), and Sharon Flake's *Pinned* (2012) are radically different in historical setting and genre, but all three suggest that the project of desegregation is still incomplete, and suggest varied responses to the accountability and choice movements as remedies for the unfinished project of *Brown*. In a brief conclusion, I return to thinking about the classroom and about how this archive of novels might be used, or misused, to open up conversations among students and between students and teachers about the realities of schooling after *Brown*.

Utopian, anti-racist educators like Patricia Hill Collins, Katherine Simon, and Gloria Ladson-Billings offer ways to make the classroom feel like a safe, rigorous, and democratic environment, even as they recognize that teachers may be constrained by time and by fear of endangering their jobs if they are seen as devoting time to critical thought and empowerment that lie outside of required state standards. Sara Schwebel's discussion of historical novels offers analysis that can help teachers to do *both* and therefore preserve their jobs. It is my hope that this book will, similarly, provide ways to think and talk about the current legacies of *Brown*—continuing segregation, disproportionate tracking and diagnosis, and anxiety about achievement—within the context of texts that "cover" important periods in United States history and that are often lauded for their literary qualities.

Notes

1 According to a 2011 report published by the U.S. Department of Education, 82 percent of public school teachers and 88 percent of private school teachers are white; overall, 76 percent of teachers are female. Goldring and Bitterman, "Characteristics of Public and Private Teachers," 3.
2 I have changed all names.
3 For histories of the multicultural turn in curriculum development, see Sara Schwebel, *Child-Sized History*, 18, 31–33; Diane Ravitch, *The Language Police*, 124.
4 *Atlanta Daily World*, quoted in Dudziak, *Cold War Civil Rights*, 2.
5 Collins, *Another Kind of Public Education*, 47.
6 Linda Darling-Hammond, for example, contends that progress was made and then lost. Darling-Hammond, *The Flat World of Education*, 18.
7 Bell goes so far as to argue that *Plessy v. Ferguson* should have been upheld rather than struck down, and that rigorous enforcement of "separate but equal" should have been the focus of *Brown*—in his words, "desegregating the money" (165) might have been a better solution than desegregating the children.
8 The terms "desegregation" and "integration" are often used interchangeably. Horsford suggests that "desegregation" ought to be used for the process of removing legal barriers to the entry of black children into a white-dominated institution, while "integration" ought to be reserved for those rare situations in which multiracial students, teachers, and pedagogies are meaningfully negotiated and given respect within a single classroom. I follow her usage. Horsford, *Learning in a Burning House*, 4; Guinier, "From Racial Liberalism to Racial Literacy," 114–166; Collins, *Another Kind of Public Education*, 109.
9 Omi and Winant, *Racial Formation in the United States*, 127.
10 Melamed, *Represent and Destroy*, "Killing Sympathies."
11 Bell, *Shades of Brown*, 136.
12 Hubler, "Girl Power and History," 99; MacLeod, "Writing Backward."
13 Trites, *Disturbing the Universe*, 21–53.
14 Egoff, *Thursday's Child*, 34.
15 Levitas, *The Concept of Utopia*, 174.
16 Tyack and Cuban, *Tinkering Toward Utopia*, 103.

17 Halpin, "Utopian Totalism Versus Utopian Realism."

18 As in Foucault's notion of disciplinarity, the school establishes normative standards that are designed to produce deviance; even if non-normative, "deviant" students choose to leave the school setting, or to reform their idiosyncrasies so as to join the mainstream, the school has nevertheless created the standards and the conditions for how all children (including dropouts) will be assessed. Despite this framework, deviant and dissident students have some agency in how they inhabit their non-normative identities, options which these novels explore. David Halperin argues that Foucault offers an ethic of *liberation*, as opposed to *freedom*. Halperin focuses on queer identities rather than on school identities, but his theorization of how to operate within an institution from which there is no exit is nonetheless germane to this project.

19 Atkins, "What's the Story?"

20 Taxel, "Children's Literature at the Turn of the Century," 173. Taxel explains that new tax laws and the pressures of fast capitalism have discouraged publishers from warehousing books and maintaining backlists. As a consequence, books have a limited shelf life and then go out of print, and publishers tend to skew their offerings toward what they think will be of immediate, "mainstream, national interest" (157).

21 Elliott, "Hot Mess."

22 Elliott, "Something Like an Open Letter." Indeed, the problem of numbers continues to be acute. Out of 3,200 new books received by CCBC in 2013, only 93 had significant content about African or African-American characters or themes; only 67 were written by African-American authors or illustrators. The numbers for other racial and cultural groups are similarly dismal. Cooperative Children's Book Center, "Publishing Statistics."

23 I am indebted to Sara Schwebel for her methodology in tracking down how widely influential particular books might be in school systems around the nation. Since I began this project, more and more states have adopted the Common Core curriculum, and previous state curricula have been taken off the web, making it slightly more difficult to track the presence of novels in older state curricula.

24 Massachusetts Department of Education, *Massachusetts English Language Arts Curriculum Framework*. The Common Core standards, which are being adopted by an increasing number of states, does not specifically mention the Newbery in the appendix of text exemplars. The authors do, however, state as part of their criteria for text selection that "While it is possible to have high-complexity texts of low inherent quality, the work group solicited only texts of recognized value." Since 1920, one of the most prominent and most-accepted ways to recognize value has been the Newbery; and indeed, Newbery winners are prominently represented among the twentieth-century texts recommended by the curriculum authors. Common Core State Standards Initiative, "English Language Arts Appendix B."

25 While Kidd argues that Newbery books tend to circulate outside the classroom rather than being heavily taught in the curriculum, medal-winning books are heavily promoted by state curricula, and are often accompanied by teacher activity packs.

26 Mikkelsen, "Insiders, Outsiders, and the Question of Authenticity," 41.

27 Diane Ravitch, representing a relatively conservative view, laments the "new canon" formed when authors like Cisneros replace Emerson in reading textbooks, and argues that students of color should be encouraged to look beyond their own experiences and those of their immediate communities

rather than to expect only books and classroom topics that are made "relevant" to them. Ravitch, *Language Police*, 128. Author Mitali Perkins voices a similar objection, but from the opposite perspective, asking, "Why should we expect white kids to want to see their own faces reflected when it comes to race and ethnicity?" Perkins, "Are Books Windows or Mirrors?" Several antiracist scholars point to the distorting quality of the mirrors offered to racially marked children in the curriculum. Beryle Banfield and Geraldine Wilson, for example, protest the appropriation of black themes by white authors, and Julius Lester criticizes "the sympathetic, cloying little books about blacks" that result. Lester and Woods, "Black and White: An Exchange," 72. Judith Thompson and Gloria Woodard suggest that children are consistently presented with selective mirrors; they are encouraged to read about role models acceptable to whites, such as Jackie Robinson and Martin Luther King, Jr., while biographies of Malcolm X and Paul Robeson are harder to come by.

28 Francis, "The Planet of Junior Brown by Virginia Hamilton."

29 Bookrags, "Social Sensitivity."

30 Simon, *Moral Questions in the Classroom*, 163, 165.

31 See, for example, Doreen Rappaport's *Nobody Gonna Turn Me 'Round*, Jacqueline Woodson's *Between Madison and Palmetto* and *If You Come Softly*, and James Howe's *Totally Joe*.

1 Scripting History and the Genre of Desegregation Stories[1]

School Stories and Consensus Memory

Children's books about the legacies of *Brown v. Board of Education* encompass all of the varied effects of that decision, including movements toward black separatism and trends toward re-segregation. Nevertheless, when most adults hear "*Brown v. Board of Education*," the stories they probably think of are a specific type of narrative I call "desegregation school stories." These are stories of a specific historic moment shortly after the *Brown* decision, when Southern white schools reluctantly, with varying degrees of violence and publicity, allowed small numbers of black students in under court order. Fictionalized accounts of school desegregation were published for children even before the historic decision (Jesse Jackson's 1945 *Call Me Charley* reflected residential segregation and token desegregation in a Northern town), though most did not appear until the late 1950s. James Miller observes in reading three of the earliest examples, which range in publication date from 1945 to 1965, that the novels tend to follow a predictable pattern: a black boy or girl enters a predominantly white school, makes a white friend who helps him or her to succeed in an extracurricular activity, faces down one or two bigoted bullies (who do not represent the majority of the white school population), and eventually achieves success and acceptance, which is contingent upon reform within the white community and an attitude of virtuous patience and hard work within the black community.[2] Later works of historical fiction, such as Jeri Watts's *Kizzy Ann Stamps* (2012) and Patricia McKissack's *A Friendship, for Today* (2007), follow a similar pattern.

Some of these plot elements are based at least in part on historical constraints. The NAACP often deliberately selected middle-class black students as test cases for desegregation, and standardized test scores were frequently used as excuses for white administrators to resist desegregation, so that only very highly performing black students were allowed to enter.[3] Narratives loosely based on these events can therefore be expected to reflect these patterns. More recent historical novels in particular, in aiming to teach history through fiction, emphasize the complex selection process as part of the history lesson about *Brown*. Nevertheless, in popular films like *Remember the Titans* and books like *Kizzy Ann Stamps*, desegregation tends to mean a unidirectional movement of black students into "superior" white schools, access to white institutions is conflated with racial justice, and achievement in an extracurricular activity is central both to interracial friendship and to the black characters' acceptance within a white institution.

In other words, the ritualized plot arc tends to support what Renee Romano and Leigh Raiford call a "consensus memory" of the Civil Rights movement, in which narratives of school struggle and temporary triumph are honored as a substitute for the accomplishment of broader racial equality and meaningful integration.[4] Moreover, fictional desegregation stories have historically been more prevalent, and more often recommended for child reading, than nonfiction about the *Brown* decision. One 1972 article for teachers recommended desegregation novels of contemporary and immediate interest to students, including Dorothy Sterling's *Mary Jane* and Natalie Savage Carlson's *The Empty Schoolhouse*.[5] The reviewer included no nonfiction titles. Indeed, though several memoirs and nonfiction titles were published from the mid-1990s on, I found no references to nonfiction texts published before that time. Students' reading about desegregation prior to the 1990s may well have been dominated by desegregation novels. In nonfiction texts of the last two decades (outside of memoirs), information about school desegregation tends to be placed in one chapter about the broader Civil Rights movement, placing the focus upon the Civil Rights movement rather than upon school desegregation specifically.[6] Memoirs such as Melba Patillo Beals' are critical of consensus memory, and are widely disseminated, but they have not stemmed the tide of fictionalized (and less violent) narratives such as Andrea Davis Pinkney's *With the Might of Angels*.

Nonfiction picture books for younger readers are popular, but they tend to emphasize a triumphant story arc even when they do not follow the detailed generic pattern of longer desegregation novels. For example, Toni Morrison's *Remember: The Journey to Integration* narrates historical photographs of classrooms with fictionalized captions, rather than with nonfictional accounts of the photographs' context, and it constructs an organizational framework of progress through sections entitled "The Narrow Path," "The Open Gate," and finally "The Wide Road" that all may walk into the happier present. The story of Ruby Bridges is another widely used nonfictional narrative for younger readers, but it is somewhat different from the experiences of the Little Rock Nine or of other desegregation pioneers like the Carter family. At the center of Ruby's story is an exceptionally warm relationship with a kind white Northern teacher. This relationship makes her narrative resonate with fictional desegregation novels, which also tend to revolve around a meaningful interracial relationship. Such a relationship also seems to support a comforting Civil Rights consensus memory; this may be one reason why Ruby's narrative has become more iconic and widely taught than nonfiction picture books that do not include a central interracial relationship, such as Doreen Rappaport's *The School Is Not White.*[7]

Nevertheless, the "typical" desegregation school story is not merely a container for consensus memory of the Civil Rights movement. It also draws upon the literary tradition of the school story and constitutes a sub-genre that extends, revises, and comments upon the existing school story tradition. As in most school stories, the desegregation story is meant to pay homage to the institution of school. Therefore, while the authors of desegregation stories do gesture to some of the more disturbing effects of Brown's implementation, these moments are contained and tamed, not only by the pressure of a celebratory Civil Rights narrative, but also by the structure of the school story genre. At the same time, the school story tradition also allows for critical portrayals of classroom pedagogy and for representations of queer interracial friendship. To the extent that desegregation stories are able to critique Brown's failure to achieve racial justice, they do so by working within and commenting upon school story tropes.

This chapter focuses primarily on three desegregation stories as examples that demonstrate the ways in which the genre of the school story imposes a common framework on representations of the *Brown* legacy: *Mary Jane* by Dorothy Sterling (1959), *Lions of Little Rock* by Kristen Levine (2012), and *With the Might of Angels* by Andrea Davis Pinkney (2011). Despite the wide variations in their publication dates and in the backgrounds of their authors, the three novels share a similar plot line, indicating the influential reach of the desegregation story genre. In each one, a pre-teenaged black girl serves as a pioneer of desegregation, copes with racist bullies, flourishes academically, and befriends a sympathetic white girl. All three incorporate even more specific tropes, which suggest a ritualized way to narrate a consensus interpretation of desegregation history. These include a depiction of pedagogical anxieties and changes prompted by the Cold War, a romantic friendship as the key to the utopian vision of desegregation, and an emphasis on a resistant racial identity that depends upon academic performance in the classroom.

These three particular novels are useful for study in part because they seem to have had some influence with young readers, although this is hard to gauge for certain. Dorothy Sterling's *Mary Jane* has been mentioned fondly by many readers who discovered it through the Scholastic Book Club flyers, and online lesson plans and teacher packs abound for Kristen Levine's *Lions of Little Rock* and Andrea Davis Pinkney's *With the Might of Angels* (in fact, Google offers to autocomplete these titles with the term 'lesson plans').[8] Furthermore, while they demonstrate the generic power of the desegregation story genre, these three novels also demonstrate the range and variety of the desegregation novel, offering examples of how differently authors may negotiate the more troubling aspects of desegregation history, even within a single genre. These differences provide insight into the degree to which direct portrayals of *Brown v. Board of Education* are managed and shaped by the publishing industry, and they also demonstrate that the school story format allows for some flexibility in telling a relatively contained consensus narrative of court-ordered desegregation.

Dorothy Sterling's *Mary Jane* was published in 1959 as the highly contentious work of court-ordered desegregation was in process. It represents a popular example of how desegregation was handled in contemporary novels. While it has much in common with other contemporary novels, such as Lorenz Graham's *Town* series and Natalie Savage Carlson's *The Empty Schoolhouse*, its publication history more clearly helps to illuminate how desegregation stories were shaped during the Cold War. *Mary Jane* is based on a compilation of student interviews Sterling had published with a photographer the year before; however, in the novel, Sterling hews much more closely to traditional school story plots. Mary Jane, the granddaughter of a prominent black biologist, elects to attend the local white junior high school so that she can gain access to their science labs. She is hounded by hostile students and hurt by the quieter racism of many teachers; but when she rescues a squirrel being tortured by some of her classmates, she befriends Sally, a lonely white girl with a similar interest in science. The two girls are unable to pursue their friendship (or to keep their new pet squirrel Furry) outside of school grounds, so they sneak off to the empty backstage dressing rooms of the school. After this hideout is discovered, they are finally allowed to form a science club that authorizes them to spend time together and to expand their circle of science-loving friends.

Kristin Levine's historical fiction novel *Lions of Little Rock*, published in 2012, offers an example of a desegregation story that veers from some of the usual elements of the genre. It follows a white protagonist, and also highlights an historical moment that runs counter to consensus memory, when the town of Little Rock closed its high schools rather than desegregate them. The protagonist Marlee is a desperately shy math whiz whose parents passively support integration but fear to speak out. As a junior high student, she attends school while her older sister is sent away to continue her education. Marlee generally does not speak to anyone outside her own family, but she is charmed by a new girl at school, who wins her trust and then is removed from school when she is revealed to be a light-skinned black girl passing as white. Marlee's desire to be with Liz leads to her increasing activism. This simultaneous battle against social anxiety and racism does not result in Liz's return, but it does result in Marlee's character development and ultimate success within the school system.

Andrea Davis Pinkney's *With the Might of Angels*, published in 2011 as part of the "Dear America" historical fiction series for girls, is an example of mainstream historical fiction about the Civil Rights era. Pinkney has authored several nonfiction books about the Civil Rights era and has both responded to and helped to create the publishing context for Civil Rights narratives in recent decades. She is also a black author whose handling of the desegregation story complicates the common trope of the interracial friendship.[9] The diary of Dawnie Ray Jones begins in 1954 with the *Brown* decision. Immediately after the decision is published, outspoken tomboy Dawnie Rae is one of three students chosen based on test results to integrate the white junior high school; she is the only one whose parents allow her to attend. From the beginning, her driving ambition is to gain the job of Bell Ringer for the school, a post that must be earned through academic achievement. She suffers through an entire semester of antagonism from teachers and students before Gertie, a Jewish girl from New York who is blissfully (and improbably) unacquainted with residential segregation or racism, moves to town and befriends her. The two girls study together for the end-of-year test that will determine who becomes Bell Ringer. Throughout, Dawnie Rae pours into her diary her other hopes and desires, which include meeting Jackie Robinson and becoming a doctor so that she can research curative therapies for her autistic brother Goober. Goober's presence in the narrative also provides a reminder that school desegregation after the *Brown* decision was hardly inclusive; this aspect of the decision's implementation is not generally highlighted in consensus memory, but underlies the structure of the desegregation novel to varying extents.

Extending the School Story Tradition

The school story genre has several permutations, depending upon the era, nationality, and type of school setting. The foundation for many school story patterns is the British boarding-school story, stemming from popular nineteenth-century British novels about boys' boarding schools such as *Tom Brown's Schooldays*. The canonical plot arc generally follows a middle-class British boy, who is good natured and athletic but not terribly intellectual, as he enters a respected boarding school with certain traditions and rules to absorb. In his early years, he makes a couple of close friends (often at least one who is able to guide him through the unwritten codes of schoolboy society), looks up to the older boys, and learns the traditions of the school, including how to learn Latin without cheating, how to answer to school authority without tattling, and how to battle the school bully. In due course, he becomes a sixth form boy, distinguishes himself in sports, and graduates with his friends to love his *alma mater* and serve the British Empire at home or abroad. Education is primarily about learning patriotism and about gender and class socialization; Latin is necessary because it is a school tradition, but it is the cricket field and not the classroom that trains men for leadership and the work of empire.

The girls' story, as it emerged in Britain and the United States at the turn of the nineteenth century, kept the framework of a little microcosmic world within which children could have adventures and develop their characters away from family, but revised some of the boys' story traditions—for example, it de-emphasized the necessity of learning how to fist-fight a bully. Most importantly for the politics of the early girls' school stories, they made intellectual excitement and opportunity central to the protagonists' development rather than depicting them as a boring distraction from outdoor games.[10] During an era when higher education for women was both increasingly common and also bitterly contested, girls' school stories celebrated their temporary freedom to learn, to pursue their own interests, and to form passionate peer bonds. By the mid-twentieth century, American writers were developing new variations on the school story, including the teen drama or junior novel, the family story that featured school adventures, and the dark, Gothic version of the boarding school story, which critiqued the elitism and the conformity of American private schools.[11] Desegregation novels are imbued with some of the sunny nationalism prevalent in the early British boarding school stories, but they are also infused with some of the emphasis on intellectualism developed in the girls' school stories and the pedagogical critiques of later American stories. They sometimes reinforce school authority in the same ways that canonical school stories do, but they also train the critical gaze of the reader on the inside of the classroom in ways that are often avoided even in canonical girls' school stories.

Some elements generally cited as key to the canonical school story are clearly retained in desegregation stories. One of the most important of these is the contest against the bully. Desegregation novels portray violence and bullying as unjust, and racist attacks against the protagonists are condemned by trusted adult characters; nevertheless, the novels construct these attacks as part of an education in character and responsibility. Historically, students desegregating schools were constantly battling the violent attacks of their peers. Melba Patillo Beals, one of the Little Rock Nine, recalls a barrage of daily violence ranging from ink on her clothes to acid in her face. Beals records that she learned not to bring complaints to the teachers and principals because they remained largely indifferent or blamed her for inciting the violence, and she credits her bodyguard from the 101st Airborne Division with showing her how to protect herself. As the title of her memoir, *Warriors Don't Cry*, indicates, she and her compatriots did indeed undergo a toughening process, becoming hardened warriors rather than innocent schoolchildren; nevertheless, she does not celebrate this transformation, emphasizing her trauma more than her resilience.

In contrast, the protagonists of novels based on Beals' travails are portrayed as learning how to work through their anger in ways that make them successful. Mary Jane, for example, refuses extra help from her sympathetic French teacher, even though it is a bully in her French class that is causing her grade to suffer, because she fears that Miss Rousseau merely pities her. Instead, she spends her lonely lunch periods studying how to say "I hate my enemies" in French, thus effectively if somewhat perversely devoting her time to her academics. Pinkney's novel links violence to character building even more explicitly. After Dawnie Rae's good skirt is ruined by her hateful science lab partner, an act that is noticed but unpunished by the teacher, she writes in her diary,

> Theresa, I will not pour anything on you. I will not, 'cause I have a better plan. ... I intend to do well in Science. I intend to be a good student at Prettyman so that I can become a doctor. I will not let you stop me from reaching my dream. ... This letter should really be a thank-you note. To you, Theresa Ludlow. Thanks to you, DAWNIE RAE JOHNSON'S INTENTION is stronger than ever![12]

Variations of this passage occur throughout the novel, as Dawnie Rae processes her anger through constructive academic activities, writing in her diary and forming metacognitive resolutions.

Despite their similar emphasis on the academic potential embedded in school violence, the two novels frame this trope in ways that reflect different historical contexts and concerns about the success of desegregation. For Mary Jane, created by a hopeful white radical in the late 1950s, building academic skills and self-sufficiency is not enough. She must then learn how to trust worthy and sympathetic whites like Miss Rousseau and Sally, in order to accomplish the ultimate goal of social as well as academic integration. Sterling, however, was also aware that the success of desegregation was threatened by the racism perpetrated by teachers and parents as well as by peers, as she recorded in *Tender Warriors*; thus, she emphasizes that the responsibility for Mary Jane's character education is shared by the adults in the school. Mary Jane can only soften after she retaliates against one of Darlene's attacks and witnesses that Miss Rousseau disciplines them both equally. In contrast, as a character created after the cultural changes of the Black Power movement, Dawnie Rae is not required to let go of her anger at whites; she merely needs to find some productive channel for it. Her self-sufficiency is a much greater concern; Dawnie Rae's diary clearly participates in the "no excuses" rhetoric of the No Child Left Behind era, when desegregation is theoretically a solved problem, and gaps in educational opportunity can be attributed to personal "choices." Thus, Dawnie Rae's science teacher is notably absent from this diary entry as a person who might share Dawnie Rae's responsibility for her performance in class, and Prettyman

Coburn School is represented as a passive structure, a well-endowed vessel of learning from which Dawnie Rae has only to "intend" to drink.

In canonical boys' school stories, the protagonist's struggle to develop the independence, discipline, and fortitude to handle a bully on his own is part of the educational opportunity the school offers; it is part of how the school helps to form a bridge between the protected world of the family and the martial conflicts awaiting adult British men.[13] True, while *Tom Brown's Schooldays* celebrates fisticuffs as the proper business of school, desegregation stories instead depict violence as a betrayal of school values rather than as its proper business. At the same time, desegregation stories still wrest a positive outcome from the bullying in the supposedly sheltered world of the school. In some of the early desegregation stories, like *Call Me Charley* and *The Empty Schoolhouse*, extreme acts of violence and exclusion catalyze a change in white attitudes when nothing else seems to work, and they provide the ultimate test of dedication and mettle for the black protagonists. In other novels, violence seems to give black protagonists the tools to succeed in a largely white world. Significantly, these tools are academic as well as emotional, so that even the brutality of the white-dominated school renders it a superior academic opportunity. In the process, the school's authority as an institution is reinforced, even if the authority of individual adults in the school is questionable. As in the canonical stories, the violent school is upheld as a worthy and noble tradition that confers not only legitimacy but also pride onto its graduates; Dawnie Rae longs to ring the bell that calls her racist classmates and teachers to school every morning, and Mary Jane is overjoyed to attend the kinds of athletic events that were sources of fear for Beals and her companions. The protagonists' school pride further serves as a bridge to their participation in nation building, just as Tom Brown and his classmates advanced the imperial expansion of Britain.

The desegregation story, however, also bends the school story genre in order to critique the school institution. One of the most notable differences is that the black protagonist of the desegregation story *must* be intellectually talented and ambitious in order to enter the white system, rather than being an unremarkable "everyboy." Like the handling of violence, this revision partly confirms the authority of the white-dominated school; Dawnie Rae, Liz, and Mary Jane's ambition prompt them to seek entry into the best school, which is of course the white one, and their intellectual ability renders them worthy of an "equal" chance at superior opportunity. Nevertheless, this revision of the canonical school story also subtly critiques the white school system. While segregated white schools are portrayed as preferable to black schools, they are also seen as unsatisfactory to smart white girls. Sally and Marlee both crave the company of intellectual equals until Mary Jane and Liz enter and provide some of the intellectual capital the "superior" white school has been missing.

A second, related difference is that while extracurricular social life is far more visible in canonical school and teen novels than classroom activities, the reverse is often true in desegregation stories. In the *Anne of Green Gables* series, for example, the reader is given to understand that Anne learns a great deal, earning a scholarship and receiving a B.A. from Redmond, yet we rarely see the inside of the classroom. Anne's extracurricular activities tend to involve poetry recitations and dramatic play in the woods rather than cricket, but they are still more central to the plot than her algebra lessons, which we see her sighing over without seeing the thing itself. In contrast, a major problem for the protagonist of the desegregation story is often that he or she is barred or at least discouraged from participating in sports and clubs, so that time spent in the classroom becomes correspondingly more central. As Mavis Reimer points out, the traditional school story maintained the mystical authority of the institution in part through the invisibility of the adults in the story. Paradoxically, the invisibility and relative unimportance of the classroom could also shore up the mythology that superior educational opportunities were offered there, in part because classroom practices were rarely exposed to the reader's view.

Desegregation stories have the potential to complicate this myth. Thus, while Dawnie Rae continues to affirm that Prettyman School is giving her a better preparation for a medical career than Mary MacLeod Bethune School would have done, she also records pointless, nitpicking English lessons in which she is asked (ironically) to regurgitate the *exact* definition of a synonym, in contrast to more inspiring lessons at Bethune in which students create presentations about notable black heroes. Similarly, Mary Jane enters Wilson believing that she will get a first-rate science education there, and finds a sympathetic haven in Mr. Stiller's science classroom. What she finds is that Mr. Stiller's assigned experiments all have pre-determined outcomes and thus are not particularly scientifically engaging or useful. Parodically lousy lessons certainly abound in earlier school stories for both boys and girls. In contemporary desegregation stories like Sterling's, however, they have more potential to dismantle the rationale for the violence the students undergo; and in historical fiction like Pinkney's, they have the potential to disrupt a consensus memory of desegregation that remembers black schooling as inferior and black students as lucky to be extended the benefits of white education.

Finally, the correspondence between the protected juvenile world of the school and the broader national arena that awaits after graduation is more fraught in the desegregation story than in the traditional school story. In British boarding school stories, the cricket field is direct preparation for the Great Game of imperial conflict, while in desegregation stories, the protagonists' parents frequently lose their jobs as a grim reminder that the character-building struggle to integrate the school may be rewarded with unemployment and poverty both before and after graduation. Reimer suggests that school stories featuring racially marked protagonists tend to present the school, not as an allegory for the wider world, but instead as a force for change, so that the changes within the "little world" of school expand into the adult world after graduation as the schoolchildren carry reform out with them.[14] Desegregation stories, however, also function within the contexts of Cold War propaganda and the multicultural curriculum, so that the influence of school upon nation is reversed; the school prepares students to do the work of a desegregated nation, true, but it is implicitly the greatness of the utopian democratic nation that enables the desegregation of the school.

Cold Warriors and Classroom Practice

British boarding school stories and their American Gothic counterparts are often told against the backdrop of war, the adult nationalist citizenship role for which students are preparing. The *Brown* decision, and its subsequent implementation, took place within the context of the Cold War; and indeed, historian Mary Dudziak argues that without the pressure of the Cold War, desegregation might not have occurred even to the limited extent that it did. In a war of ideas against the Soviets, with both sides seeking to influence newly decolonized nations in Africa, the Caribbean, and Southeast Asia, the United States' treatment of its nonwhite citizens at home was seen as an indication of how it would be likely to treat nonwhite nations under its sway. The *Brown* decision, and Eisenhower's 1957 intervention in the Little Rock crisis, were thus used as propaganda tools to demonstrate the nation's commitment to justice, its willingness to openly discuss and heal its flaws, and its use of federal force for the protection of its most vulnerable citizens. As in earlier school stories, the structure of war is also seen to shape the pedagogy and nationalist training of budding soldiers. And indeed, the Cold War did affect pedagogy. Most notably, the Soviets' 1957 launching of *Sputnik* crystallized already existing anxiety over the quality of math and science education in American schools. The following year, Eisenhower passed the National Defense Education Act, channeling federal money to schools solely in order to improve the areas judged most necessary to Cold War national security: math, science, and foreign language education (even for girls, who had traditionally been excluded from math and science fields). The impetus to beef up American national security through the schools was also reflected in a push toward stricter, more traditionally authoritative teaching, as the Progressive, child-centered philosophies of the 1930s and '40s were increasingly dismissed as overly soft and feminine.[15] Depictions of such pedagogical changes, often portrayed in desegregation novels, reflect the genre's connection to utopian educational philosophy as well as to Civil Rights memory.

The Cold War backdrop of desegregation novels tends to reinforce the idea that the United States offers an ideal of prosperous equality, even if this ideal is not yet realized. Indeed, because the nation is falling short of its ideals, the stakes of a successful ending for desegregation stories are dramatically high. This was clearly the case in the decade immediately following the *Brown* decision, when information about desegregation was being managed and edited for international consumption; thus, in contemporary novels like *Mary Jane*, the backdrop of the Cold War is evident in the kinds of characteristic violent events that were edited out of the narrative before its publication. The stakes of successful desegregation stories are different in more recent historical novels like *The Lions of Little Rock*, published after the end of the Cold War. Nevertheless, as Raiford and Romano point out, the nation has an interest in managing historical memory, even when wars and conflicts are over, and memories of the Civil Rights movement continue to be used for nation building and consensus building projects.[16] Later novels need not censor violence in the same way as earlier ones, but despite this historical distance, they reflect less criticism of mid-century pedagogy or of U.S. participation in the Cold War than one might expect. Despite the variation in historical context, therefore, the structure of the school story shadowed by war establishes a common vehicle that upholds the public, state-sponsored school and its meritocratic, teacher-centered pedagogy.

Images of desegregation were tightly managed in the years following 1954, in ways that seem to have affected at least some desegregation novels. In some novels, only oblique signs of pressure are evident. Graham's *South Town*, for example, encountered resistance from publishers and librarians, and his earlier children's books set in Liberia (inspired by his experience as a teacher there) were also rejected by several publishers; his characters were considered inauthentic, too much like white people in their speech, in a political climate that tied anti-racist activity to Communism.[17] In later books in the *Town* series, the protagonist David explicitly reiterates his American loyalties on the football field and then at the much more troubling scene of an urban uprising. *Mary Jane* provides a much more direct example of the pressures the Cold War exerted upon desegregation novels. *Tender Warriors*, Sterling's 1958 collection of photographs and interviews with students in newly desegregating schools, went quickly out of print in part because it was disapproved for export and refused for the Informational Media Guaranty Program that would have made it lucrative for sale abroad. *Tender Warriors* includes blunt statements from children about being pelted with books and eggs and threatened with knives, nooses, and ice picks. It ends with a condemnation of continuing adult interference, racist teaching, and the exclusion of black students from extracurricular activities. *Mary Jane*, which was published in seven European countries, presents only selective information from these interviews. Mary Jane and Fred are permitted to join extracurricular activities, which Sterling knew very well was unrepresentative if not inaccurate, and the violence they encounter is mostly verbal, with occasional episodes of being tripped in aisles and hallways.

In a speech to educators, Sterling openly questioned her decision to censor *Mary Jane*:

> When you begin to write the truth, you bump into all sorts of obstacles. Consider the rule of the happy or at least upbeat ending. Should we tell children that in real life people do not always live happily ever after? I faced this problem in *Mary Jane* and didn't really solve it properly. I compromised by letting her make one friend in school and ending with the hope that she would make more next year. When the book was published, the bright, warmhearted little girl who lives next door asked, "Is it really that bad?" "Much worse," I answered. "Why, today's paper tells about the bombing of the home of an eight-year-old boy because he went to a 'white' school." "Oh, don't tell me about it!" she said and ran home. Should she be told? I think so.[18]

Sterling emphasizes not only that publishers and federal agencies pressure authors to present falsely innocent stories to children, but also that such cumulative pressure has destructive consequences. Her young neighbor has been so conditioned not to expect disturbing information that she seems likely to grow into an adult who refuses to hear or to acknowledge it. Nevertheless, in this speech as in *Mary Jane*, Sterling frames her blistering critiques of white supremacy as serving the ultimate good of the nation. She asks, "Increasingly isolated from their darker contemporaries, how well are these white children being prepared for the larger adult world in which they are globally a minority?"[19] She thus makes the case that open and democratic airing of the nation's sins will ultimately prepare white children to function as part of a better, more fulfilled American democracy abroad—just as Dudziak demonstrates the Cold War propagandists argued.

Sterling's ambivalence about tempering violence in *Mary Jane* only obliquely translates to her portrayal of the Cold War classroom, which emphasizes the educational success of desegregation. The two teachers who appear most often in the text are also those who treat Mary Jane fairly: her foreign language teacher Miss Rousseau and her science teacher Mr. Stiller. These subjects, not coincidentally, are two of the areas identified as necessary for national security and resource building, and they are also places where Sterling can suggest her own more radical utopian goals for desegregated education. The fiery Miss Rousseau is named for a philosopher whose work on political liberties and republican education influenced the French Revolution, and she teaches Mary Jane a language spoken in many decolonizing nations of Africa. Science, too, had a special valence for radical Leftists as well as for conservative education critics. Julia Mickenberg notes that Leftist and Marxist children's authors, including Sterling (who wrote science picture books as well as novels and black history books), believed that the principles of rational scientific reasoning could empower children to look critically and dispassionately at social problems and to embrace change as an inevitable part of life, including antiracist social change. And yet, as Mickenberg also emphasizes, science books were solicited and distributed precisely because they "fit into a larger educational, military, and corporate scheme."[20]

Mary Jane's founding of the science club is thus a highlight of the book, demonstrating how she confers benefits upon the school as well as receiving them. In the process, however, utopian classroom models are sacrificed to the needs of the desegregated national institution. In fact, Mary Jane comes to school already fairly knowledgeable in science because her grandfather is a distinguished biologist known for his work on agriculture and conservation. During her summers on his farm, she learns an approach to science that involves open-minded experimentation and appreciation for natural cycles; for example, Grampa feeds the weeds in his garden, having discovered ways to extract rubber and oil from the wild plants other farmers see as useless, and he allows the presence of garden pests that have a valid place in the larger ecosystem. In contrast, at Wilson High, Mary Jane and Sally follow steps set out in a textbook for experiments with predetermined, predictable ends. Grampa's farm teems with all kinds of animals, both tame and wild, but Mr. Stiller's science classroom cannot accommodate the girls' half-wild, unpredictable squirrel Furry. In the end, the girls must substitute their care of Furry, whose injury brought them together and prompted them to observe veterinary care, feeding, and animal behavior, for controlled experiments in which they train white mice to run through a maze.

In some ways, this experiment seems to validate Sterling's faith that science education can address social problems like racism. The girls are aided in their project by Randall, an avid science enthusiast who stares at Mary Jane, like a dispassionate scientist observing an unfamiliar specimen. Despite this rudeness, his rational approach leads him to accept and even welcome Mary Jane's presence, as he shares his resources with the girls and helps them build their maze. When the girls realize that winning the science fair will force the newspaper to print a photo of interracial friendship on the front page, it is Randall who suggests that they post a big sign above their experiment reading, "IF WHITE MICE CAN LEARN, SO CAN YOU."[21] The other white students in the Science Club laugh; they, like the white mice, have already learned to overcome their fear and confusion in response to change. The novel closes with a contained utopia of rational scientists democratically overcoming racial prejudice in the classroom; nevertheless, running white mice through a maze to fetch a treat is a troubling metaphor for successful classroom education.[22] In order for Mary Jane to train white mice (and white scientists) in the service of her country, the novel not only leaves behind Grampa's wild Nature's Classroom, it also celebrates this substitution as a successful experiment, reassuring anxious domestic audiences that desegregation will support the educational front of the Cold War. A similar pattern is evident in the earlier novel *Call Me Charley*. Charley's engineering prowess contributes to a proposal to benefit the town, and also convinces a racist neighbor boy to trust his own observations rather than his father's second-hand bigoted assumptions; at the same time, Charley's seat in a desk in the front of a class in which students are seated according to their current grade averages is highlighted in the novel as meritocratic teaching, making it easy for all observers to see when Charley does well and when he slips.

Historical novelists do not face the same kinds of publishing pressures as Sterling and Graham did. Pinkney, for example, is able to depict the kind of classroom violence that was excised from *Mary Jane*. Historical desegregation stories do not, however, generally take this license from explicit censorship to interrogate the U.S. participation in the Cold War or its pedagogical philosophies. Instead, they tend to uphold the notion that a meritocratic approach, weeding out the racist and the underperforming, was a fitting weapon in the war against historical racism.

This pattern is most clearly evident in *The Lions of Little Rock*, which is an unusual desegregation novel in that it very directly discusses the Cold War's competing rhetorics of post-Sputnik anxiety and segregationist anti-Communism. Marlee watches Governor Faubus on television declaring the desegregation of Little Rock's Central High to be a Communist plot, and at the same time recalls her teacher's injunction for more students to study math to fight the Communists. She is blunt about her observations in a way that Sterling's novel only hints at:

> When our teacher told us last year that our country needs more of us to study math, I think she meant more boys. I watched all those talks on TV about the satellite really closely, and I didn't see any experts who were women.[23]

Later, when she learns that Liz's mother is also a math whiz, she realizes that she has seen no black science experts, either. This conclusively establishes for young readers that both segregation and sexism were holding the nation back in its war against Communism. As Marlee learns to separate false anti-Communist, anti-integration rhetoric from the more pressing wider war of the Space Race, so too does the reader learn that school desegregation and rigorous pedagogy were positioned as tools for both national idealism and national security. Despite the novel's distance from its events, however, the overall goals of the Cold War are never questioned, in the way that many historical novels do question the Vietnam War. No mention is made of the fact that American Communists were, in fact, quite active in the fight against segregation. Nor is the worthiness of American scientific supremacy ever interrogated; despite the many references to the satellites and spaceships Marlee will build, there is not a single mention of a nuclear weapon. Her father is fired by the state for his participation in an interracial organization, but the House Un-American Activities Committee is completely absent from her family's conversations, even those in which her father educates her about the complexities of current events. Instead, the structure of the desegregation story preserves the framework of a valid war that gives meaning to the school enterprise in general, and to the success of Civil Rights victories in particular.

To Levine's credit, she avoids a celebratory ending, qualifying the sense of victory the readers can feel. Marlee realizes at the end that after exhausting and anxious months of activism, only five black students are allowed to attend white schools, and only at the high school level. As in *Mary Jane*, much of the sense of hope and progress the reader feels comes from the scenes in the classroom. The classroom is clearly much improved for Marlee when it is desegregated by Liz, but the bracing pedagogy she experiences also helps her to grow into the kind of anti-racist, feminist math star her country needs. Mr. Harding, her new young math teacher, injects some needed academic rigor into Marlee's flabby American math education. Mr. Harding's class is portrayed as an accessible meritocracy; Marlee immediately notices that he calls on the girls as often as the boys (she counts). When she avoids the cafeteria after Liz's departure, he eagerly adopts her as his protégée and teaches her high school algebra during lunch, a kind of intellectual nurturing she clearly craves. In the meantime, Marlee's tall, athletic crush JT, who barely knows his times tables, has finagled her into doing his math homework for him so that he won't have to repeat seventh grade. Strangely, despite his obvious enthusiasm and strong work ethic, Mr. Harding at no point offers the struggling JT extra help. His spare time is reserved for Marlee, who deserves it due to her natural ability.

As Andrew Hartman argues, the meritocratic division of educational resources was called for in the years after Sputnik as the best way to address the perceived mediocrity of American schools. Even at the time, this approach was criticized as legitimizing inequality and leading to the exclusion of "inferior" students, setting up citizenship status as a competition rather than a birthright.[24] In the decade leading up to the publication of Levine's book, however, some policymakers have expressed concern about a perceived "excellence gap," fearing that with more attention given to students who are "left behind," fewer resources are available for students who might advance both themselves and the nation.[25] In a similar vein, educational critics like Amanda Ripley have raised alarms about American youths' poor educational performance, and low standards, in comparison to other nations struggling with economic and social diversity. In this climate, Levine's matter-of-fact depiction of Mr. Harding's devotion to Marlee at the expense of JT gestures not only to Cold War-era beliefs about meritocracy, but to present-day anxieties about the perceived loss of such classroom meritocracies, and to the relevance of historical desegregation novels that emphasize them.

Other historical novels, such as Pinkney's and Watt's, celebrate the competitive, meritocratic classroom. In addition, they tend to soften their portrayals of Cold War pedagogy, depicting antiracist reforms as occurring alongside ample classroom opportunities for racially mixed groups of students to work together. In *Mary Jane*, the *Town* books, and *Call Me Charley*, students sit in rows and demonstrate their knowledge when the teacher asks them questions. In *Kizzy Ann Stamps* and *The Lions of Little Rock*, students do group work, and in *With the Might of Angels*, they have open-ended discussions in history class. Contemporary readers of Sterling's, Graham's, and Jackson's books may well have experienced these pedagogical methods, but such methods are not often depicted in contemporary novels. In historical novels, they are commonplace. It is through these group activities and discussions that students begin to soften toward each other, so that in the historical novels, progress toward American nationalist goals is imagined not only through an historical legal decision, but also through the lens of an educational philosophy that combines an admiration for tough meritocracy with an acknowledgment of recent student-centered methods. In the process, American participation in the Cold War is softened. Indeed, in Levine's novel, JT's racist, violent brother Red is sent to the Army in order to remove him from the character's lives and make their community safer. The novel does not mention that, given the era, Red would likely be deployed to countries in Southeast Asia, South American, and Africa, ostensibly to protect people he viciously hates from Communism by engaging in violent conflicts.

Romantic Friendships and White Desires

Much segregationist resistance to *Brown* crystallized around fears of interracial dating and sex. In response, many black students who participated in integration argued that their desires were solely educational and not social—a plausible claim, considering the formidable loneliness they were prepared to endure in order to desegregate hostile schools. Footage of Ernest Green shows him telling a group of white students that he does not attend school to socialize.[26] James Baldwin, asking the mother of another student why she has chosen to have her son attend the white school, quotes her as saying,

> "Well, it's not because I'm so anxious to have him around white people." Then she laughed. "I really don't know how I'd feel if I was to

> carry a white baby around who was calling me Grandma.... White people say," the mother went on, "that that's all a Negro wants. I don't think they believe that themselves."[27]

At the same time, many activists, both black and white, argued that the situation for white students was different; they *ought* to be coming to school to socialize with black students, and the knowledge of their own racism and privilege they might gain through interracial conversation would further American education more than any shiny new textbooks might.[28]

Children's literature in general, and historical fiction in particular, tends to heavily censor representations of sexual desire.[29] For this reason, desegregation stories would seem to offer an ideal combination of the denial of interracial desire on the one hand, and the need for interracial emotional connections on the other. Girls and boys form same-sex friendships across interracial lines that often provide the emotional core of the narrative and the happy ending of the successful desegregation story. Once the special friendship is formed, both black and white protagonists feel more at home in the school, and consequently benefit more from their education. These relationships are never openly queer; as Kathryn Bond Stockton observes, children are compelled either to be asexual or to be budding heterosexuals, so that the same-sex friendships in these novels can be read as attempts to avoid confronting the possibility that students attending desegregated schools might want to date each other.

Nevertheless, even before the recent advent of more explicit "problem novels" and coming-out stories for gay teens, school stories widely read by both boys and girls were always charged with homoeroticism through the portrayal of special chumships. In girls' stories, literary critics and historians have pointed out that these friendships have functioned politically to construct the girls' school as a place where girls and women might avoid the constraints of heterosexual marriage and housekeeping and instead grow and develop intellectually with a community of like minds. The connection between education and same-sex love is not coincidental, but mutually constitutive. Lillian Faderman suggests that women who loved other women sometimes chose higher education precisely because that path would lead to a career, ruling out marriage and legitimizing the life choice to form a household with another career woman. Conversely, Diana Fuss suggests that desire moves through "channels of group identification," so that sharing a teacher's passion for learning also opens up passions for the teacher herself and for the other students who share the same goals and enthusiasms.[30] A successful education—one that awakens intellectual desires—will inevitably awaken sexual desires as well.

Romantic friendships in girls' desegregation stories sometimes function similarly to establish a politically contentious institution as an idyll;

the fearsome desegregated school, like the suspect girls' college, is represented as a haven for shared intellectual excitement, which both nurtures and naturalizes the friendships formed under its roof. Nevertheless, the desegregation story also alters this trope. Whereas the school in the earlier girls' stories enables alternate lifestyles and loves for the women under its roof, the school in the desegregation story instead tames and domesticates the more radical desires and alternatives it stimulates. Furthermore, the structural power imbalance between black girls and white ones in desegregation stories alters the trope of the romantic friendship. In white-authored stories, the romantic friendship seems much the same as it does in the earlier girls' school narratives, in which passion is fully reciprocal. In black-authored novels, however, the white girl is portrayed as far more desirous and invested than her black friend. Baldwin's interviewee says that whites don't even believe their own rhetoric about black desire. Desegregation stories open this statement up further, suggesting that white liberal protagonists' desires go beyond a simple wish to diffuse fear and misunderstanding. These characters also want to imagine that their own desire for black contact is reciprocated.

Kathryn Bond Stockton observes that proto-lesbian children are often paired with dogs, suggesting that "animal/child affectionate bondings can offer opportunities ... for children's motions inside their delay, making delay a sideways growth the child in part controls for herself, in ways confounding her parents and her future."[31] In both Sterling's and Levine's novels, animal/child bonds not only facilitate queer interracial loves and help the protagonists to alter the national future, they also function to make school seem the "natural" place for these "natural" interests. Nevertheless, these animal bonds are not with dogs, as are the relationships Stockton discusses, but with wild and potentially destructive animals that the children cannot control. Moreover, while Stockton cites animal care as one form of delay, school is famously another form of childhood delay, one that is controlled (tenuously) by adults and by institutional traditions. In girls' school literature as described by Fuss and Faderman, girls use *voluntary* school attendance as Stockton's lesbian children use their dogs. In Sterling's and Levine's novels, *compulsory* school attendance reinforces heterosexual delay, but also tames dangerously unpredictable interracial loves.

In *Mary Jane*, it is Furry, and not academic excitement in the classroom, that brings Mary Jane and Sally together. In fact, it is their joint effort to care for Furry that leads to the discovery of their shared interest in biology, and not the other way around. Although it is Mary Jane who rescues Furry from bullying boys and splints his leg, Sally quickly assumes equal responsibility for his care, defying the racist Mothers' League that she had previously been afraid to confront. After the Mothers' League protests Furry's being used as the school mascot, Mr. Stiller ejects him from the Science Room where he had been allowed to convalesce. Mary Jane asserts that she will return to Grampa's farm and take Furry with her, leaving Wilson altogether, but Sally insists that Furry is a shared problem. From this point on, the goal of the novel becomes, not for Furry to have a home (which he eventually finds), but for the girls to have a home *in the school*; ejecting Furry might have driven Mary Jane back to the segregated system and scored a victory for the Mothers' League, but Sally's assumption of shared responsibility renders Furry a subject of interracial concern who cannot be properly cared for under segregation.

As a result, Mary Jane and Sally infiltrate the school with Furry, as an illicit black-white-animal threesome, hiding during lunch and after hours in a backstage dressing room and pretending to be outlaws for justice and equality, like Robin Hood. They jointly furnish the room with comforts and treats, so that Sally says,

> It's like this is our home, yours and Furry's and mine ... I mean, everybody's against the three of us being together. Your mother, I don't think she really wants me to come to your house, and mine –.[32]

This outlaw school "home" is where they discover that they both like biographies and folk songs, where they envision their future lives as a biologist and a doctor who will live together on an animal farm, and where they discuss the problems of racial prejudice. Their cozy extra-curricular idyll functions much as the earlier girls' school story friendships did; as critic Deyonne Bryant notes, it is both "puppy love" and also meant "to establish the black girl's budding feminist identity and reinforce the idea that girls could and should pursue educational opportunities and careers established traditionally for men."[33] The language of "home" and family resonates not only with queer love, but also with the language of antiracist activism during the early Civil Rights movement. Historian Phyllis Palmer observes that the activists who ran interracial Brotherhood Camps encouraged the formation of intense emotional bonds, believing that only when interracial friends thought of each other as family would they be willing to defend each other against slurs and injustices. Similarly, this section of the novel establishes a utopian vision of what the school ought to be—an intellectually charged, homelike place where the natural bonds between black girls and white girls and the animals they love can be nurtured and thrive. In the literal sense, the school already is this place, since the girls have no other space in their heavily segregated town to sit together and talk. Nevertheless, their outlaw status cannot continue, as Furry grows increasingly restive. In moving their friendship from the margins of the school to the center, the school benefits both intellectually and socially, and so, in a sense, do the girls; however, their bond with Furry cannot survive this move, and neither can their exclusivity.

The mechanism for transforming the girls from outlaws to legitimate friends is the Junior Science Club, which Mr. Stiller helps them to start explicitly as a way for them to spend time together without getting in trouble. As it turns out, a number of other alienated students share their intellectual interests, so that their social and academic worlds expand while the school is able to offer more academic rigor in a much-needed area. At the same time, Furry is exiled to Grampa's farm, where Sally is not allowed to visit, and the Science Club and the tame white mice that replace their outlaw home are clearly a second-best solution. Legitimizing interracial friendship within school walls, like learning science in school, comes at a price, as the girls substitute participation in the more regimented science club for what they really want, which is open and flexible time to spend time together with Furry. Like the ending of the novel, this solution to the girls' problems echoes Sterling's stated ambivalence about desegregation. On the one hand, she deeply desires it, and on the other, she recognizes that it has not sufficiently addressed the deep-seated problem of racism. In *Mary Jane*, thus, the school is the starting point for interracial conversation and friendship, but it also fails to sufficiently sustain and support the specific kind of interracial relationships needed, promoting tame contact instead of the kind of loving, passionate family Sally and Mary Jane want.

In *The Lions of Little Rock*, the girls' trajectory is the opposite. They are exiles moving to the margins of the school, rather than outlaws being incorporated. It is in the portrayal of their friendship that Levine betrays ambivalence about the school as a utopia. Marlee and Liz do form a friendship through a classroom project, pairing up for an Arkansas history presentation. Liz diversifies the curriculum, even when she is passing as white, suggesting that they research the Quapaw tribe rather than the colonial white history of Arkansas. The two girls meet at the zoo so that Marlee can practice giving her presentation to the animals, and Marlee recognizes her affinity with Liz when they talk about how they both like to listen to the lions roaring at night. She has already identified with the lions, telling the reader that she imagines what it might be like to "just yell out whatever I was thinking or feeling and not care one whit who heard.... But by the time I wake up in the morning, the lions are always silent, and so am I."[34] Throughout, the lions reflect the girls' friendship, and facilitate their bond. After Liz has been exposed and their friendship forbidden, they "accidentally" meet sometimes in front of the lion cage on Tuesday afternoons, having just happened to visit the zoo at the same time. When Liz ends their friendship due to a bomb threat, the girls meet one last time on the bench in front of the cages. In this scene, the lions themselves are never even mentioned, and their disappearance as a shared concern reflects the erasure of the girls' special bond. And finally, after Marlee has effectively lost Liz, but gained her voice, she conquers her fear of the high dive at the still segregated pool by pretending that Liz and her family's black maid are at the pool with her; after she jumps, she hears the lions roaring, in an imagined scene of desired communion. Thus, Levine's novel both illustrates the American school's distance from the earlier utopian girls' colleges, which bring smart (white) girls together in a way that segregated schools cannot, and also reinforces the ideal of the school as a place where that kind of intellectual bond might happen.

In both of these novels, the desire for access to white education begins the desegregation story, but what sustains desegregation efforts through obstacles and violence is the desire to preserve the nurturing power of an interracial friendship. Pinkney's novel comments upon this trope by presenting it in a very different way. Dawnie Rae and Gertie are, according to form, both smart and ambitious girls who question gender norms as well as racial barriers. In contrast to the other pairs, who concoct elaborate plots in order to be together and who share stimulating conversations about their self-directed academic interests, Dawnie Rae's friendship with Gertie is quite lukewarm both intellectually and emotionally. Dawnie writes often in her diary about her dream of becoming a doctor, and Gertie intrigues her in part because she has witnessed black accomplishments that Dawnie herself would like to see; Gertie has seen Jackie Robinson play in Brooklyn, and she has met black doctors, talking of these things in a way that seems to make Dawnie's dreams real and reachable. Yet Dawnie never records any conversations in which she and Gertie actually discuss their aspirations. The two girls study together for the single comprehensive year-end test that will determine their classroom jobs for the following year, but outside of baseball, they never spontaneously share their interests with each other in the way that Sally and Mary Jane discover each other's enthusiasm for animals or Liz and Marlee explore math and Quapaw Indian culture together. Their intellectual partnership is governed and overshadowed by a high-stakes examination. After Gertie gives the Bell Ringer job to Dawnie, she writes in her diary, "Gertie Feldman will be my true good friend for a long time," but this is the most affectionate statement she ever makes.[35] It is a far cry from the longing expressed by Marlee or the cozy family romance shared by Mary Jane and Sally. Despite Dawnie Rae's liking for Gertie, she never invites her over or wishes to have more time with her. Gertie, in contrast, is continually making overtures to Dawnie Rae, offering her candy and finally even her coveted Bell Ringer job.

A number of black writers commenting on the legacy of segregation and racism note that whites often perceive reciprocal friendship and open dialogue where there is, in fact, suspicion and suppression. James Baldwin writes in 1965 that

> a great deal of one's energy is expended in reassuring white Americans that they do not see what they see.... What they see is a disastrous,

> continuing, present condition which menaces them, and for which they bear an inescapable responsibility. But since in the main they seem to lack the energy to change this condition they would rather not be reminded of it.[36]

In Sterling's and Levine's novels, as in other white-authored novels like Jeri Watt's *Kizzy Ann Stamps* and Natalie Carlson's *The Empty Schoolhouse*, friendships may go through periods of suspicion and white avoidance of responsibility, but white characters are capable of correcting their ignorance and learning to change conditions of racial injustice. These narratives imagine that interracial friendship will inevitably produce honest dialogue, and that such dialogue will result in healing on the one side and forgiveness on the other. This vision, in fact, is one of the utopian desires that drive these novels. In contrast, black novelists writing about school desegregation have consistently chronicled uneven dialogue between interracial friends. Lorenz Graham's *North Town* (1965) and *Whose Town?* (1969), Mildred Pitts Walter's *Girl on the Outside* (1982), and Patricia McKissack's *A Friendship, for Today* (2007) vary widely in their publication dates; but all depict interracial relationships in which whites are somewhat needier than their black counterparts, and in which blacks accept white overtures of friendship with a certain degree of coolness and distance—as necessary to surviving desegregation gracefully, but, McKissack's title indicates, as temporary, for "today." Pinkney's novel offers a very clear example of this alternate view of how interracial friendship can be driven, not by the desire for dialogue, but the desire for consumption.

In her study *Racial Indigestion*, Kyla Wazana Tompkins argues that the white body politic in the United States is in part constructed through fantasies of edible nonwhite subjects, which are desired, consumed, and digested by white citizens. She also, however, traces strategies of resistance. For example, mouths are used for talking as well as for eating, and scenes of eating are also comic scenes of sociality in which class, race, and even species boundaries are often upended and inverted. "Sauciness" from a black subject, then, becomes one way in which black subjects "feed" white ones ideas they do not want to consume and statements they find hard to digest.[37] Tompkins focuses on the nineteenth century, but her formulations of consumption and dialogue are useful for thinking about the dynamics of romantic friendship in desegregation stories. Not only are these narratives saturated with white desire for healing and well-being through communion with a black subject, they often feature scenes of interracial eating as a way to emphasize how the friendship upends well-established racial taboos that prevent black and white subjects even from mingling the food that enters their bodies.

In their handling of this trope, the three novels differ markedly. In *Mary Jane*, scenes with Mary Jane and Sally are almost entirely dominated by dialogue. The two sip soda together and eat in the school cafeteria, but sharing food is secondary to sharing talk. Bodily mingling is not entirely metaphysical, but it is envisioned as elevating and as equal—in one of their conversations, Mary Jane puts her brown arm against Sally's pink one and tells her about a family genealogy of black, Indian, and white ancestry. It is Mary Jane who directs the conversation here, looking at two different skin colors and conjuring up a history of racial mingling with her words. In *The Lions of Little Rock*, Marlee imagines that every person she meets is a kind of drink—those she finds easy to talk to are milk, juice, or soda, and those who make her nervous are coffee or tea. People exist for her to consume, or not, as she chooses. Her friendship with Liz, however, corrects this tendency somewhat. Marlee cannot identify Liz as a drink, so instead of a food to be consumed, Liz becomes a talking partner who openly chides Marlee for "forcing [people] into one cup."[38] In Tompkins' formulation, Liz is "saucy" and does not go down easily. Nevertheless, Marlee ingests her sauciness and absorbs it, becoming more and more saucy herself as Liz becomes more and more controlled.

Dawnie Rae's diary, in contrast, is dominated throughout by descriptions of food and hunger, rather than dialogue. Despite her having ample food, her diary reveals her as constantly hungry. She gets double the food anyone else in the school cafeteria does, courtesy of the black lunch ladies, but does not enjoy eating it all alone; and when her father is fired from the dairy company for sending her to the white school, the entire black community boycotts dairy products and Dawnie Rae fills pages of her diary with her longing for milk, butter, and cream. Furthermore, she understands that she is being consumed by the same people who refuse even indirect bodily contact with her. Her mother pays money to a white store to buy Dawnie Rae a dress labeled "Peach Melba" which she is not allowed to put on her body in the store and which does not fit her. Later, she and her mother bake non-dairy cookies to raise money for the new school bell, which she bitterly reflects she will not be allowed to ring. She may have successfully gotten white students to eat food adapted from a boycott of white goods, but she is still feeding white mouths and raising money for the benefit of white students, who will get a symbolic new bell while the students at Bethune lack books.

If Dawnie is consumed and hungry, Gertie is a voracious eater who observes no boundaries in either her choice of food or eating companions. When she sees Dawnie Rae's overflowing cafeteria plate, she demands the extra portions that Dawnie Rae gets, and then plunks herself down next to Dawnie in the cafeteria. Gertie claims both black and white food cultures as a matter of course, provided that they involve privilege and not deprivation. In addition to claiming the extra portions of food Dawnie receives due to the black lunch ladies' support, Gertie also sees her empty cafeteria table as an expansive space all for herself and Dawnie, a gain of property rather than a loss of companionship. On the one hand, this attitude indicates Gertie's extreme racial innocence, as it does not even occur to her that Dawnie is being ostracized and that she, Gertie, will be so too if she sits with Dawnie.[39] On the other hand, her transcendence of racial boundaries is predicated on her being able to consume whatever Dawnie has, *and* whatever the white students get. While eating her extra portion and chatting with Dawnie about Jackie Robinson, Gertie slurps chocolate milk, a drink that the lunch ladies will not even put on Dawnie's tray lest she be tempted to break the boycott. Her innocence of racial boundaries and taboos thus does not manifest as a politically motivated selection of nourishment, but only as an extension of resources. To be fair, Gertie does feed Dawnie Rae in return, both with food and with company; her pockets are always filled with licorice and gumdrops that she shares liberally. Nevertheless, Dawnie Rae's constant evocations of being hungry and being an edible product for white consumption highlight the extent to which Gertie's racial innocence prevents her from being an equal partner in dialogue and simply renders her another kind of white consumer.

Dawnie Rae, as a heroine in an extremely lucrative history series, is the subject of another kind of consumption, too. Hazel Carby points out that black female characters have become commodities in texts for the school market, and worries that "for white suburbia ... these texts are becoming a way of gaining knowledge of the 'other,' a knowledge that appears to satisfy and replace the desire to overcome existing frameworks of desegregation."[40] Pinkney works within this framework, both offering a black female subject for consumption and also shaping her in ways that comment upon this process. In addition to authoring several novels, picture books, and biographies featuring black characters, Pinkney has had an extremely influential career in the children's book publishing industry. She founded the first imprint for African-American children's books at a major publishing house, Jump At the Sun for Disney's Hyperion books; and after fuming in the early 1980s that there were too few materials available for black children, she has been instrumental in acquiring and editing a wide range of black-authored children's books for the imprint.[41] The black female literary subjects Pinkney collaborates in producing are clearly not intended only for consumption by white readers. At the same time, publishing teams often have limited ideas about what kinds of black subjects they feel they can offer for consumption by a school market that is perceived to be dominated by white purchasers. *With the Might of Angels* offers, in many ways, a black female subject acceptable to white palates. Dawnie Rae is spicy, saucy, and outspoken, but in moderation. She takes as her role model Jackie Robinson, a man chosen to integrate the major leagues in part because he was seen as being able to control his speech and temper, and she works hard to express her anger in ways that will shore up the white academic system rather than openly speaking her rebellious thoughts. At the same time, the prevalent metaphors of food and eating work as a counternarrative, dramatizing Dawnie Rae's feeling of being consumed and forcing readers to share it. Furthermore, while Dawnie Rae does accept Gertie's friendship, she withholds the easy comingling and the overflowing bounty of love and forgiveness that is imagined, and desired, by writers like Sterling and Levine.

School Performances: Race, Gender, and Ability

The final trope important to understanding desegregation stories is performance; schools (both in stories and in life) train students to adequately perform both designated academic skills and designated social roles, including gender, race, and class. In girls' stories like *Rebecca of Sunnybrook Farm* and *Anne of Green Gables*, creative, self-conscious performance of both kinds of tasks is made an explicit concern. The heroines often have dramatic tendencies and talents that need to be channeled into safe and productive formats like school recitations, instead of poetic re-enactments that result in near-drowning (Anne) or melodramatic destruction of personal property (Rebecca). In these stories, however, the girls' performances are presented as "natural," even as they are problematized and seen as needing shaping and instruction. In contrast, desegregation stories make performance an explicit concern, forming the conditions for the desegregation process itself and setting the political framework for how desegregation can be seen as a success. Academic performance, in a "successful" desegregation story, provides a fluid, malleable identity that appears to offer a meritocratic way to resist, or to revise, a pejorative, essentialist racial identity. At the same time, academic performance establishes a narrow parameter for acceptable performances of racial identity.

The concept of race as performance rather than essence has the potential to destabilize racial binaries and disrupt the logic of inherent white superiority. Nevertheless, many scholars also note that racial performances can be compelled and scripted. Kenneth Clark, a leading advocate of school desegregation, notes in a 1955 parenting manual that the black community enforces specific and stringent racial scripts in order to counter white prejudice. Middle- and upper-class black parents, he says, demand that their children "be a living refutation of the stereotyped picture of the primitive and inferior Negro," expecting sexual moderation, cleanliness, and very high achievement.[42] While Clark lauds the gains made through high expectations, he also laments the pressure placed upon children to perform success and respectability at all times. Catherine Rottenberg further points out that the adoption of such white-associated scripts also reinforces their desirability and circumscribes the kinds of performances resistant black subjects are permitted to give.[43]

Black students desegregating white schools were often selected precisely because they were seen as capable of performing a demanding and narrow script. Academic achievement as measured by grades and tests was one requirement, but Carlotta Walls LaNier, one of the Little Rock Nine, records that they also had to pass a "Jackie Robinson test" ensuring that their personal appearance, conduct, and family backgrounds would render them acceptable to white administrators.[44] As historian James Patterson points out, this kind of desegregation by typecasting meant that these "ambassadors" had limited ability to open the way for others in their community, as in effect, each incoming student had to audition anew for a role that never changed. Moreover, for the benefit of the black community, they had to prove at all times, through their grades, conduct, and public statements that desegregation was succeeding. To Walls LaNier, this meant a constant stream of public interviews and televised events in which the nine students were expected to downplay the constant violence and suffering they experienced, and to "[reassure] television viewers that we lived in a great country and that all was well at Central."[45] In this historical context, academic performance was only one aspect of an overarching racial script that aimed to counter claims of black inferiority. Nevertheless, the need for a "Jackie Robinson test" indicates that there were other kinds of resistant performances available, ones that adults controlling the desegregation process attempted to weed out.

In *Mary Jane*, some of these alternate resistant roles are briefly presented. Red Anne, Mary Jane's great-grandmother, is a revered figure in Mary Jane's life due to her commitment to education and her skillful role playing. As an enslaved woman, Red Anne secretly teaches herself to read and write, but feigns ignorance and stupidity to evade censure from her white mistress. When she finds a letter indicating that she is about to be sold down the river, she forges a pass and escapes North. Her son, Mary Jane's distinguished grandfather, studies with his books tied to the handle of a plow, works nights scrubbing floors, and takes pride in an all-black education that has enabled him to work with black farmers around the state, reminding Mary Jane that attendance at a white school is not the only way for her to achieve dignity and success. The reader is encouraged to share Mary Jane's conviction that the role of a bright and ambitious middle-class black student ought to be readily available to her. Nevertheless, Sterling avoids packaging academic performance, gentility, and resistance inextricably, acknowledging the work of many of Mary Jane's elders (and Sterling's own peers) who crafted multiple modes of resistance. Graham's *Town* series similarly depicts several forms of resistant performance, and emphasizes that participation in resistance might automatically nullify whites' perceptions of academic performance and gentility.

In historical novels about desegregation, however, academic performance and resistant racial performance tend to be depicted as mutually constitutive. Furthermore, both resistance and academic achievement are depicted as being enhanced by, if not dependent upon, desegregation, reinforcing an historical narrative in which, as Capshaw asserts, "school integration enables social integration."[46] For example, in *A Friendship for Today*, Rosemary fights against her principal's attempts to put her in a remedial class, and also coaches her friends to maintain confidence in their academic abilities and prove themselves despite prejudiced teachers. For Halloween, she dresses as Harriet Tubman, about whom none of her classmates, or even her teacher, has learned. This incident subtly demonstrates her resistance to racism through a performance of historical acumen that allows her to educate her white class. Nevertheless, performances of resistant black identity in these novels that would not pass the "Jackie Robinson test" tend to be invalidated as less desirable academically.

In Pinkney's novel, this narrowing of performance parameters happens in two ways: first, with the contrast between Dawnie and her brother Goober, and second, with the contrast between Dawnie's two year-end performances. Dawnie is as conscious of herself as a performer as Walls LaNier records having been. She avoids direct retaliation against her tormentors and instead is careful to perform gentility, opting to resist by proving her academic qualifications. She also is keenly aware that any lapse in deportment and grooming will count against her; Dawnie may hate the girly Peach Melba dress, but she is even more upset when her mother puts Vaseline on her face in the cold weather and rubs her with camphor after she is sick, as this provides the white girls with reasons to believe that her body is an object of disgust.

In contrast, Goober is presented as a kind of holy fool who is incapable of understanding any kind of racial performance, resistant or otherwise. In the process of narrating her sibling relationship, Dawnie projects a role for herself within the black community as someone willing to recognize and protect seemingly valueless and vulnerable members of the community, but simultaneously casts Goober in a passive role, writing him out of active or conscious participation in antiracist action. When Goober insists upon drinking from the "Whites Only" fountain, even after being warned off by a gang of hostile white boys, Dawnie Rae equates Goober's disability with complete racial innocence, assuming "he doesn't know nothing about colored water fountains, or those marked 'Whites Only.'"[47] This is one possible interpretation of Goober's actions; however, exaggerated performances of ignorance, in which resistant black subjects deploy stereotypes of slowness in order to thwart white desires, have a long history in black resistance, and Goober's behavior might also be interpreted in this way.[48] Instead, Goober's actions are framed as entirely naïve. Dawnie's academic ability is clearly a performative quality rather than a wholly natural one. She works hard at her role, and she is aware of factors like stereotype threat that might impact her performance. And it is because she can perform in the academic realm that she is able to perform racial resistance. In contrast, Goober's disability is represented as essence rather than performance, and it thus renders him incapable of other kinds of resistant identity performances. Along the way, paths of conscious resistance not tied to normative academic achievement are eliminated.

Another kind of resistant performance, one that might have highlighted Dawnie's academic talents, is also edited out. Before Dawnie desegregates the Prettyman Coburn School, she is designated as the sixth grade valedictory speaker for her class's Stepping Up ceremony to mark their transition to junior high. Dawnie has plenty of thoughts concerning this event, noting bitterly, "We're not really stepping *up* to anyplace … we're staying at Bethune, like all the other colored kids in Hadley. We're stepping *over* to more chewed pencils, more stinky bathrooms, more books with missing pages."[49] The shopping trip that precedes the Stepping Up also prompts a chorus of internal questions about the prejudice Dawnie Rae witnesses in the store, and the quiet, servile roles they are pressured to assume. Conceivably, she could use the speech to voice some of the persistent questions her mother stops her from asking. The Stepping Up speech calls to mind other examples of black intellectual resistance staged through the drama of the graduation speech. In Richard Wright's *Black Boy*, and Patricia Hill Collins's *Another Kind of Public Education*, black narrators recall being challenged to censor their ideas for the comfort of white listeners. Wright's speech draws down retribution and Collins opts not to serve as a docile, censored symbol of integration, but in both cases, black intellectuals have the chance to perform roles and speak lines that are threatening to white audiences. Dawnie Rae, however, does not refer in her diary to any collective history of graduation speeches and their censorship; she does not write her *how comes* into a speech and then debate whether to deliver it; she does not receive advice from any adult in her segregated and heavily policed community who is worried about what she might decide to say. She simply has no ideas at all, never writes a speech, and is saved from humiliation on the day of the Stepping Up by a wardrobe malfunction when her Peach Melba dress splits down the sides. Thus, not only is her intra-diegetic audience prevented from seeing her in the role of outspoken black intellectual (an elision which would have been quite historically accurate), her reading audience is also shielded from the knowledge that such a performance might have been possible or had any historical precedent.

Instead, Dawnie's climactic performance of resistance is the ringing of the bell at the Prettyman Coburn School, a performance which involves answering test questions created by her teachers and answered in private, rather than showcasing her intellect as a student-written speech would do. Dawnie clearly feels that she rings the bell as a performance of resistance; she writes,

> I'm sure Mr. Lloyd didn't expect that I'd pull on that bell's handle twenty times over. But I was there to introduce that bell. Mr. Lloyd could not stop *me, me, me*. I *claaaannnggged* that bell for Mama and Daddy. I *claaaannnggged* for Jackie Robinson and Mr. Dunphey. I *claaaannnggged* for Mr. Williams, Miss Cora, and Miss Billie [the black custodian and lunch ladies who help Dawnie]. I pulled on that bell's handle doubly hard for Gertie and Goober, who both see things in ways others don't.... Most of all, I christened that pretty Prettyman Bell for myself. Dawnie Rae Johnson.[50]

Dawnie Rae feels that she is taking an opportunity to publicize injustice in a forum where white authorities are unable to silence her, similar to other black intellectuals' use of the graduation speech. However, she is *not* giving a speech, having ceded that opportunity. She is instead performing in a non-speaking role, her thoughts about racial injustice voiced only through the clanging of the bell; and in doing so, she is testifying to the success of desegregation through her physical presence but not her words. The only mode of resistant performance available to her in the novel is thus one in which she proves the inclusivity of the racist white school, speaking through a symbolic medium (the bell of freedom, rung by a black female) that can easily be interpreted as national triumph instead of protest. This kind of visible, scripted performance echoes both Collins's experience, and also earlier desegregation novels, such as *Call Me Charley*. Charley's triumphant acceptance is heralded, not by his engineering project, but by a school play in which he is allowed to speak exactly one line in a walk-on part, an offer that lures him back to the white school after he makes the administrators look bad by dropping out due to ill treatment.

For black protagonists, the desegregation story tends to narrow resistant performances to visible demonstrations of academic engagement. Nevertheless, racial performance in the context of the classroom is also depicted as helping students discover resistance through trying on fluid identities. The more idealized classrooms in these novels not only accommodate, but actually elicit diverse racial performances. The Halloween parade in McKissack's novel offers Rosemary this opportunity, and in Watt's novel, a mixed-race Greek myth project prompts a reconsideration of white beauty norms when Kizzy Ann's black classmate argues (successfully) that Kizzy Ann, not the white girl in the group, should portray Aphrodite. In the process, however, because racial performance seems to grant fluidity and agency to the performers, disability is also framed as an identity that is subject to performance decisions—specifically, as a role that ought not to be chosen.

The implications of fluid identity performance are most evident in *The Lions of Little Rock*, with a white protagonist who has more leeway than Dawnie Rae to perform a range of resistant roles. The novel begins with Liz passing as white. Under cover of whiteness, she is able for a limited time to needle the daughter of a prominent racist in town. She is discovered, and pushed into a quieter role. Nevertheless, the exposure of Liz's identity as a performance teaches Marlee that her own identity can be fluid. After Liz is driven out, Marlee is given the option of writing out a report instead of delivering a presentation by herself; she has been so adamant about staying in her longtime role as the silent girl that the teacher accepts and accommodates it. Instead, Marlee goes to the bathroom, and narrates, "I was careful not to glance in the mirror and see my brown hair and brown eyes that looked so much like Liz's. Could it be true? Can a girl be white one day and colored the next?"[51] Marlee might avoid looking in the mirror, but she nevertheless "sees" that she looks like Liz, and resolves not to lose her. Back in the classroom, she announces that she intends to do the presentation, and pulls out the black feather that serves as her good-luck charm. In a telling reference to *Dumbo*, Liz had earlier found the feather on the ground at the zoo and given it to Marlee, reminding her of the magic "Jim Crow" feather given to Dumbo so that he will believe that his large ears can help him fly. Before giving her presentation, Marlee sticks the feather in one of her braids, "like an Indian headdress," as a talisman of her Jim Crow friend while she talks to the class about the Quapaw Indians.[52] As she speaks, she imagines that the white schoolchildren are animals and that the classroom is a zoo.

The dizzying number of shifts in this short section seems to answer Marlee's previous question: a girl *can* be white one day and colored the next, and if Liz can effect this transformation, then so too can Marlee. At first, this possibility appears as a threat, so that Marlee avoids the gaze of her colored self in the mirror; but it very soon becomes a chosen act of resistance. If Jim Crow laws are meant to keep Liz away from Marlee, then Marlee will perform a "colored" identity that symbolically brings Liz back into the classroom. Clearly, this is a stylized performance of non-white identity, haphazardly mixing the Jim Crow feather with an appropriation of stereotyped "Indian" costuming. As Eric Lott notes, stylized "Indian" costuming has historically been adopted as an expression of political resistance in the United States and Europe, most famously during the Boston Tea Party.[53] Marlee's performance of "native" nonwhite identity thus echoes a founding moment in American mythology, when "native" colonists asserted the American ideals of justice and redistributive equality. As the classroom transforms into a zoo, it evokes one of the threats feared by opponents of desegregation—that primitive nonwhite bodies will turn the transmission tool of civilization into a "blackboard jungle." For Marlee, though, the zoo is a utopian learning environment, where both Jim Crow and her paralyzing shyness can be sidestepped for a time. Racist white children transforming into animals might be an improvement. Phyllis Palmer argues that "civil rights inspired some white Americans to become new kinds of white people," and this is certainly the ultimate point of the novel.[54] Marlee does not continue to perform a nonwhite identity, but her temporary performance of "color" allows her to envision performing her white identity differently. This effect of Indian performance also surfaces in *A Friendship for Today*; during the Halloween parade, Rosemary's erstwhile racist enemy Grace signals her shifting allegiances and politics by wearing an Indian princess costume.

These episodes of cross-racial performance help to destabilize a narrative of desegregation in which black students became the beneficiaries of white education and culture in a one-sided exchange. At the same time, such visions of how classrooms might ideally help desegregation efforts to succeed also construct classrooms with a narrow range of academic identities available even for white students. Catherine Rottenberg argues that "performativity all too often gets conflated with the notion of an autonomous agent who can choose identities at will or with rather simplistic notions of identity as fluid."[55] Subjects who make conscious performance choices so as to rise up the class ladder or to forge a new kind of racialized identity also, in the process, tend to reinforce the "mythical norm" of the white, able-bodied, determined, independent, sexually restrained, genteel, young, heterosexual male as the highest ideal to emulate.[56] Thus, Marlee may appropriate stereotyped nonwhite costume props in order to help herself "fly," but in order to become a "new kind of white person," she must overcome the muteness that marks her as socially limited, but also politically cowardly. One sign of her political progress is performing in the school's mainstream, rejecting the accommodations teachers have allowed her in order to give presentations and eat in the lunchroom with everyone else. Goober, who is seen as incapable of understanding scripts, is excluded from resistance through the desegregated school. Marlee, who is capable of emulating ability, must repudiate disability if she wants to perform a more ideal version of whiteness. Otherwise, her brief encounter with desegregation will not be legible as a "successful" schooling experiment.

Temporary Alternatives and their Potential

The novels in this chapter are variations on the school story, and therefore focus on how the institution of the school can be maximized as an instrument for training citizens. This is the function of the school story genre. Therefore, while these novels expose many of the problems that occurred during the implementation of the *Brown* decision—daily violence in the hallways, social ostracism and loneliness, and intense public pressure for the chosen students, among others—the format in which the stories are told frames and softens how these problems are portrayed. Violence becomes character building; inclusion and participation in the white classroom substitutes for unpredictable interracial connections outside the classroom; academic achievement becomes the primary mode of resistance; and if the protagonists are not always happy at the end, they at least affirm that the trials they have undergone for the sake of desegregation have been worthwhile for themselves, for the school, and for the nation. Because of their adherence to school story tropes, it would be difficult for these novels to measure the success of desegregation in any way other than normative academic achievement. Any sprouts of utopian educational reform must be made to fit into the framework of traditional school achievement in order to be recognizable and justifiable.

Nevertheless, these desegregation stories also demonstrate that the school can allow for and even produce a range of utopian forms of resistance. While the generic plot arc tends to domesticate or eliminate visions of racial justice that would not produce a protagonist happily incorporated into a traditional nationalist school institution, along the way these stories elicit and even encourage alternate, unmeasurable kinds of emotional connection, political solidarity, and intellectual quests. Perry Nodelman suggests that while children's books usually resolve stories of topsy-turvy child-directed exploits by restoring a safe adult rule of law and reinforcing the immaturity of children, it is nevertheless the mayhem and role reversals that occupy the brunt of the stories and that often prove more memorable and appealing for readers than the tidy endings. Similarly, while the critical moments and radical educational alternatives in desegregation stories may be tamed by the end, they nevertheless appear as attractive possibilities. Furthermore, while the desegregated school characterized by normative academic achievement and national absorption should not be seen as the only path to either "successful" racial justice or "successful" education, there is no question that many generations of students have desired exactly this option. Some of the protagonists I discuss in later chapters learn, as part of their utopian educations, to desire other models of education and national citizenship. Nevertheless, because the school story model of utopia has been so attractive to readers for so many generations, it is important to acknowledge the possibilities for resistance that it does allow. In the next chapter, I explore how the desegregation story is further revised by black authors seeking to openly question the consensus memory of *Brown*. Within some of the same generic constraints of the school story, these authors open up some alternate visions of utopian classrooms, even as they hew to some of the same limitations for defining success.

Notes

1 An abbreviated version of this chapter was previously published in *Children's Literature in Education* under the title "Scripting History: The Genre of Desegregation Stories." It is reprinted with permission of Springer.
2 Miller, "Black Images," 107. He reviews Jackson's *Call Me Charley*, Graham's *Town* series, and Carlson's *The Empty Schoolhouse.*
3 Guinier, "From Racial Liberalism to Racial Literacy," 96–97; Patterson, *Brown v. Board of Education*, "Southern Whites Fight Back."
4 Romano and Raiford, "Introduction," xiv.
5 Schulte, "Today's Literature for Today's Children," 356.
6 Examples include Milton Meltzer's *There Comes a Time*, Ellen Levine's *Freedom's Children*, and Casey King and Linda Barrett Osborne's *Oh, Freedom!* While these texts do not focus on school, all three do challenge consensus narratives to some degree.
7 Significantly, Robert Coles's picture book version of Bridges's story predates, and often eclipses, Bridges's own more ambivalent version for children in *Through My Eyes*; it was Coles's book that served as the basis for a Disney movie. *Separate Is Never Equal: Sylvia Mendez and Her Family's Fight for Desegregation*, by Duncan Tonatiuh, is another example of a nonfiction picture book that does not include a warm interracial relationship, and that is less widely known than *The Story of Ruby Bridges.*
8 Bryant, "A Moral Compass"; Patricia, "Book Review: 'Mary Jane'—Dorothy Sterling." Levine's novel is recommended on California's searchable state curriculum literature list. Common Core lesson plans for her novel are provided by Penguin publishers, but also by other sites, such as teachingbooks.net. Pinkney's novel is part of the popular and widely publicized *Dear America* series. Scholastic offers a teacher's guide, but her novel has also been picked up for lesson plans on the Kidsread blog site.
9 With the exception of *Hand in Hand*, Pinkney's nonfiction narratives of the Civil Rights movement largely parallel her treatment of the subject in *With the Might of Angels*; the nonfiction works appeal to a broad audience by focusing on iconic moments within the consensus narrative of the Civil Rights era, but also incorporate subtle adjustments to consensus views. For example, *Boycott Blues* celebrates the progress made through the well-known Montgomery bus boycott, but also emphasizes the collective determination of Montgomery's black citizens over long, weary months, rather than attributing the success of the boycott to singular heroes Rosa Parks and Martin Luther King, Jr.
10 Beverly Lyon Clark, "Cracking the Code"; Gill Frith, "The Time of Your Life."
11 Mavis Reimer, "Traditions of the School Story;" Anne Scott MacLeod, *American Childhood*, 53; Thomas Atwood and Wade Lee's "The Price of Deviance."
12 Pinkney, *With the Might of Angels*, 155; emphasis in original.
13 Beverly Lyon Clark discusses how the girls' school and cross-written stories revised (and largely eliminated) this tradition of character-building violence, which is brought back in the desegregation story. "Domesticating the School Story," 327; *Regendering the School Story*, 104, 182.
14 Reimer, "Traditions of the School Story," 223.
15 Hartman, *Education and the Cold War,* 4–6, 73–91. Hartman also notes that widespread fear of Communism led to purges of teachers suspected of Leftist or Communist leanings. Due to the American Communist Party's history of anti-racist efforts, those teachers most active in redressing racial inequality in the schools were also those most likely to be fired. This aspect of Cold War schooling is not reflected in desegregation novels.

16 Romano and Raiford, "Introduction," xvii.
17 Walter M. Brasch, *Black English and the Mass Media*, 240; Margaret Alic, "Lorenz Graham Biography." Dorothy Sterling, when interviewed by Julia Mickenberg, did not confirm that she had been a member of the Communist party, but "suggested, only half-jokingly, that any book published by a white writer before 1965 and sympathetic to African Americans was probably written by a Communist or former Communist, so constricted was the political climate." Mickenberg, *Learning From the Left*, 10.
18 Sterling, "The Soul of Learning," 234.
19 Ibid., 233.
20 Mickenberg, *Learning From the Left*, 179.
21 Sterling, *Mary Jane*, 218.
22 Contemporary education critic Paul Goodman also noted, and lambasted, the replacement of an open and playful approach to science education with one governed by pre-determined results.
23 Levine, *Lions of Little Rock*, 6.
24 Clark, *Prejudice and Your Child*, 61–75; Samuel Bowles and Herbert Gintis offer similar critiques in the 1970s.
25 Plucker et al., *Mind the (Other) Gap*, 1.
26 *Eyes on the Prize*, "Fighting Back."
27 Baldwin, "A Fly in Buttermilk," 190.
28 Dorothy Sterling's "Soul of Learning" speech indicates this position, and Baldwin also suggests it.
29 Sara Schwebel points out that historical fiction often avoids the censorship and criticism directed at other young adult fiction, because of its relative lack of sexual content. Schwebel, *Child-Sized History*, 26.
30 Fuss, *Identification Papers*, 123. Marah Gubar also suggests that school delays marriage in the *Anne of Green Gables* stories in a way that allows for passionate and romantic friendships between women.
31 Stockton, *The Queer Child*, 90.
32 Sterling, *Mary Jane*, 148.
33 Bryant, "A Moral Compass," 111–112.
34 Levine, *Lions of Little Rock*, 20.
35 Pinkney, *With the Might of Angels*, 286.
36 Baldwin, "White Man's Guilt," 320. bell hooks comments on a similar phenomenon decades later, in "Representations of Whiteness in the Black Imagination."
37 Tompkins, *Racial Indigestion*, 9.
38 Levine, *Lions of Little Rock*, 272.
39 Robin Bernstein's concept of racial innocence is crucial to Gertie's characterization; she suggests that white children's color-blindness involves an "active state of repelling knowledge," which is idealized and used to promote political reforms. *Racial Innocence*, 6.
40 Carby, "The Multicultural Wars," 197.
41 "Andrea Pinkney Profile" and "Andrea Pinkney."
42 Clark, *Prejudice and Your Child*, 58.
43 Rottenberg, *Performing Americanness*, 102, 112. Katherine Capshaw Smith, in "Childhood, the Body, and Race Performance," offers an alternate view and suggests that white norms are used to reinvent black public identity.
44 LaNier and Page, *A Mighty Long Way*, 60.
45 Ibid., 109.
46 Capshaw, *Civil Rights Childhood*, 218.
47 Pinkney, *With the Might of Angels*, 57.
48 See Glymph, *Out of the House of Bondage*, 70–73; Ellison, *Invisible Man*, 16; Clark, *Prejudice and Your Child*, 58.

49 Pinkney, *With the Might of Angels*, 30.
50 Ibid., 289.
51 Levine, *Lions of Little Rock*, 64.
52 Ibid., 64.
53 Philip Deloria traces distinct movements in Indian appropriation. In the 1950s, the setting of Levine's novel, Indian hobbyists were countering inauthenticity and conformism, appropriately for Marlee's growth into personal voice; more recently, and more pertinent to the novel's publication date, Indian hobbyists sought social harmony, appropriate in a different way for the novel's presentation of desegregation.
54 Palmer, *Living as Equals*, 13.
55 Rottenberg, *Performing Americanness*, 7.
56 Ibid., 112.

2 Counternarratives and the Persistence of White Privilege

Desegregation stories commonly end with a successful event that ends the school year, featuring a hopeful scene of interracial friendship as a signal of the direction American schooling is headed. This common literary structure, however, projects an optimism that is not supported by actual historical events. While desegregation programs did move forward in the South after the passage of the 1964 Civil Rights Act, school desegregation in the North did not; and in the 1974 *Milliken v. Bradley* decision, the Supreme Court limited the scope of voluntary desegregation programs that sought to address residential segregation by busing black students from the cities into the white-dominated suburban schools, and vice versa.[1] During the busing controversies of the 1970s, many white parents protested the ways in which desegregation legislation attempted to address the effects of white flight from cities. Black parents, teachers, and school staff, however, also expressed disillusionment with school desegregation. A 1971 NAACP pamphlet on busing records that black parents in one Florida county began to protest because their children were assigned the longest bus rides, and attended white-dominated schools for ten of their twelve school years; and in Thomas Cottle's 1976 series of interviews about busing, he records black parents and teachers who are concerned that their children are being implicitly taught that their own communities are inadequate and inferior.[2] By the 1990s, historians began to construct narratives that countered the consensus stories of *Brown*, emphasizing stories of cherished black schools closed or taken over by whites, and of dedicated black teachers fired, in the process of desegregation.[3]

While many desegregation novels continue to present a story of progress, a second, much smaller, set of desegregation novels mediates this thread of discontent and historical loss for young readers, beginning in the late 1970s and early 1980s. A few novels, like Katherine Paterson's *The Great Gilly Hopkins* (1978), Mildred Pitts Walter's *Because We Are* (1983), and Cynthia Voigt's *Come a Stranger* (1986), reflect contemporary struggles to manage racism in the classroom decades after the *Brown* decision. More often, these critical counter-narratives are filtered through more recently published historical novels and nonfiction that incorporate facets of the 1990s historiography about proud black schools. In fact, many texts published in the twenty-first century attempt, at the very least, to acknowledge a tradition of excellence in black schools, even when they are otherwise celebratory. In Watts's *Kizzy Ann Stamps*, for example, Kizzy Ann visits her former teacher to thank her for sacrificing her job for the sake of desegregation, and Andrea Davis Pinkney's biographical sketch of Thurgood Marshall notes both that black students had the opportunity to learn black history in segregated schools and that the Supreme Court reversed its commitment to desegregation in *Bakke v. Regents of the University of California*.[4] Nevertheless, many nonfiction pieces that emphasize the failures of *Brown*'s implementation, such as Ishmael Reed's "Color Blind" and Joyce Carol Thomas's "Who Is Linda Brown?," tend to receive little attention, while novels like Watts's and picture books like Robert Michelson's *Busing Brewster* gesture to alternate historical narratives and then return to a plotline that reaffirms the success of desegregation and the triumph of the interracial friendship.[5]

By contrast, the novels in this chapter are relatively unusual, because their protagonists actively choose predominantly black schools over desegregated schools; to the extent that successful desegregation is referenced, it involves white students entering predominantly black schools rather than the other way around. These novels not only reference a history of strong black schools, but also outright suggest that black schools are preferable to white ones, and that aspects of the *Brown* decision itself, as well as its implementation, were flawed. *Because We Are*, by Mildred Pitts Walter (1983), *Fire From the Rock*, by Sharon Draper (2007), and *Feathers*, by Jacqueline Woodson (2007), are published at different times, and they also represent the difficulties of desegregation at three different time periods. Walter's novel depicts its contemporary publication moment of the early 1980s, while Woodson's historical novel recalls the persistent segregation of the 1970s and Draper's looks all the way back to 1956 to reinterpret the era of the Little Rock Nine. Within these various publication contexts and settings, all three novels rewrite the desegregation story to suggest that black schools offer love instead of violence, and build community and responsibility for all instead of sorting students within a meritocracy, *creating* merit rather than just rewarding it.

Like the desegregation novels of the previous chapter, these counternarratives rely upon school story plots and tropes in order to comment upon how the pedagogical practices of desegregation are crucial to the success or failure of education for racial justice. Loving, predominantly black classrooms replace the competitive, individualist pedagogical methods that the novels' contemporary readers may be experiencing. Like the consensus-narrative desegregation novels, the counter-narratives also reinforce the public school as a necessary, central source of justice and reform. In all three novels, pedagogy within an institutional setting provides a more effective force of justice than any found outside the school; however, ideal classrooms can only be found outside the time of the novelists' (desegregated) moments of publication. Walter's contemporary novel imagines better pedagogy in the future, while Draper's and Woodson's historical novels look to the past for inspiration. This displacement works in contradictory ways; it allows the novels to elide the question of how effective the school can actually be, but it also denies the reader the complacent sense that he or she is living in an era of enlightened utopian progress.

Because We Are: Cultural Immersion for the Post-Civil Rights Generation

In *Because We Are*, Mildred Pitts Walter directly addresses the *Brown* decision's failures to achieve its goals in ways that are unusual in children's fiction. Although it won the Coretta Scott King Honor Award in 1984, unlike many award winners (and unlike several other books by Walter), it appears on few recommendation lists, and is currently out of print. Walter notes that some teachers were unhappy with how teachers were represented in the novel, and recalls that while she received many letters from children about her novels, she did not receive them from teachers.[6] *Because We Are* is not representative of contemporary school stories about the aftermath of the *Brown* decision, and adult gatekeepers seem to have been ambivalent about the extent to which they wish children to read it. Nevertheless, it is noteworthy because it provides an example of how blunt critiques of racist pedagogy are still shaped by the school story genre.

Walter's novel dramatizes the reasons that the push to desegregate education has not sufficiently accomplished the goals of *Brown*, primarily by highlighting the absence of a wider commitment to eradicating inequality. Historians and legal scholars who critique the effects of the *Brown* decision often draw a distinction between the overarching goals of the decision and the strategy chosen by the NAACP and the Legal Defense Fund for implementing those goals. The goals, according to Jerome Morris and Derrick Bell, were, first, eventual racial integration and equality in all areas of society, and second, high-quality education for all black children, including those in low-income and rural communities.[7] The strategies chosen to achieve these ends—legal desegregation and the creation of racially balanced schools—became adopted as ends in themselves, but in fact were chosen from a number of possible strategies. In practice, both the wording of the *Brown* decision and its implementation limited the effects of this strategy so that the original goals of racial justice and high-quality education were not achieved. One of the most often criticized aspects of the *Brown* decision was the famous footnote eleven; this footnote incorporated the well-known doll experiments of Kenneth and Mamie Clark, among other psychological studies, which appeared to demonstrate that segregation instilled a sense of inferiority in black children.[8] Many scholars argue that the decision's emphasis on feelings of inferiority in black children was one of its most destructive aspects, reinforcing a "cultural deprivation paradigm" that assumed black communities were completely devoid of educational support and that black children must absorb white culture if they were to succeed.[9]

Furthermore, as historian James Patterson notes, Chief Justice Warren did not, in writing a decision that overturned *Plessy v. Ferguson*, reinforce one of the key ideas in Justice John Marshall Harlan's dissent to *Plessy*. Harlan had asserted that the Constitution was "color-blind"; Warren stated merely that education "is the very foundation of good citizenship," thus limiting his call for racial justice and equality to the realm of education and specifically omitting the idea that such justice should extend to the Constitution, and the state, as a whole.[10] Substituting the institution of education for the whole apparatus of the state has had far-reaching implications; as James Patterson notes (and as contemporary critics like Paul Goodman lamented), liberal reformers concerned about racial equality have tended to funnel attention into compensatory education for black students rather than directing it toward other areas of inequality.

Because We Are focuses attention on how concern for schooling supplanted a desire for broader equality in ways that divided the black community. The protagonist Emma not only struggles against the white power structure in her school system, but she also finds herself at odds with black adults of her parents' generation, who celebrate legal access without protesting the price they and their children are paying for desegregation. Walter's novel draws a clear distinction between legal desegregation and meaningful integration, and suggests that privileged members of the black community should insist that all members of the community have the same opportunities, rather than being content to serve as symbols of racial advancement.

The novel combines elements of the teen "problem novel" and the school story. It invites the reader to consider contemporary social problems besetting teenagers, including drug use, divorce, and conflicts over popularity, but it primarily follows a school story plot in which a new student is inducted into a hostile new school, faces a bully, develops school pride, and graduates to be a credit to the nation. Emma begins the novel as an "opportunity transfer student" at a desegregated school. She is a National Honor scholar and a student government leader, and she hopes to pledge an elite black social club, but she encounters such persistent racism from white teachers and students that she erupts in rage. As a consequence, she is removed from the school and sent back to finish her senior year at her neighborhood all-black school, a move that ruins her chances of being a debutante and disappoints her parents—especially her upwardly mobile father, a doctor who has divorced her mother and replaced her with a younger white woman. The new school has several problems, including stark class divisions, crowded facilities, and an egregiously racist English teacher. Nevertheless, the novel depicts Emma's growing acceptance that she belongs at this school and not the desegregated one, and highlights her developing commitment to uniting the school community in resistance to the racist teacher. Like the desegregation stories that narrate *Brown*'s immediate aftermath, *Because We Are* asks readers to hope for a more utopian school in the future; unlike those novels, it refuses to accept the victories of the Civil Rights era as sufficient, instead urging on a new generation of activists. Nevertheless, the school story plot still shapes the novel's critique; its vision for change depends upon the reformation of the white-dominated school system, and the protagonists have natural ability which grants them the privilege and responsibility to fight for their less fortunate brethren.

Because We Are begins by highlighting the isolation and exclusion experienced by black students attending nominally desegregated schools. Entering the cafeteria, Emma heads for the tables where the other black students congregate together, and where she feels at home. Yet there are signs that this community's warmth and safety is contingent at best. As she walks through the section, she hears another black student call her "'white-girl lady,'" because "[it] was well known that she maintained a four-point average, was the only Black on the student council, and that she had white friends. Would she forever have to prove her Blackness?"[11] As a result of this remark, Emma decides not to tell her friends that she has just been elected to the National Honor Society. From the outset, the desegregated Marlborough High School is depicted as a white-dominated, hostile place. It resembles the environments described by psychologists like Beverly Daniel Tatum in *Why Are All the Black Kids Sitting Together in the Cafeteria* and by scholars like Signithia Fordham, John Ogbu, and Stuart Buck. These scholars cite ethnographies of high-achieving black students criticized by their peers for "acting white" as evidence that black students, in the years following desegregation, have come to see school as a domain established, defined, and controlled by white society—even in schools mostly attended and taught by black students and teachers. While many texts for children emphasize that desegregation disproved the myth of white intellectual superiority for black and white students alike, others highlight the damage done to formerly high-achieving black students who desegregated schools and internalized racist messages about their abilities.[12] Walter's novel begins by revealing the damage done to black student achievement, as Emma's peers feel threatened by academic prowess.

The character of Ms. Simmons is used to exemplify how black students in desegregated schools can be led to internalize racism. Ms. Simmons,

Emma's white English teacher and the faculty advisor for the Student Council, both discourages her from associating with her black peer group and also fails to step in when white students target Emma with racist comments. She consistently praises Emma's intelligence and leadership ability, but also sets the terms for her success, saying: "'I can get you into the mainstream, but I can't keep you there. *You have to want to be there.* I know your parents don't approve of you isolating yourself with hall walkers ... with riffraff.'"[13] In other words, Emma is to depend upon (and presumably give credit to) Ms. Simmons to "get" her into the (white) mainstream, and she is to give up the black community that Ms. Simmons views as both threatening "riffraff" and as antithetical to achievement. Tatum suggests that white school staff feel threatened by seeing black students sitting together in desegregated schools because the phenomenon visibly challenges the notion that color-blind equality has been achieved in the post-Civil Rights era. Further, it implicates white administrators in creating an environment that is not safe or "color-blind" for black students. In *Because We Are*, Ms. Simmons' emphasis on "color-blind" meritocracy only exacerbates the hostility experienced by the black students. When Emma refuses to accept this form of color-blindness (which would require her to agree that her friends are "riffraff"), Ms. Simmons has her removed from the desegregated "mainstream" school and returned to her segregated neighborhood school.

Walter's narrator does not believe that Emma's friends deserve the label of "riffraff," and certainly critiques the ethos of exceptionalism practiced by Ms. Simmons; but she also exposes the ways in which this peer group is a flawed, tenuous shelter from white hostility. The depiction of this peer group echoes much older critiques of internalized racism made by black scholars such as W.E.B. Du Bois and Carter G. Woodson. Well before court-ordered desegregation, they took the black community to task for passing on internalized racism through education, establishing a long history for the practices Walter criticizes in the 1980s. In Du Bois's 1935 essay, "Does the Negro Need Separate Schools?" he defends the right of black students and citizens to combat segregation. At the same time, he critiques the "utter lack of faith on the part of Negroes that their race can do anything really well," and he suggests that the black community is so focused on gaining access to white knowledge and culture that they neglect how they also have unique contributions for the intellectual resources of the nation.[14] As a result, he says, they put their energy into fighting for desegregation rather than into fighting for better pay for their teachers, respect for their own institutions, and a more appropriately inclusive curriculum nationwide. Woodson, in his 1933 collection *The Mis-Education of the Negro*, goes even further and argues,

> Negroes ... are anxious to have everything the white man has even if it is harmful. ...The author, however, does not have such an attitude.

> He considers the educational system as it has developed in both Europe and America an antiquated process which does not hit the mark even in the case of the needs of the white man himself.[15]

He says that after passing through a degree process which elevates the achievements of Europe while suppressing the culture of Africa, "The Negroes thus placed in charge [are] products of the same system."[16] In other words, educational institutions that serve black students and are staffed primarily by black teachers are not necessarily ideologically black institutions, no matter how warm and loving a shelter they may aim to create.

Within the desegregated setting of Walter's post-Civil Rights novel, these same problems continue to haunt the extracurricular social clubs that ostensibly promote black pride. Despite the black students' reluctance to be identified with "white" academic activities, they attain status primarily through proximity to whiteness. Attending an integrated school signals that they have enough "class" to be chosen as nominal participants in white institutions, and they use the same measures in determining the criteria for their own institutions.

This internalized racism is passed on, not only directly through the white-dominated school, but also through black leaders of their parents' generation who have fought bitterly for desegregation and who have ended by becoming products of the white-dominated system they fought to join. Thus, when Emma is rejected from the Golden Slipper debutante club for attending a segregated school, her father is unsupportive:

> Blacks who have *class* are no different from any other people with class—thank God for that—and anybody wanting to be considered by those with class has to measure up.... Whether Emma is a good girl, or bad, Manning girls are not considered Golden Slipper material. That's that.[17]

Emma's mother reminds him of his experiences of racism in the 1960s; but from his new perspective as a wealthy doctor with a white wife, integration has succeeded, and further investment in black community building is an anachronism and a shame to be overcome.[18] He adopts the tenets of color-blind racism, maintaining that class and merit know no color. In the meantime, the black Golden Slipper society depends directly on the approval of the white school for its criteria; if a girl has been deemed worthy to attend the desegregated school, she can be considered for the society, and if the white administrators refuse her entry, then she is not "material" for the black upper crust. With the exception of the "self-segregation" their parents abhor, Emma's peers seem to be passively adopting their parents' values, as her boyfriend Marvin enjoys attention from a wealthy white girl and her friends sympathize with her rejection but do not fight on her behalf. The black middle class, therefore, has adopted an ideology of merit and has identified merit as being proximity to whiteness, rather than as the kind of quality education sought by the initial architects of the *Brown* decision. Meanwhile, Walter suggests, *real* merit, the academic achievement that Emma pursues and her classy friends reject, is neglected.

Walter's scathing critique of desegregation, and of the Civil Rights generation, is especially poignant because she is commenting upon her own legacy as an activist; in 1968, together with her husband Earl Walter, who was the head of CORE's Los Angeles chapter, she helped to file the lawsuit that desegregated the Los Angeles school system. In an interview conducted in the 1990s, however, she reflected on her disappointment with the results of desegregation: "We felt we had no other choice but to try to become a part of the total system. We tried and saw that it was just not working for us even though we tried. Our children took the brunt of a lot of mental abuse to make the nation whole. The nation didn't want to be whole. And it still doesn't want to be whole."[19] Thus, in *Because We Are*, Emma's task is to figure out the other choices Walter and her compatriots overlooked, taking as a starting point a nation that does not want to be whole.

The first step in this process is for Emma to continue down the same path that has gotten her removed from Marlborough; rather than protecting her access to the "mainstream," she must increasingly identify with the "riffraff," the segregated black students who apparently lack the potential to be adopted by white society. This portion of the novel uses a key school story trope to uplift the dignity of the segregated black school. The protagonist enters a school that signifies shame and social demotion, rather than one whose association confers pride; yet the trajectory of the school story plot remains the same. Emma, for whom being a "Manning girl" is a disgrace, still needs to *become* a "Manning girl." If Manning lacks the kind of virtuous school spirit engendered by the institutions of classic school stories, then it is incumbent upon Emma to create a new school spirit as a symbol of a resurgent community identity.

Her guide in this process is Allan, another star student, who has turned down prestigious white-dominated schools in order to attend the all-black Manning. Consoling Emma after her rejection from the Golden Slippers, Allan tells her, "'Out there I was chosen. Here I can choose,'" thus directly refuting her father's logic of needing to "measure up" in order to be accorded full opportunities to participate.[20] Nevertheless, Allan's insight is the exception and not the norm at Manning, where the students' behavior continues to reflect the kind of internalized racism described by Carter Woodson and Du Bois a half century earlier. The students still clump into cliques according to class status, and resentment between the different groups prevents them from working to solve the common problems that diminish the quality of their school. School spirit is needed for Emma and for the Manning student body.

This new school spirit is developed through the classic school story event of standing up to the bully, a trial that teaches Emma to, as Allan says, "choose" her values for herself and prioritize her own judgments. The occasion for this moral lesson occurs in precisely the area for which she was ridiculed by her black peers—her desire to excel academically. In this instance, however, the bully is not another student, but a teacher, and Emma passes her test of character, not by demonstrating individual grit, but by insisting upon an environment in which all of her classmates have the opportunity to achieve.

For her final graduation credit in American literature, Emma is unable to secure a spot in the class she wants, taught by a new African-American teacher who is the only faculty member to include the work of black writers in his course. Instead, she must take the course with Mr. Kooner, an ineffectual white teacher who seems fearful of his own students and who makes no attempt to teach. In contrast to Ms. Simmons, who did not believe in equality but who did cultivate a few star students, Mr. Kooner announces, "Your chance of holding a book is as good as anyone else's in the room. I see to that. No one can say I do not believe in equality of opportunity."[21] In effect, what this means is that he provides opportunity for no one. Mr. Kooner's class is dominated by the "scramble"; he provides only seventeen books for thirty-five students, and begins each class period by tossing piles of books on the floor and watching the students fight each other to get one. By the time they regain their seats, the class period is over and no work has been done. Worst of all, Emma sees a boy split his pants open while fighting for a book and realizes that Mr. Kooner feeds on the performance of mayhem and sexualized shame. Although he tells the students that the problem arises from simple lack of materials (a lack that Emma did not experience in racially mixed classrooms), he has actually constructed the shortfall so as to reinforce the students' sense of scarcity and to provide himself with a spectacle; as the students eventually realize, with just *one* more book for the group, each pair of students could share a book, use class time for learning, and preserve their dignity.

As Walter notes in an interview, the scramble scenes recall a history of similar incidents, such as those represented in Ellison's *Invisible Man* and Wright's *Black Boy*, and provide a reminder that education for black students was always overseen at some level by a hostile white power structure. In another interview, however, she also states that the scramble was drawn from stories told her by the high school students she tutored, and represented an actual classroom practice in a post-Civil Rights era high school.[22] Michael Omi and Howard Winant suggest that ideas about white superiority have never gone away, but have simply been redefined in response to changing circumstances. In the decades since the 1960s, they argue, "Racial equality had to be acknowledged as a desirable goal. But the *meaning* of equality, and the proper means for achieving it, remained matters of considerable debate."[23] In other words, inequality and racism remain, as the reasons and strategies for fighting it change. Just as Omi and Winant suggest that the language of equality is repurposed to justify old injustices, so Mr. Kooner continues a history of inadequate and racist education for black students by ironically mocking the language of opportunity.

The adults Emma consults try to redress the problem by trying to repeat their own histories and strategies of redress—namely, by trying to secure access for Emma without addressing the root problem of Kooner's racist power trip. The principal advises her to find a handsome swain to scramble on her behalf; her father gives her money to buy her own textbook; and her mother checks out a copy of the textbook from the library. Instead, Emma insists upon solidarity with the "riffraff"—until they all have books, she will not use one. Allan suggests a new strategy inspired by the African proverb from which the book takes its title: "'*Because* we *are, I am* … The *I* is always included in *we. We,* never in I.'"[24] Instead of embracing the "mis-education" of her parents and teachers, which has led to internalized racism, Emma instead adopts Allan's return to African roots and pride. Proponents of Afro-centric education, such as Jawanza Kunjufu, argue, as Woodson did, that black schools can only nurture proud, able, and resistant students if they convey the idea that intellectual achievement historically *belongs* to black students and is not merely borrowed or imitated from white culture. In a similar way, Allan's Afro-centrism offers a way for Emma to recover, not only her origins of academic excellence, but also the original goals of her parents' battle for desegregation—good education, dignity, and widespread equality. Emma organizes the students in the class to boycott the scramble until Kooner finds sufficient books; and while this tactic is not exactly radically different from those of the Civil Rights generation, the strategies are repurposed for a slightly altered goal. Instead of insisting on the opportunity to access books, the students insist upon their actual physical delivery. Furthermore, the novel reframes the philosophies of education that are needed to produce racial justice. Instead of racist teachers being told they ought to expect and demand excellence from their black students, the students demand more excellence from the teacher; instead of white liberal teachers and activists studying how best to produce results from passive students, the black student body identifies its own needs and goals and determines how to milk an education from an unwilling teacher.[25]

This temporary collectivity points the way to utopia, but it does not create a utopian segregated school or a haven from white power. In Walter's novel, there is no haven, and the utopian classroom is a psychological commitment to collective justice rather than an actual place where the community can be free of oppression. The white world is omnipresent; it looms after graduation, and is even present in Emma's own family, in the form of her friendly but alien stepmother. Belief in white superiority persists in the black community in the form of her father's and Marvin's pursuit of status and white approval. Thus, Emma, Allan, and the students in Kooner's class must be prepared to survive continued assaults on their psyches, their values, and their sense of unity. In this context, the novel distances itself from the character-toughening brutalities of the desegregation story genre, suggesting that the racially just classroom can succeed only through collective love and support for all its members, building strength only when each individual's needs are met and skills are strengthened.

Emma's efforts toward equality and community building, nevertheless, remain centered around opportunities for academic achievement, rather than around the issues of poverty and unequal employment that affect many Manning students. This focus opens up a conceptual gap between earlier goals for black education and post-*Brown* conceptions of its importance. Writing in an era before desegregation, Woodson and Du Bois were not concerned with combating a scourge of underachievement. They argued that increased literacy and knowledge of black history might produce more proud, resistant students and cohesive communities, but they did not argue that it would, in itself, result in more citizenship rights being granted. In contrast, the era of legal access since *Brown* emphasizes equal education as foundational to citizenship, and racial inequalities in academic performance (or, at least, test scores) are framed as the primary ongoing barrier to equal citizenship rights.[26] Abigail and Stephan Thernstrom, advocates for accountability reforms, write, "Racial equality will remain a dream as long as blacks and Hispanics learn less in school than whites and Asians. If black youngsters remain second-class students, they will be second-class citizens."[27] Walter's novel does not make quite such a strong causal connection; however, the structure of the plot does suggest that the remedy for second-class citizenship is the achievement of first-class student-ship.

Indeed, Walter's novel slips away from its commitment to collective accomplishment to reinforce a conception that academic achievement ought to be the condition for inclusive citizenship rights. This happens mainly through the celebration of the protagonists' academic talent and the rewarding of their merit. Emma and Allen, the star students who had the possibility of choosing to join the white world, are the enlightened leaders who organize the less talented brethren given no such choice. Allan, as valedictorian, National Honor Student, National Awards winner, and University of Southern California music scholarship winner, delivers a speech at graduation. So does Emma; despite being sabotaged by Mr. Kooner for a speech competition, she wins the honor of being class speaker, and is additionally introduced to the assembly as a National

Honor student, National Merit scholar, and soon-to-be Stanford freshman. Emma's speech "declare[s] her proud to be a Manning Girl, … certain that she now ha[s] the desire and will to help make earth a safer and healthier place for *all* living things."[28] This resolution, which celebrates the protagonist's school spirit and the preparation for service she has received through the institution, reinforces the school story frame that constrains the impact of the text's many innovative critiques.

While Allan and Emma have worked for community unity and collective opportunities for expression, the plot device of the successful graduation speech means that they voice their thoughts and insights *on behalf of* the community, whose voices are still not heard and whose destinations and aspirations remain unstated. Furthermore, the celebration of their school successes works to undermine the alternate conceptions of citizenship developed earlier in the text. In the battle against the bully Kooner, academic opportunity is treated as a universal entitlement of citizenship regardless of apparent "merit" or talent. Upon graduation, however, academic achievement is the ticket to a more fully realized public citizenship role, and Allan and Emma are claimed, over and over, as *national* scholars who receive the state's bounty and recognition for their success. Thus, despite the narrative's overarching message of unity and its pessimism about the nation's ability to meaningfully integrate any part of the black community, the structure of the school story works to separate Allan and Emma from the rest and to reinforce individual academic merit as the way to advance in the white-dominated nation.

Fire From the Rock: Recovering History, Rewriting *Brown*

The publication context of *Fire From the Rock* is quite different. As a result of the kind of disillusionment voiced by activists like Walter, beginning in the late 1980s, the idea of immersion schools for black students (especially boys) became increasingly popular. As Gloria Ladson-Billings notes about this movement, "African Americans already have separate schools. The African American immersion movement is about *taking control* of those separate schools."[29] At the same time, the changing historiography of the *Brown* decision told stories of cherished black schools closed or taken over by whites in the process of desegregation; these narratives seemed to offer models of proud institutions from the past that might be recreated in new and perhaps better forms.

These counter-histories carefully trace how black communities had, since Reconstruction, invested in education, and consequently had built a network of all-black institutions, staffed by committed and well-respected black teachers who worked to instill, not only knowledge of literacy, math, and history, but also ambition, community responsibility, and knowledge of how to succeed in a hostile white world. Ironically, during the time lapse between the *Brown* decision and its reluctant implementation, these black institutions were developed even further. Historian David Cecelski writes that many local school boards attempted to fend off desegregation by finally funding black schools so that the black students would prefer to stay segregated.[30] When desegregation plans were implemented, however, white school boards generally continued to operate on the assumption that the black schools were inferior and unfit for white students. Local school boards shut down historic black schools, crowded black students into white schools, and fired black teachers, rather than utilize the resources of the black community for the benefit of an integrated student body. In many districts where historically black school buildings were used, their names were changed in an attempt to erase the history and the pride celebrated by naming schools after black heroes like Frederick Douglass and Paul Laurence Dunbar. Even trophy cases were removed, so that white students would not be confronted with the symbols of black achievements in athletic and debate competitions.

Many alumni of these formerly black institutions, as well as others who witnessed the closures and the firings of black teachers, felt an overwhelming sense of loss as a result of such racist implementation plans, so much so that that Lani Guinier argues, "There is an eerie nostalgia for the feeling of community that was destroyed post-*Brown*";[31] indeed, this sense of lost community is the element of counter-consensus historiography most often incorporated into recent historical novels for children. *Fire From the Rock*, in particular, gestures to "eerie nostalgia," mediating between the need to depict the very real violence of segregation and the need to combat a history of erasure.

Of the three novels in this chapter, *Fire From the Rock* is the most explicit about revising desegregation stories and offering a counter-history of *Brown*. While Draper discusses the many ways she feels that the story she tells is relevant to her present-day readers, the novel is set in the 1950s, not in her readers' contemporary moment as Walter's is. Perhaps as a result, unlike Walter's novel, *Fire From the Rock* is required reading in many secondary schools, including most of the ones in Little Rock.[32] It imagines a protagonist, Sylvia, who is on the NAACP's list of potential students to integrate Little Rock's Central High, but who elects not to join the Nine. Sylvia's brother Gary wants desperately to be on that list, but is disqualified due to his fiery anger and his sympathy for militant tactics; in contrast, her little sister, Donna Jean, speaks of desegregation as a fearsome threat rather than as an opportunity for a better education or for justice. All three children struggle against the strictures laid down by their cautious and conservative parents, who are torn between their fear of violence and their desire for their children to inherit a more just world. The plot spans the school year prior to the desegregation of Central High (with a brief epilogue showing the beginning of the Little Rock Nine's travails), and it traces Sylvia's gradual decision to work for racial equality from the vantage point of the black school.

Draper is not involved in reform movements like the immersion school movement, but she is engaged with similar projects of fostering educational success for students through a nurturing approach and an emphasis on pride. She was a secondary school teacher for thirty years, and states that she thinks of herself as continuing to teach through her writing, both by explaining ideas so that young readers can understand them and by appealing to reluctant readers so that they can improve their literacy skills.[33] Over and over, in published interviews and biographical anecdotes, Draper establishes her beliefs that high expectations and copious praise garner good results from students, that tracking and ability grouping damage them, and that effective literary study must involve interdisciplinary historical investigation and must feel relevant to students' lives. She emphasizes the effect that the publication of Alex Haley's *Roots* had upon her and her students, crediting the book and the miniseries with transforming both her view of history and also her teaching. When *Roots* first aired, she was teaching at a desegregated junior high school, and witnessed how the series raised the students' awareness of racial tension, as their discussions about the series spilled into the classroom. Crucially, however, as she describes how she responded to these classroom incidents and began to incorporate Haley's work into her units on American literature, she emphasizes that it increased student achievement by engaging them in a cross-curricular, challenging study "with no pain and much gain."[34] Thus, the process of reclaiming a formerly shameful and occluded history is linked both with a vibrant, responsive pedagogy and with academic success.

Draper's historical fiction has a similar pedagogical focus.[35] *Fire From the Rock* echoes Draper's classroom use of Haley and also extends the new *Brown* historiography into a format for use in the secondary classroom. The novel suggests that learning buried and redemptive aspects of history will be helpful for students' achievement; but furthermore, past philosophies and methods of education are recreated in a way that offers correctives for the present. Draper directly reverses the trajectory of the desegregation story in order to evoke what was lost for many black students (and thus to raise the question of what is now lacking). Her novel offers a thoughtful counter-history to the narratives generally told about *Brown*, filling in perspectives and complexities that are often omitted. Nevertheless, in order to portray the segregated black school as a utopian, nurturing cradle of academic success, Draper must portray the classroom as being more independent and self-contained than it has ever been, then or now. Furthermore, while the whole black community is portrayed as deserving citizenship rights, and as being driven to fight for these rights in a variety of ways, black youth in this novel must still earn their citizenship through good student-ship.

Fire From the Rock explicitly evokes many of the generic conventions of the desegregation stories discussed in the previous chapter. Like the protagonists of those other stories, Sylvia is an ambitious and talented girl from a middle-class family. She has a white Jewish best friend, Rachel Zucker, who has been her playmate from childhood and whose parents are among the few white people who treat black adults with respect. Like the interracial female friends of other desegregation stories, she and Rachel notice and question norms of gender as well as race; and, of course, Sylvia has the opportunity to be a pioneer in school desegregation. Instead of telling the story of a child who becomes a Civil Rights hero for desegregating the schools, however, Draper suggests that Sylvia becomes just as worthy a participant in Civil Rights history by deciding *not* to do so. In large part, this is due to her embrace of the benefits she can gain from the segregated black school. In the process of deciding against desegregation, Sylvia comes to a series of understandings: effective citizenship is nonviolent; school is both a form of citizenship and also a preparation for further action in the world; the best schooling is therefore nonviolent; so, finally, the loving and safe black school provides a better opportunity for development than the violent white one.

From the beginning, the three Patterson children establish a continuum of approaches to dealing with racism and fighting for civil rights. Gary, the oldest, leans toward militancy, and gathers around him a group of like-minded militant youth who debate the use of violent tactics and sabotage. Gary is an impatient student and hates whites, but he passionately desires to integrate Central precisely *because* it represents the kind of violent fight for which he longs. At the other end of the spectrum is Donna Jean, the youngest, who cannot for the life of her understand why anyone would want to brave daily violence simply to go to school with white children, whom she can see are not particularly special. In the middle is Sylvia, who is increasingly impatient with her parents' cautionary proverbs and pessimism, but who is also reluctant to undergo the pressure and daily harassment she knows she would face as a visible Civil Rights symbol. The inclusion of Gary and Donna Jean as advisors and models represents an important revision of the desegregation story, as neither perspective—the militant approach nor the separatist—is adequately represented in most desegregation stories. In many desegregation novels, members of the protagonists' communities castigate them for being "uppity" or for bringing danger to the community, but they do not simply shrug off white people altogether as Donna Jean does—and the militant perspective is written out entirely. Ultimately, like Emma in *Because We Are*, Sylvia must find her own approach, which is neither completely separatist, nor militant, nor heroically and symbolically integrationist in the way that the NAACP advises—even as she expresses respect and admiration for all of these tactics. In this way, school desegregation is unusually, and perhaps daringly, constructed in the novel as a strategy for moving toward racial justice, not as the endpoint or accomplishment of racial justice. At the same time, the strategy Sylvia eventually chooses is still based in institutional schooling.

The climax of the novel occurs when Sylvia's boyfriend Reggie, who has been attending Gary's militant meetings, throws a firebomb into the Zuckers' store when Sylvia just happens to be there visiting Rachel. The two girls are nearly killed in the fire that results, and both the Zuckers' store and the adjacent black-owned business, Miss Lillie and Calvin's flower shop, are completely destroyed. As it turns out, Reggie was attempting to bomb the barbershop across the street, owned by the vicious Crandalls who are responsible for many of the scariest racist incidents in the novel. Unfortunately, his aim is so epically terrible that he lands the bomb 180 degrees away from its target. The lesson against violence is clear; Reggie's bomb has left the racist business intact and instead harmed not only a white business that has been fairly helpful to the black community, but also a black business owner. Nevertheless, the racist police response to the bombing, on top of previous violent incidents, also makes Sylvia so angry that she cannot simply dismiss the issue of integration and retreat to the comfort of the black community as Donna Jean would like to do. Instead, as she processes her reaction to the bombing, she says,

> "What terrified me when I was lying on that floor is that I'd never get the chance to learn what I needed to learn, never have the time to do what I needed to do. ...I need what the colored school will give me for the next four years. I have to suck up as much pride and dignity as I can while it's there for me. Integration will happen eventually, and we're gonna lose something when it does—that feeling of being special when we walk in the school just because it's us.... I want to go to college. I want to be a teacher like Miss Washington—only with better clothes," she added with a laugh, "so little colored girls like me can grow up to be proud of their brown skin and fuzzy hair. I don't think I can suck that in like I need to from teachers and kids at an all-white high school."[36]

Good education, for Sylvia, comes from love, pride, and feelings of specialness rather than from the shiny science labs desired by the integrationist protagonists of the desegregation stories. It is, in fact, incompatible with the violence that will accompany the desegregation of Central High. That kind of violence, she suggests, is necessary for a certain kind of civil rights fight—namely, the one being fought at that moment in her town—but it is not *her* civil rights fight. Hers will be fought on a delayed schedule, through the transmission of education.

Sylvia's experience of education is shaped by the classroom culture created by Miss Washington, the teacher she takes as a role model.

Miss Washington is a no-nonsense teacher who wears stiff, dark-colored, respectable dresses. When the reader meets her, she is reprimanding the class clown, Calvin; however, her discipline is not portrayed as unnecessarily harsh or unproductive. She uses the opportunity as a teachable moment to make him demonstrate his knowledge about the recent Supreme Court *Brown* decision and to encourage him to study and achieve. In fact, Sylvia writes in her diary that while students do not like Miss Washington, they do recognize her commitment to them, drilling them in civics and grammar and forthright lessons in surviving racism, saying

> that we have to be better prepared than the white children so that we can compete for jobs and opportunities. She told us she refuses to send incompetent, unprepared Negroes into a world that expects us to mess up in the first place.[37]

Miss Washington is immediately recognizable as the kind of respected pillar of the segregated school described by numerous observers and scholars, who insisted upon achievement for all students and who delivered explicit messages about how to combat the white world's low expectations.[38]

Moreover, although she insists that the students be able to display knowledge valuable to the white world, like Shakespearean passages and the conjugations of irregular verbs, she seems to avoid the mis-education in white superiority decried by Woodson and Kunjufu; she also teaches the poetry of Paul Laurence Dunbar and Langston Hughes and requires research projects investigating topics in contemporary black culture: Jackie Robinson, Fats Domino, and the decolonization of Africa. When Miss Washington asks Sylvia why she chose Africa as her topic, Sylvia replies, "'I read an article in the World Book encyclopedia and it made me angry.... I wanted to find something that would make me feel proud.'"[39] As a result of her research paper on Africa, Sylvia begins following news stories about Ghana with increasing interest and understanding, thus drawing upon the knowledge gained in school to further her emotional involvement with the international Civil Rights movement. Miss Washington's teaching thus models for readers of *Fire From the Rock* what their own reading of historical counter-narratives ought to do—namely, to reach for corrections to the dominant historical record to find a source of pride.

One of the greatest causes for pride to be excavated from the history of segregated black schooling is the cultivation of achievement in "troublesome" or "at-risk" students. Before 1975, education law did not provide for students with disabilities to be educated in the general classroom. Nevertheless, in pre-*Brown* segregated schools, one former student recalls, "'We didn't have special ed, because the children weren't allowed to be that dumb.'"[40] This sense of inclusiveness is echoed by scholars like

Gloria Ladson-Billings and Sonya Ramsey. The passage of Education for Handicapped Children Act of 1975 (EHA), later renamed the Individuals with Disabilities Education Act (IDEA), required that students with disabilities be educated in the "least restrictive environment." This law was implemented in a climate of continuing white resistance to racial desegregation, however, so that in practice, the "least restrictive environment" for black students was disproportionately found to be a segregated special education room or a vocational track. Re-segregation through tracking, in fact, predated EHA, but this process rarely gains visibility in desegregation novels; McKissack's *A Friendship for Today*, in which Rosemary's principal pushes to have her placed in a remedial class, is a rare exception. Draper writes on her website of her frustration with this approach to sorting and designating students for failure. In *Fire From the Rock*, rather than represent this process, she instead depicts a utopian alternative historical approach in Miss Washington's class.

The characters of Calvin Cobbs and Candy Castle exemplify two types of worrisome students whom Miss Washington brings up to the mark. Calvin Cobbs is the kind of mischievous class clown who is identified in books like Kunjufu's as being at risk of under-performing, and in books like Gloria Ladson-Billings's as likely to be sent to the office by fearful white teachers. Yet, under Miss Washington's tutelage, he can recite the Gettysburg Address and define vocabulary words. Moreover, as the novel continues, it becomes increasingly clear that Calvin's goofiness would only be a deficit to be overcome in a white classroom; in a loving black community, it offers the gift of laughter and lightheartedness during a stressful time. His mischief may be distracting, but it is ultimately compatible with achievement and ethical citizenship; Calvin announces his pride in Sylvia and his determination to support her (by calling her to tell her dirty jokes after a hard day at Central), and when his mother's flower shop burns, he tries to run into the burning building to find her and then cheerfully helps her rebuild her business. Candy Castle, aptly named for her delicious appeal and lack of substance, is a different kind of "at-risk" stereotype; she is the precociously sexual teenaged girl who uses school as an opportunity, not to learn, but to flirt with boys and to flaunt her curves in revealing clothing. As with Calvin, Miss Washington cares enough about Candy to try to discipline her, rather than dismissing her as "riffraff" or taking her boy-craziness as a given, as the white teachers and administrators in Emma's schools do. While Candy does not respond to discipline with the same alacrity that Calvin does, she does appear to develop a more serious attitude over time, appearing at school in a modest, dark-colored dress and demonstrating an awareness of Civil Rights conflicts.

Nevertheless, Miss Washington's reclamation of Candy also points to the idealized black school's limitations in imagining inclusive citizenship. The black school may be able to nurture a wider range of personalities, abilities, and interests than the white school, but it is still a state institution that functions to create normative citizens. As numerous scholars observe, sexuality in adolescents is consistently portrayed as destructive to character and achievement, posing an aggregate threat to the state by spoiling the quality of its human resources.[41] Beyond this, the sexuality of black women in particular is portrayed as especially non-normative, excessive, and incompatible with other qualities of citizenship such as middle-class values and able-bodied independence.[42] Thus, in order to be a powerful and influential citizen in the black community, Miss Washington must wear dark and drab clothing, and Candy must learn to correct her own wardrobe; in fact, when she gets serious about school, she does not demonstrate her change by actually reciting her knowledge as Calvin does, but by wearing the kind of dark colors and plain clothing that Miss Washington favors. Similarly, Sylvia's desire for Reggie threatens her academic ambitions; before she chooses the segregated black high school, she must break with Reggie so that she can choose the school solely for academic, and not social, reasons. While *Fire From the Rock* does not end with Sylvia and her friends' triumphant graduation and entry into adult nation building, it does culminate with the anticipation of their successful and public-spirited future, a future that depends upon delaying sexual desire and framing it as antithetical to the desire for learning.

This careful monitoring of sexuality provides one of the few indications that the resistant black school system of the novel remains ideologically (in addition to physically and financially) constrained by the racist white world outside. Critic Robert Stepto coins the term "ritual grounds" to describe enclosed, circumscribed spaces that function in black literature as cradles of community, protection, and learning; schoolrooms are one of his primary examples. Nevertheless, he stresses that the ritual grounds provide nurturing only within the confines of a white world that surrounds and threatens it. Thus, in Mildred Taylor's award-winning and popular children's novel *Roll of Thunder, Hear My Cry*, the only "safe space" for learning is the black-owned and operated Logan family farm. The segregated school is taught mostly by black teachers who fear white authority and who consent to teach racist versions of history. Mary Logan, the protagonists' mother, represents the kind of demanding, resistant teacher described by counter-historians who point to the black school as a community center; yet when her resistance attracts the notice of white authorities, her adjustments to the state curriculum come under scrutiny and she is fired. Only on the shelter of the Logans' land, with Mrs. Logan working as an unpaid volunteer outside of the state's employ, can the children in the community come to her unofficial school to be educated in literacy and pride.[43] Similarly, *Because We Are* imagines that no ground is truly safe or sheltered; community cohesion can provide a psychological, but not a literal "safe space" for resistance.

In Draper's novel, however, written during the No Child Left Behind era of increased top-down requirements for standardized testing and accountability, black schools of the past are nostalgically imagined as exempt from the oppressive requirements of the novel's 2007 publication (even as they contend with historic forms of oppression). This nostalgia sharply contrasts with novels written before the Afro-centric immersion school movement. In *Roll of Thunder, Hear My Cry*, Mrs. Logan is fired because T.J., a class clown who *fails* to achieve in her class, retaliates against her discipline by reporting her resistant teaching methods to the white authorities. In Taylor's novel, not all students achieve simply because they are expected to; failure is still a part of school life. Moreover, when T.J. does fail to achieve, the costs of his failure are disastrous not only to him (he ends up on trial for murder) but also to the project of subversive black education. In contrast, Miss Washington never has to defend her curricular choices or her teaching methods to a white administrator, even though historically, the kind of resistant teaching she exemplifies was sometimes constrained by a white supervisory structure. Nor does she seem to contend with dismal employment prospects for students who wish to pursue white-collar jobs.

In various ways, then, the novel's selective depiction of an historical classroom idyll leans toward the "eerie nostalgia" observed by Lani Guinier. Draper highlights aspects of *Brown* historiography, not merely for the sake of historical education, but also in order to envision reforms for many of the institutional constraints she finds damaging to teaching and learning for democratic citizenship. Her vision of antiracist educational reform offers a model of citizenship that does not depend upon surviving brutality, and acknowledges that young people may find many ways, and many timelines, for supporting the struggle for justice. Miss Washington's self-contained classroom probably has few, if any, actual precedents in mid-century United States education; in order to offer such a vision as a hopeful alternative, one *must* venture into the realm of nostalgic fantasy. Nevertheless, like the more "typical" desegregation stories of Chapter 1, *Fire from the Rock* depends upon a narrative of triumph and success in order to make its point. Just as the students, both black and white, of the forced desegregation stories must succeed academically in order to prove the worthiness of the desegregation project, so Sylvia and her companions must perform academically in order to demonstrate the validity of the supportive Afro-centric alternative to desegregation. As a result, there is no room for a citizen who is not also a good student, and good students must adhere to normative timelines of sexual delay in order to succeed.

Feathers: Finding Hope in the Past

Jacqueline Woodson's 2007 novel *Feathers*, published in the same year as Draper's book, offers a different kind of classroom haven from whiteness, one that redefines what academic achievement and ability mean.

Feathers represents a third approach to counter-narratives of desegregation, occupying a middle ground between the status of Draper's historical novel, which is explicitly designed as a Civil Rights teaching text and is taught as such, and Walter's radical contemporary critique, which quietly went out of print. Woodson is a prominent author whose books are widely circulated, and *Feathers* won a Newbery Honor award. At the same time, *Feathers* has received less attention than Woodson's more recent texts like the picture book *Each Kindness* (2014) and the verse memoir *Brown Girl Dreaming* (2014); these address the issue of bullying and the struggles of children who learn slowly, but do not focus on classroom dynamics and pedagogy to the extent that *Feathers* does. Unlike many of Woodson's novels, which focus on contemporary issues, *Feathers* is a work of historical fiction. Unlike Draper's novel, it does not explicitly engage the Civil Rights era. This setting in a past that is both distant from the reader's own time and distinct from the usual time frame of Civil Rights consensus history allows for a creative re-invention of desegregated education that neither repeats consensus narratives nor closes off the potential for meaningful desegregated education.

Feathers departs from several desegregation story conventions.[44] Its protagonist, Frannie, is an indifferent student, hardly the shining star that other black protagonists are. The narrative covers only part of a school year, so that the plot arc of the school story is cut short; the novel does not end with Frannie's being recognized by the school for her contributions. Moreover, she faces no clear-cut decision between a desegregated community and a segregated one; her community is clearly segregated, but she never has any desire to participate in the white world across the highway and in fact spends much of the novel wondering why her friends are so discontented. The novel is set in the early 1970s, against the backdrop of the Black Power movement. At the beginning of the school year, Frannie's warm, encouraging teacher reads them the famous Emily Dickinson poem about hope, and she struggles to understand its metaphoric imagery of feathers. She begins to understand the poem better as she observes that her deaf brother Sean,[45] who attends a separate school, wishes he could participate in the hearing and white worlds from which he is barred; that her mother, who has miscarried many pregnancies, fears to lose another; and that her classmates talk about Black Power but long for what they see on the white side of the highway. In a reversal of the typical desegregation story, a white-appearing boy joins Frannie's classroom and is quickly nicknamed the Jesus Boy by the class bully, due to his resemblance to traditional white pictures of Jesus. The Jesus Boy, an adopted son of a black family, has been harassed and tormented at schools on the white side of the highway, and his parents assure him that the black community will be more welcoming. They are wrong; most of Frannie's classmates take out their frustrations on the Jesus Boy, and only Frannie, secure in her own sense of safety within the black community, is willing to befriend him.

This novel explicitly evokes the typical desegregation stories of the previous chapter in that its action revolves around the entry of a single racially different student who forges an interracial friendship, stands up to a bully, and achieves some measure of classroom acceptance. Rather than assuming that black students wish to integrate white schools, however, Woodson imagines a white boy who wishes to integrate into the black community. She thus explicitly pushes the counter-narratives of Walter and Draper a step further; not only are black schools superior for black students, they may also be more desirable for white students. Nevertheless, just as the desegregation of the white school in the desegregation story pushes white society to develop toward a more inclusive form of democracy, so the desegregation of the black school in *Feathers* also demonstrates where the black community falls short of utopian fulfillment.

Unlike in other desegregation novels, the plot is not structured by the school year, so that there is no graduation or stepping-up ceremony at the end that renders the students up to the service of the nation. These departures from the generic conventions of school stories allow the novel to open up some innovative critiques of the school system, most importantly the demand that learning occur according to an inflexible timeline. Nevertheless, as in Draper's novel, the novel's nostalgic setting both allows for some of its utopian educational visions to be presented as "realistic" and also limits these utopian solutions. Woodson's idealized classroom breaks fairly entrenched institutional linkages between academic achievement and speed of learning, and it allows for a black "safe space" that may be integrated by white students willing to recognize the benefits of the black community; however, it is set during a period when students with disabilities remain excluded from the utopian classroom.

From the beginning of the novel, a schoolroom drama of racial integration is framed by an academic lesson on the Emily Dickinson poem, "'Hope' is the thing with feathers." The issue of integration and the poem are both, in turn, connected with the experience of time as a political rather than natural force. Some characters seek hope by looking forward to changing times; others cling to their own past and to a history of segregation; and Frannie struggles both to encode memories and to allow herself to hope for the future. Ultimately, as she lives with the poem in her consciousness, she facilitates both classroom integration and her own academic understanding by attending to each moment as it passes, rather than focusing either on the past or on the future.

The day the Jesus Boy walks in is the day after Ms. Johnson reads the Dickinson poem to the class. Frannie is thinking about the poem as the Jesus Boy is introduced to the stares of her classmates and the hostile comments of the class bully Trevor. She makes a face at him, then looks down at her notebook to face the immediate reminder of the poem and her mother's response to it:

> When I told Mama about the poem, she'd said, Welcome to the seventies, Frannie. Sounds like Ms. Johnson's trying to tell you all something about looking forward instead of back all the time. I just stared at Mama. The poem was about hope and how hope had these feathers on it. It didn't have a single thing to do with looking forward or backward or even sideways. But then Sean came home and I told him about the poem and the crazy thing Mama had said. Sean smiled and shook his head. You're a fool, he signed to me. The word doesn't have feathers. It's a metaphor. Don't you learn anything at Price? So maybe the seventies is the thing with feathers. Maybe it was about hope and moving forward and not looking behind you.[46]

This passage establishes a few crucial concepts. First, Frannie is introduced as a character who is attracted to words and poetry but who struggles to understand her lessons "correctly"; Sean's remark suggests that she is somehow lagging, not learning what she ought to know at her grade level. This characterization is sustained throughout; Frannie frequently remarks that she has trouble remembering vocabulary words and schoolwork, and she knows that she takes longer than her classmates to grasp her lessons. Nevertheless, this passage also emphasizes that understanding Dickinson's poem will not involve merely the academic skills of memory and retention. Moving forward, Mama says, will mean letting go of some aspects of the historical past. Frannie may have difficulty retaining her lessons, but the flip side of this seeming limitation is that she also releases bad memories.

This ability turns out to be crucial to her willingness to accept the Jesus Boy's attending a residentially segregated black school. When Frannie's classmate Maribel Tanks—a middle-class girl Frannie despises—complains that the Jesus Boy belongs on the other side of the highway with the white people, Frannie replies, "'It's the nineteen seventies,' I said. 'Not the fifties. There's no more segregation, remember?' 'Try telling that to the people on the other side of the highway,' Maribel said. 'Or the people on this side.'"[47] Maribel has a point; while nobody else specifically references the history of segregation, many of the people Frannie knows cling to the past in small ways as well as historically consequential ones. Maribel, for example, still wears her outgrown sweatshirts from a private school she attended as a constant reminder of her past status. Trevor, who was teased as a younger child for being light-skinned and having an absent white father on the other side of the highway, continues to be alert to insult, lashing out and terrifying his classmates with his angry words and his fists. Conversely, her peers assert superiority as a way to protect their future status. Maribel anticipates inheriting her mother's store, and replicates her disdain for poorer classmates; Frannie's best friend Samantha, a devout member of a fire-and-brimstone church, insists that she is holy and (unlike Frannie) will not have to worry about her afterlife. Samantha is briefly willing to welcome the Jesus Boy, but only because she hopes he really is Jesus, come to bring a better future; once she realizes that he is not, she loses interest in him.

These classmates function more "normally" in school than Frannie does; implicitly, through Frannie's outsider point of view, readers experience their sense of time, normative development, and expectations through a critical lens. While Frannie is not an openly queer character, her narrative perspective frames time in ways that resonate with Judith "Jack" Halberstam's concepts of "queer time," and indeed with Woodson's many novels that highlight the concerns of queer youth. Halberstam argues that the concept of normative time tends to pressure citizens to reproduce according to a biological clock and to pass along an inheritance to offspring. He goes on to say, "It also connects the family to the historical past of the nation, and glances ahead to connect the family to the future of both familial and national stability."[48] Thus, a strong sense of historic time shapes the future by framing capital, genetic material, and—crucially—normative values, as important pieces of inheritance that must be preserved for future generations. In Walter's and Draper's novels, a sense of normative time is powerful; black schoolchildren must recover their lost inheritance in order to create a better future. In *Feathers*, by contrast, a concern with inheritance is seen to be an obstacle to racial justice and equality. In part, this is because the children seem to have adopted a belief in white superiority along with a capitalist sense of time; thus, investing in national values of heteropatriarchal inheritance also means investing in a history of segregation that marks black cultural inheritance as inferior.

Similar to the middle-class students at Emma's desegregated school, Frannie's peers mouth Black Power and anti-white sentiments, but prize their own inheritance of community very little. Maribel straightens her hair. Other kids carry Afro picks in their pockets, but their stance toward the Jesus Boy reflects some critiques of Black Power economic separatism during the 1970s, as activists who encouraged self-sufficiency were nevertheless invested in the white-dominated U.S. capitalist system.[49] The students don't want the Jesus Boy in their school, but neither do they want to be where they are, adopting both white attitudes toward desegregation and white attitudes toward their own community. Frannie's brother Sean imagines building a bridge from his own window to the other side of the highway, and Trevor tries to swing high enough to fly over the fence. The other kids have internalized what Frannie has trouble grasping; when she asks her mother why no white people live on their side of the highway, she says, "*They don't want to live over here.*

And the way she said it made me wonder what was so wrong with *our* side of the highway."[50] Frannie wonders this because she seems to live outside of normative time and sees no better future (or present) on the other side of the highway. Rather than wishing to cross her brother's imaginary bridge to the white side of town, she looks out the same window he does and sees the beauty of the bright graffiti art that the adults complain about. Like Donna Jean in Draper's novel, Frannie feels she has everything she needs right in her own community.

Frannie's contentment with living in the present conflicts with the goals of the school, which are to preserve the nation's cultural inheritance through the transmission of knowledge and to increase its capital inheritance through the development of its human resources. Educational discourse sometimes emphasizes this alignment; Stuart Buck, for example, says,

> Education is like money in the bank. Someone who starts with ten thousand dollars will earn more interest from day one than someone who starts with ten dollars, and the spread between the two accounts will only grow larger as the interest is compounded over time.[51]

In *Feathers*, this approach to education is echoed ironically. When Frannie cannot remember a vocabulary word, she thinks,

> I tried to find the word *surreal* in my mental vocabulary bank where Ms. Johnson had said we should save vocabulary words so that we could grow up and have rich brains, but it wasn't there. Ms. Johnson said that the only way you can deposit a word in your bank is by committing it to memory. I hadn't deposited *surreal*. I guess I must have spent it somewhere.[52]

Arguably, of course, when one spends a thing, it means that one uses it. In the case of a vocabulary word, spending it through common use is presumably the purpose of learning it in the first place; however, the metaphors of depositing, saving, and spending here suggest that Frannie is supposed to save her knowledge rather than spend it. Educational philosopher Paolo Freire famously attacks the "banking model" of pedagogy for making students into passive safe-deposit boxes for inert bits of knowledge and thereby making them more compliant and oppress-able. Frannie's disingenuous comment about her failure to deposit rich vocabulary words suggests a further critique of this method—that school learning is to be hoarded for personal gain rather than circulated for the common good.

In addition to wantonly spending her inheritance of learning, Frannie is out of step with normative time in another key way. Achievement within the state-sponsored school system depends, not only upon learning, but also upon learning within a certain time frame. Abigail and Stephan Thernstrom draw upon this discourse in arguing for increased accountability for standardized testing:

> "In education, the time we waste today can mean a lifetime wasted tomorrow," Lyndon B. Johnson said in introducing Title I in 1965. "Wasted" was a bit of hyperbole, but as long as the typical black or Hispanic student knows much less than the average white or Asian, racial and ethnic equality will remain an elusive goal.[53]

Developmental time thus becomes a resource to be controlled and husbanded as part of the nation's capital inheritance, and national progress toward racial equality must inexplicably be determined according to an age-graded academic schedule or not at all.[54] Frannie, who needs more time to understand material, thus is framed within educational discourse as "wasting" the future lifetime belonging to the nation.

Frannie's and Sean's black schools, however, operate according to a different philosophy and a different sense of time, one that might allow for meaningful racial integration precisely by *avoiding* normative capitalist constructs of time and achievement. Frannie's teacher, Ms. Johnson, is a gentler and hipper version of Sylvia's teacher Miss Washington, expecting all of her students to succeed and providing constant support for them to do so in the form of discipline, snacks, and encouragement. Frannie says, "[Ms. Johnson] doesn't just teach us and if we don't get it, she keeps on moving. She really cares about us understanding things and she'll take a real long time explaining something until she's sure everybody's got it."[55] Notably, Ms. Johnson's flexible approach to the time of achievement does not seem to result in Frannie's learning any less, even though she may appear to cover the material more slowly.

Frannie learns in her own time, but she does learn. In a debate with Samantha, she surprises both Samantha and herself by rapidly spitting out several pertinent historical examples that she seems to have absorbed without realizing it. Then, months after Ms. Johnson first reads them the Dickinson poem, Frannie continues to reflect on the metaphor of feathers, developing expanding interpretations. At one point, the Jesus Boy faces down Trevor in the schoolyard and humiliates him. Frannie thinks about the poem, and about Trevor wanting to fly over the fence and rejoin his white father, and she and the Jesus Boy both pull Trevor out of the snow and dust him off. Because of Frannie's reflection on the poem, both Trevor and the Jesus Boy are thus reclaimed and redeemed for the community rather than abandoned for their transgressions, just as Frannie is redeemed as a learner despite her slowness.

This scene both revises and continues traditions of the desegregation school story. Unlike in other desegregation stories, the bully is not ejected or dismissed as marginal to the majority community. The Jesus

Boy's desire to join the black community signals its utopian potential, but its rejection of him also signals its failure; the community must be made more worthy of his desire, and must also recapture Trevor's strayed desire. The success of this integration effort is not demonstrated by Frannie's, or the Jesus Boy's, academic success in the form of high grades or test scores. Nevertheless, some form of school learning is necessary in order to catalyze the success of integration, as it is only when Frannie thinks about the poem that she realizes that Trevor needs to see some hope on his own side of the highway. Ms. Johnson's warmth and flexibility allows Frannie to absorb the poem more deeply; in turn, she internalizes not only the concept of metaphor, but also a community ethic that shapes the school as a loving rather than violent or vengeful place. If Ms. Johnson's method is meant to make Frannie's test scores equivalent to those of the kids on the other side of the highway, it may have failed, due to her "wasting" of time; but it may have made Frannie successful in the integration (pun intended) of meaningful learning.

The reader learns less about Sean's education, given Frannie's limited window into it; she knows mainly that he excels at math. Sean attends the Daffodil School, a neighborhood special education facility with a counterpart on the white side of the highway called the Starship Academy. The contrast between the names of the two schools illustrates the greater potential of black neighborhood schools:

> Mama said even if we lived on that side of the highway, she'd cross it every day to come to the Daffodil School because there was no way on God's green earth she'd send Sean to a school that sounded like it was for people from outer space.[56]

The Daffodil School evokes a kind of Romantic, Progressive philosophy from the turn of the twentieth century, when discourse about learning frequently compared children to plants that needed to be nurtured to full growth and allowed to unfold according to Nature's timeline.[57] The white Starship Academy instead gestures toward the rhetoric of "reaching for the stars" and recalls the national achievement of space exploration; but it also, as Mama recognizes, positions students with disabilities as aliens who are shot into the outer spaces of the school system. Mama—and, she believes, her neighborhood schools—consistently revalue the polarities of black/white and abled/disabled.

Nevertheless, protected disability segregation is questioned in the novel just as protected racial segregation is. Frannie's loving school can expand to include Trevor, who has a white father, and the Jesus Boy, who chooses the black community despite his white appearance, but racial ambiguity proves easier to include than disability. When two hearing girls approach Sean and flirt with him on the way to school, they make hurtful comments when they realize he is deaf, before losing interest entirely. Frannie is furious, but Sean tries to explain why he remains interested in the hearing girls:

> *When we were sitting at the window that day and I said what if we could build a bridge from every window.... The hearing girls are the bridges. They're the other worlds. They're the worlds I can't just walk across and into, you know.... I don't just want my world. I want everybody else's world too.*[58]

According to the ethos of Walter's or Draper's novels, Sean should not experience black hearing girls as "other worlds"; as part of the black community, Sean ought to be in the same world. He is aware that he is not; and Frannie says, "I watched him walk away, all dressed like a Black Panther but looking a little bit smaller than when we'd left the house that morning."[59] Sean may dress like a Black Panther and attend a school that nurtures him like a daffodil, but he is still thrust to the margins of the black community. This exclusion partly accounts for Woodson's ambivalent incorporation of the Black Power movement in the novel. Black Power, in the sense of Frannie's embrace of her community, is celebrated, but Black Power is also diminished when Sean, who ought to be part of its strength, is made to feel small.

Sean's exclusion from full membership in the black community points to one of the contradictions in the novel's utopian vision of education. Considering how much emphasis is placed upon Frannie's ethical wisdom in living fully in the present, the novel's setting in the historical past of the 1970s is remarkable. In an interview on National Public Radio, Woodson explains that the overarching idea driving the book is one that she feels is necessary and pertinent to contemporary readers; she feels that we live in a society dominated by fear, and she wanted to think about the many different ways that children can find small moments of hope in their everyday lives. The historical setting does allow for Frannie's school to be hopeful and utopian in ways that are increasingly difficult for schools in the era of No Child Left Behind; it also places Frannie's school out of reach of another kind of reform, that of disability inclusion.

The key to Frannie's learning, and to the desirability of the black school and community, is the abandonment of the normative timelines of inheritance and achievement—timelines driven by individualist or capitalist goals—in favor of a flexible timeline guided by hope, love, and communal service. This kind of flexibility is precisely what is targeted by the move toward accountability and standards since the 2001 No Child Left Behind Act. The accountability movement regards achievement as valid only in comparison with white norms. In addition, it enforces a strict timeline according to which a student has failed if she is not able to demonstrate the knowledge that is determined to be standard for a fourth grader (or fifth grader or eighth grader)—regardless of how much he or she has learned since the start of the school year.

This timeline is an important part of how schools are assessed and punished under the No Child Left Behind law; Jim Horn, in an article published in 2007, the same year as *Feathers*, notes that the ticking clock of impending consequences for failing Louisiana's LEAP test greatly altered how teachers in New Orleans schools led their classes. In interviews, teachers complained of the "unyielding scope and sequence that [left] little latitude for dealing with the many students who are not on the fourth-grade level."[60] Principals had trouble staffing their fourth-grade classrooms or mentoring teachers due to time pressures, and fourth-grade students were throwing up and becoming sick from anxiety before the test. Horn offers statistics suggesting that this time pressure disproportionately affects black students; he cites studies which demonstrate that none of the ten states with the lowest proportion of black students require high-stakes grade-level tests of this kind, but all ten of the states with the highest proportion of black students do. The disparities are similar in looking at high school exit examinations.

Especially when written within such a context of fear and anxiety, Ms. Johnson's approach to education seems preferable ethically and practically. The nuanced understanding of hope and its relation to time that Frannie gains as a result of this unhurried, nurturing approach can be read as a direct comment upon the pressured conditions under which the novel's readers must find their own hope. Like Draper, Woodson reaches back to the past for an alternative model of schooling and citizenship. At the same time, her interview suggests that Frannie's expansive, reflective time sense can serve as a model for her young readers, who may see their worlds as being as closed and unyielding as Trevor and Sean do. This provides an important reminder that Frannie is not entirely dependent upon Ms. Johnson for her approach to learning; she has, after all, had other teachers, who proceeded through material regardless of whether the students "got it," and yet she has continued to learn, and to reflect, at her own pace. Frannie's neighborhood school does not look utopian to all the students who attend it; it is, in part, her vision that makes it so. In this respect, Woodson both opens a door for readers to escape to a freer, more utopian past, and simultaneously reminds them that the past rarely felt like utopia to those living through it. Utopian learning and citizenship, therefore, always require a willingness to resist normative pressures, during any time period and under any institutional structure.

And yet, as readers can see in *Feathers*, institutional structures do matter. Setting the novel in the early 1970s makes Frannie's freedom to learn at her own pace (at least, in Ms. Johnson's exceptional classroom) more believable. Setting the novel before the passage of EHA, however, means that an environment that allows for Frannie's learning style will also inevitably divide the nurturing black community and deny Sean a similarly utopian environment. Considering how much Frannie loves her brother and how much pain his alienation causes her, a school that excludes disability is not entirely utopian for Frannie, either. Resistant learning *can* take place within any structure; conversely, as the novel makes clear in its depiction of desegregation, legalized structural change is no guarantee of progress toward more democratic or utopian communities. Nevertheless, the ubiquity of the structural constraints that overshadow Frannie's (and readers') experience of school raises the question of why a school-based utopia continues to be the desired end of so many novels, even when those same novels critique the exclusionary nature of most "real" school utopias.

The Appeal of the School Story

Children are compelled by the state to spend six hours a day in school, and so attempting to improve both their present and the nation's future by envisioning more utopian schools is both logical and attractive. It matters to children how they spend six hours a day. Not all children wish to spend that chunk of their lives in daily resistance and struggle; while much utopian educational theory necessarily places a high value on everyday acts of resistance,[61] theorists tend to aim these messages of resistance at teachers. Defining ideal citizenship as a daily exercise in pain, insecurity, or isolation would be a heavy burden to place on children, or adults either, for that matter. The Gothic school stories discussed by Thomas Atwood and Wade Lee do frame citizenship education as a series of lessons in pain and fear, and they also highlight the costs of this approach; Cormier's *The Chocolate War*, for example, ends in the nearly fatal beating of a resistant student. By contrast, even the character-building violence of the classic school stories emphasize straightforward moral and physical challenges that are clearly supported by structural mores, rather than asking protagonists to pit their own values against those demanded by the institution. This is the great appeal of many school stories, both classic and revisionist; they hold out the hope of a world in which the ethical goals and values of the children, the teachers, the institution, and the wider democracy might be in harmony rather than at odds—even if this world can exist only within the temporary, limited space of an exceptional utopian classroom.

This is the kind of hope that the three novels in this chapter evoke. Each of them counters the assumption that the *Brown* decision produced a utopian school system; but rather than looking away from the school as a source of utopian reform, each looks to practices from black schools rather than white ones as sources of hopeful reform. Specifically, all three counter the idea that the classroom ought to be a competitive meritocracy and instead offer the belief that merit, ability, and achievement can be developed through the nurturing of loving teachers or through the unification and pride of the students themselves. All three suggest important ways that the entrenched racism in the *existing* system might be decreased, whether by valuing student learning on its own terms instead of by comparison to white students, by eliminating pressured timelines for achievement, or by empowering students to insist upon gaining knowledge from racist teachers determined to withhold it.

Nevertheless, in countering the claims of inferiority propagated by *Brown*, these novels also reinforce the idea that the quality of a school, and the achievement of the students it produces, are the truly crucial questions in considering the citizenship rights and abilities of voting adults. Granted, the institutional values of a school can be extremely flexible; schools can define "success" through cricket games, tests of character, or academic performance, can set a strict or a loose timeline for the required learning, and can incentivize individual competition or community cohesion. Regardless of how they define success or what conditions they place upon its achievement, however, schools do exist to promote whatever kind of achievement they deem necessary; and school stories aim to give the reader the vicarious satisfaction of experiencing the protagonist's success within a given school setting.

This is a real satisfaction (whether vicariously or directly experienced), and it often carries real, positive consequences; achievement is often a worthy goal, and good student-ship can provide one route to ethical citizenship. Nevertheless, many models of utopian education and citizenship are ruled out even by resistant school stories. The structure of most school stories does not allow for consideration of how failing students might have something valuable to contribute to the nation—even those who "fail" to be rescued by the school. Nor do they always account for how successful students might fail to fulfill their ideals of racial justice within a wider society where racism is continually mutating. In the next chapter, I examine constructs of disability and academic failure as fruitful alternatives for thinking about citizenship and racial justice.

Notes

1 Nikole Hannah-Jones, in "Choosing a School for My Daughter," gives a concise and clear overview of this process.
2 NAACP, "It's Not the Distance"; Cottle, *Busing*, 77.
3 See Fairclough, "The Costs of *Brown*," 43–44; Walker, "Second-Class Integration," 272–273; and Cecelski, *Along Freedom Road*, 8–9.
4 Pinkney, *Hand in Hand*, "Thurgood Marshall—Mr. Civil Rights." Further examples include Patricia McKissack's novel *A Friendship for Today*, in which Rosemary's friends clearly learn less after desegregation, and Ellen Levine's collection of interviews, *Freedom's Children*, in which at least one student recalls wanting to attend Tuskegee after desegregation because of her sense of pride (41).

5 Other novels that do so include McKissack's *A Friendship for Today* and Andrea Davis Pinkney's *Hold Fast to Dreams.* Within the nonfiction collection *Linda Brown, You Are Not Alone*, reviewers Fenly and Henderson specifically praise white-authored selections by Jerry Spinelli and Katherine Paterson, and criticize Reed's and Troupe's selections for "open[ing] old wounds" (Fenly).
6 Mildred Pitts Walter, email message to author, May 25, 2013.
7 Morris, "Research, Ideology, and the *Brown* Decision;" Bell, *Shades of Brown*, 115, 135.
8 Robin Bernstein explains how the doll experiments were manipulated to achieve the desired results. Specifically, the Clarks changed the order of the questions so as to produce emotional distress that had not been present in earlier experiments. Furthermore, during the *Brown* hearings, they downplayed the differences they saw between Southern and Northern black children; Northern children, who experienced integrated settings more often, showed more distress and displayed more preference for the white dolls than the more strictly segregated Southern children did. See also Derrick Bell for a critique of how the deleterious effects of segregation on white children was notably absent from the *Brown* decision. *Shades of Brown*, 19–23.
9 Morris, "Research, Ideology, and the *Brown* Decision."
10 Patterson, *Brown v. Board of Education*, 66.
11 Walter, *Because We Are*, 8.
12 Paterson's *The Great Gilly Hopkins* and Troupe's "St. Louis" both highlight the demystification of white superiority; McKissack's and Watts's novels both allude to black students who internalize racism, and Pinkney's *Hold Fast to Dreams* references the trap of "acting white."
13 Walter, *Because We Are*, 13.
14 Du Bois, "Does the Negro Need Separate Schools?," 330.
15 Woodson, *The Mis-Education of the Negro*, xii.
16 Ibid., 23.
17 Walter, *Because We Are*, 84–85.
18 Andrea Simpson traces divisions between the Civil Rights generation, who tend to be more optimistic about opportunity, and the post-Civil Rights generation of the 1980s, who tend to see decreasing opportunity.
19 Jordan, *Broken Silences*, 281.
20 Walter, *Because We Are*, 99.
21 Ibid., 134.
22 Walter references the history of forced boxing in her interview with Shirley Jordan, and her experiences in tutoring high school students in the interview "Profile: Choice, Courage, and Change."
23 Omi and Winant, *Racial Formation*, 117. Lani Guinier suggests a similar reason for the failures of *Brown*'s implementation, and Roderick Ferguson traces a similar process in higher education in *The Re-Order of Things*.
24 Walter, *Because We Are*, 170.
25 Educational philosophers, antiracist activists, and disability activists often share a critical stance toward the pattern of the white, active, adult studying the minoritized, passive, immature 'problem' subject. See Dewey, *Democracy in Education*, 25; Linton, *Claiming Disability*, 25–28; Lewis, *Race in the Schoolyard*, "Struggling With Dangerous Subjects."
26 Omi and Winant's theory of racism as a mutating structure might predict that when testing gaps are narrowed, disparities in employment, wages, and living conditions will likely continue, and some other reason will be found for those inequalities. Nevertheless, many antiracist scholars, such

as Jawanza Kunjufu and Amanda Lewis, hold to the hope that closing the achievement gap is a way to eliminate racism and structural inequality.

27 Thernstrom and Thernstrom, *No Excuses*, 3.
28 Walter, *Because We Are*, 192.
29 Ladson-Billings, *The Dreamkeepers*, 3, emphasis in original. Jawanza Kunjufu also testifies to the benefits of Afro-centric schools.
30 Cecelski, *Along Freedom Road*, 27.
31 Guinier, "Racial Liberalism to Racial Literacy," 98. Patterson records similarly ambivalent statements of nostalgia. *Brown v. Board of Education*, 194.
32 Sharon Draper, personal email to author, February 22, 2013.
33 Hinton, "Reaching Reluctant Readers." Draper also explains her sense of educational mission on her website.
34 Draper, "Digging Deeper."
35 Draper discusses this in her interview with KaaVonia Hinton, "Reaching Reluctant Readers."
36 Draper, *Fire From the Rock*, 200.
37 Ibid., 38.
38 See, for example, Ramsey, "We Will Be Ready," 37–39; Kunjufu, *To Be Popular or Smart*, 15.
39 Draper, *Fire From the Rock*, 92.
40 Buck, *Acting White*, 117.
41 Nancy Lesko traces this discourse in Chapter Five of *Act Your Age!*. Mike Males also suggests that teenaged sexuality offers an excuse for scapegoating teens (242–269).
42 Rottenberg discusses the constriction of sexual norms for "respectable" black women (*Performing Americanness*, 102). In Ferguson's *Aberrations in Black*, the chapter on *Invisible Man* similarly analyzes how non-normative sexuality is portrayed as incompatible with black citizenship.
43 This occurs in *Let the Circle Be Unbroken*, the sequel to *Roll of Thunder, Hear My Cry*.
44 Woodson's earlier novel about contemporary desegregation, *Maizon at Blue Hill* (1992), also departs from generic conventions, but less so. The novel depicts the isolation of a black student at a prestigious desegregated boarding school. Maizon struggles to feel comfortable in white-dominated classrooms and feels constrained by the social rules of her small black peer group. She is a gifted student, not a struggling one like Frannie, and the novel portrays the teachers and administrators as being relatively well meaning and inclusive. Like Frannie, though, Maizon values her own urban community in Brooklyn, and leaves the white school despite her academic success and despite the friendliness of her white roommate.
45 People in the Deaf community make a distinction between deafness and Deafness, with the change in orthography signaling the difference between an impairment and a cultural orientation. I use the lower-case form of the word when discussing Sean. Vivian Yenika-Agbaw argues, in her analysis of *Feathers*, that the novel offers a social model of disability, but does not position Sean within Deaf culture or even portray Deafness as a resistant culture. Therefore, I indicate Sean's position by describing him as deaf rather than as Deaf.
46 Woodson, *Feathers*, 3.
47 Ibid., 11.
48 Halberstam, *Queer Time*, 5.
49 Dubey, *Black Women Novelists*, 21–22.
50 Woodson, *Feathers*, 16.

51 Buck, *Acting White*, 28.
52 Woodson, *Feathers*, 35.
53 Thernstrom and Thernstrom, *No Excuses*, 247.
54 Michel Foucault's *Discipline and Punish* details how time becomes a national resource; Vinovskis, Angus, and Mirel trace the development of age-graded schooling and the standardization of learning timelines.
55 Woodson, *Feathers*, 23.
56 Ibid., 18.
57 The title of Kate Douglas Wiggin's *Garden of Childhood* indicates one example of this Progressive-era parallel between children and natural plant growth. Dewey, in *Democracy in Education*, also expounds on the idea of education as a process of unfolding in Chapter 5.
58 Woodson, *Feathers*, 83.
59 Ibid., 85. Wendy Rountree notes that Woodson consistently highlights diversity within the black community.
60 Horn, "The LEAP for Accountability?," 129.
61 See Giroux, *Theory and Resistance*, xxvii, 36; Freire, *Pedagogy of the Oppressed*, 46–47, 126–128.

3 Pedagogies of Desegregation

Narratives of Disability and Giftedness

School Resegregation and Parallel Spaces

One legacy of the *Brown* decision is seldom discussed openly in children's literature. The implementation of *Brown* has had, and continues to have, a complicated effect upon the school system's mechanisms for diagnosing, sorting, and educating students with disabilities. On the one hand, as Beth Ferri and David Connor point out, the activists who pushed for the passage of the 1975 Education of Handicapped Children Act (later named IDEA), which provided for the inclusion of students with disabilities in the "least restrictive environment," drew inspiration from the legal precedent of *Brown*. On the other hand, they also note that placement in special education has been consistently used as a mechanism to re-segregate children placed in racially desegregated schools. Since at least the late 1960s, African-American and Latino children have been disproportionately diagnosed with mental retardation or have been tracked into remedial programs. After the passage of IDEA, this re-segregation continued, and has persisted into the twenty-first century, in both Northern and Southern states. White children with learning difficulties tend to be diagnosed as learning disabled (LD), and placed in the "least restrictive environment" of the general classroom; African-American children with similar profiles are three times more likely to be diagnosed with mental retardation and twice as likely to be diagnosed with emotional disability, labels which more often lead to placement in a separate classroom.[1] In practical terms, this means not only that classroom segregation has continued to be an issue even within nominally desegregated schools, but also that problems with disability education are simultaneously problems of racial justice. Movements for desegregation and inclusive education are entwined both in their common goals for a more just and humane educational system, and also in seeing these goals stymied and distorted in similar ways upon implementation.

This legacy of *Brown*—re-segregation through tracking and diagnosis—is one that schoolchildren across the United States have personally witnessed for decades; unlike the story of Ruby Bridges or the struggles of the Little Rock Nine, it does not occur in a seemingly faraway time or place. Nevertheless, it is rarely represented in texts for children in any genre, in striking contrast to the many picture books, novels, and memoirs that tell children about Bridges, the Nine, and various other examples of black students struggling simply to enter white schools. Some texts briefly reference the intersection of race and disability. In McKissack's *A Friendship for Today* (2007), Rosemary is nearly placed in a remedial track by default, but her mother fights for her to join the regular classroom and so the reader leaves special education behind as a threat successfully averted. In John Waters's 1988 film *Hairspray*, set in the 1960s, Tracy Turnblad directly tells the principal that she knows he is using special education as a tool to re-segregate the newly desegregated school; however, Waters's film is not intended for children. The 2007 remake of the film, in a musical form more friendly to young adult viewing, removes the reference to special education and instead shows Tracy meeting black dance partners in detention (where she has been legitimately sent for tardiness).

Conversely, children's texts that critique tracking and labeling tend to bypass the issue of race. In Disney's 2005 film *Sky High*, for example, the practice of sorting future superheroes from sidekicks is depicted as unjust, but both tracks are multiracial. In Miriam Cohen's 1980 picture book *First Grade Takes a Test*, an African American student is led away from her classroom and separated after the first graders take their standardized test; however, though academic sorting is clearly critiqued, and racial segregation is implied, Anna Maria is being led to the *gifted* program, not diagnosed as mentally retarded like many of her real-life counterparts. In fact, children's stories that explicitly focus on racial mixing in the school tend to highlight the dilemma of the gifted black child, and assume that once access to a properly supplied and humanely taught classroom is secured, highly able black students will inevitably shine. Disability, or at least the lack of ability, is the threat that hangs over these texts; Goober's slowness in *With the Might of Angels* nearly damages the powerhouse image Dawnie Rae works to project, and Emma's parents and teachers fear her association with less talented peers. Thus, young media consumers tend to be shielded from representations of how tracking and special education diagnosis tend to operate for children from different social strata, indicating perhaps the extent to which this is a live issue that cannot be safely contained in hopeful historical desegregation stories or contemporary teen school stories.[2]

The novels I discuss in this chapter, Virginia Hamilton's 1971 *The Planet of Junior Brown* and Cynthia Voigt's 1980s Tillerman series, are thus among a small handful of texts that address this important long-term legacy of the *Brown* decision. Like the others, they represent the intersection of race and disability only obliquely. I choose to focus on these because, unlike the others, they engage in some depth with the struggles students with disabilities face in the school system, rather than referencing these issues and then returning the characters to the "mainstream." Indeed, even their characterizations of "gifted" characters emphasize the non-normative school experiences of these characters, rather than using "giftedness" as shorthand for "able to be desegregated." In doing so, the novels stringently critique mainstream education. Researchers who write about culturally sensitive pedagogy or about strategies for disability inclusion sometimes assume that teachers and systems are serving their "central" populations—the white, the abled, and the middle class—appropriately, and primarily need assistance in serving their more marginalized students.[3] Voigt's and Hamilton's novels demonstrate otherwise. Draper's and Woodson's novels suggest that historically black institutions offered pedagogy and opportunities superior to white ones; Hamilton's and Voigt's extend this critique, exposing how white-dominated schools (white, that is, either in ideology or in population) were failing even to give many of their white students an appropriate education. Moreover, these novels offer a collective disability identity as an alternative form of successful citizenship. Rather than asking for acknowledgment of hidden gifts, several characters in these novels claim the stigma of disability as a way to radically reshape the concept of a utopian educational community. They form coalitions in order to develop alternate systems of pedagogy that serve them all better than the official school systems they attend. While these coalitions do reach across identity categories, they do not present the children as innocent and transcendent, but instead as modeling the kind of fraught, sometimes tense, commitment to dialogue and conflict resolution (outside of the school) that was desired by many of the early proponents of legal desegregation (inside of the school).[4]

Significantly, both Hamilton's and Voigt's texts straddle the boundaries of the school setting and highlight learning that occurs in homes, neighborhoods, and community spaces that are outside of the state's sphere of influence. While they portray classrooms and school personnel in extremely critical ways, they are not easily classifiable as desegregation stories, or school stories, and therefore do not obviously criticize the implementation of *Brown* and the ongoing issue of segregation through disability. Because of this departure from genre, they can treat issues of racist and able-ist pedagogy as entwined rather than separate issues without directly accusing contemporary school systems of racism. In fact, through their holistic criticisms of pedagogy, they push even further, and question the moral value of success within the school system. The generic conventions of the school story insist that the protagonist ultimately achieve some kind of school success in preparation for contributing to the nation as an adult citizen. Ideal education—and utopian national identity—therefore depends upon access and is measured by student achievement. In contrast, Voigt's and Hamilton's approach to realism allows them to question how desirable access and achievement are, and what they cost students. Instead, they illuminate the possibilities of failure, asking what alternative rewards students might gain by failing according to the norms of the school. The protagonists of these texts turn away from the institution of school as the site where the nation might be healed, and in the process, imagine other goals for education besides nation building and alternate ways to define citizenship and community membership.

In doing so, Hamilton's and Voigt's novels offer alternative routes to citizenship besides school success. In fact, school success in these novels often involves moral passivity and abandonment of democratic values. Characters become worthy of democratic citizenship, not by preparing themselves for future compliance and productivity, but by taking on a responsibility that many of the adults in their lives have abandoned, to uphold democratic ideals in the present.

Including Junior Brown: Disability in the Black Community

Virginia Hamilton's novel *The Planet of Junior Brown* was published in 1971. Only the year before, the Supreme Court had decided in *Swann v. Charlotte-Mecklenberg Board of Education* that school districts must remedy school segregation caused by residential patterns rather than by legalized exclusion, and Mississippi Senator John Stennis had proposed that desegregation measures be enforced in the *de facto* segregated areas of the North and West as well as in the *de jure* ones of the South. According to education policy critic Linda Darling-Hammond, the period of time between 1965 and the early 1980s saw more advances in desegregation and equity than any period before or since; Great Society programs to address community poverty, combined with busing programs and increased funding for urban schools, narrowed achievement gaps dramatically.[5] At the same time, Ferri and Connor note that the early 1970s was when the dismal statistics about disproportionate tracking and diagnosis began to be gathered and criticized on a large scale. A range of critics argued that the ineffective teaching and curricula reserved for students *labeled* as less abled succeeded in *producing* students with less academic ability than their peers in higher tracks.[6] Education scholars Gwen Meyer and James Patton sum up the problem quite neatly with the derisive comment, "[We are] suggesting a new category of disability called 'ABT,' which translates into 'ain't been taught.'"[7]

The Planet of Junior Brown predates the passage of IDEA, and neither of its protagonists is diagnosed; both are nominally assigned to mainstream, or general education classrooms. Buddy and Junior live and attend school in Harlem, and they inhabit a social world that is almost entirely black. The advances in equity and child poverty that Darling-Hammond observes do not seem to have reached Buddy and

Junior's neighborhood; their school building is relatively new, but it is also noisy, overheated, smelly, and so overcrowded that the stairwells must be lined with prison mesh to keep students from falling over the banisters between periods. Thus, while the setting does not openly critique the failures of *Brown*'s implementation in the North, neither does it celebrate progress. Instead, the novel can be read as a text about disability in schools, as it highlights the dilemma of students attending a school in which a majority "ain't been taught."

When the reader meets Buddy and Junior, they have segregated themselves from the other students, although they are officially assigned to general education. Instead, alienated by the chaos of the school, they play hooky in the basement of the building, where Mr. Pool, a teacher turned custodian, teaches them math and science. When the novel begins, they are building a scale model of the solar system. Each is a refugee for a different reason: Buddy is homeless and trying to avoid being placed in the state social system, Junior is a talented pianist who is ostracized for being fat, and Mr. Pool has exiled himself from the teaching he loves because of his frustration with the school system. As the novel continues, Junior is denied his usual outlets of making music and art, and he has a psychotic break and runs away from home. Rather than let Junior be institutionalized, Buddy reveals his secret; he helps to run a network of underground shelters for homeless children, known as "planets." Despite the risks involved in including Junior in his secret community, Buddy asks Mr. Pool to help him lower Junior into a relatively inaccessible hideout, and he reframes his philosophy of individual survival to one of community caring. Junior is not specifically identified as a character with disabilities until the end, and Buddy prides himself on his able-bodied status, but both boys move in and out of situations in which they are assumed to be impaired, incapable, or dangerous. Thus, Lennard Davis's concept of disability as a "modality" or "moment" is helpful for understanding how both Buddy and Junior can be read as disabled characters; disability is not an essence, embedded in a clear binary of abled/disabled, but a way of temporarily living in the world.[8]

In fact, nearly every character carries some kind of stigmatized identity on top of a racialized black identity. Buddy is homeless. Mr. Pool has been demoted from teacher to school custodian. Junior's mother Junella suffers from chronic severe asthma, and it is unclear whether her husband has left her or whether he is simply always away on business. Junior's piano teacher Miss Peebs lives in a filthy, roach-infested home and hallucinates. And Junior, by the end, seems to be a dumping ground for everyone's stigma; he is fat, fatherless, homeless, and hallucinating.

Each character also possesses some form of privileged identity and clings to it. The teachers and assistant principal at the school are middle-class citizens proud of their achievements. Miss Peebs is from an elite family who had never been enslaved. Mr. Pool is well educated. Junella is cultured and has money enough to lead a middle-class lifestyle despite her husband's absence. Buddy is healthy, strong, and independent. For most of the novel, these characters put significant energy into protecting themselves from being contaminated with each other's stigma. Junior alone seems to insist that his stigmatized qualities be seen and acknowledged. He refuses to diet. He draws himself into paintings of street scenes his mother finds disreputable. He runs away from home. Thus, from the beginning chapter of the novel, when Buddy adds an additional planet resembling Junior Brown to his model of the solar system, to the end, when Junior has run away, the guiding concern of the novel is what will happen, not merely to a classroom, but to a society that includes Junior Brown. Just as the gravitational pull from the imaginary additional planet must be accounted for and managed, so Junior's multiple stigmas threaten the orbits of the other characters and thus call for management. In the beginning of the novel, both Buddy and Mr. Pool do what the other characters do, and try to cling to their own orbits of privilege; at the end, they elect to place themselves in danger and rebuild the solar system.

In desegregation stories, the performance of respectability—the construction of an apparently privileged, or at least destigmatized, public identity—was essential for black students trying to gain access. As early as 1955, Kenneth Clark warned that this strategy had limitations, resulting in tremendous psychological pressure.[9] Hamilton's novel further suggests that choosing to identify with and showcase privilege rather than stigma may also reinforce stigmas of race, poverty, and disability. Moreover, individuals who carry a stigma are discouraged from making common cause with other communities, as they might suffer further loss of status.

This process has certainly impeded antiracist and inclusive education reforms sought by proponents of desegregation and IDEA. Antiracist educator Lisa Delpit, for example, reacted against the assumptions of racial inferiority and deficit she saw as a teacher in the 1970s, and instead began to frame black students as privileged, rather than as damaged, bringing knowledge and skills to the classroom, rather than deficit. Similarly, Mike Rose, in chronicling his experiences teaching so-called remedial students in the 1960s and 1970s, reframed the writing and reading struggles of lower-tracked children as signs of creative experimentation and cognitive growth. Nevertheless, the strategy of claiming hidden gifts for marginalized students has had the unintended effect of reinforcing deficit models of both disability and race. The disability community has not always extended the assumption of hidden gifts, or the social construction of disability, to the African-American community; in fact, Meyer and Patton argue that "over time, the terms 'difference,' 'culture,' and 'disability' have become linked so that children's cultural 'differences' may, as a result of this association, contribute to a diagnosis of 'disability.'"[10] Indeed, Natasha Warikoo and Prudence Carter argue that, not only are individual students marked as deviant and diagnosable, but African-American culture as a whole is infantilized and depicted as "subtractive from the goal of academic mobility."[11] Race, in other words, becomes inappropriately constructed as a form of disability. Conversely, researchers Davison and Ford found that after decades of black students being denied access to gifted programs, shunted into lower tracks, and disproportionately diagnosed as emotionally disturbed or mildly mentally retarded, many parents, teachers, and activists in the black community are understandably reluctant to identify with disability movements, even though their children are disproportionately affected by deficit models of disability. Hamilton's novel both attests to the pressures placed on intersectional alliances, and also critiques respectability politics and its effects upon students' educational experiences and daily lives.

Junella and the school personnel are the characters who most obviously dissociate themselves from stigma. They are also the characters most obviously critiqued by the narrator as chasing respectability at the cost of others in the community. Junella tries to uplift both herself and Junior by taking them to plays and concerts, cultivating the acquaintance of elites like Miss Peebs, and setting her dinner table with tablecloths and napkin holders. Her son, however, poses a problem. Her claim to privilege is being a respectable middle-class wife and mother, so that Junior's achievements reflect her own;[12] however, his deviations from the norm also reflect her failures and necessitate her intervention. Thus, she can take pride in providing her son with a well-cooked turkey dinner served in a mannerly way, but she also tries to take Junior to Weight Watchers and to place him on a restricted diet. She gives Junior piano lessons, but takes the strings out of his piano at home so that his sound will not disturb her rest. She discourages Junior from befriending Buddy because he is poor; and when Junior insists upon bringing Buddy home, she cooks the fancy turkey dinner in part to shame him. (Ironically, it is after this dinner that Junella's own stigmatized identity appears, when she has an asthma attack and coughs sputum all over the dinner dishes.) And finally, when Junior uses the paints she has provided to create a picture of everything in the neighborhood Junella has tried to exclude from her life—street crime, sex, drug abuse, poverty—Junella burns the painting and removes Junior's paints.

Significantly, her rationale is framed, not in terms of silencing Junior's expression, but in terms of helping him uncover his true potential for achievement. She imagines telling him,

> *"I destroyed that painting, Junior, because I know you weren't yourself when you thought to paint it. ...You can never have materials for painting, Junior, until you can demonstrate to me you will*

> *occupy your mind with thoughts proper and normal for your age group."* Yes, she could say that. Junior had always been the kind of boy who was obedient, who listened to his parents.[13]

She believes that when Junior is being deviant, he is not being "himself"; underneath, he is a different "kind" of boy, one who is properly obedient and normal. The reader is meant to feel critical of Junella's response, which echoes the respectability strategies of desegregation, and also the hidden giftedness strategies adopted in later decades to manage stigma. Junior does have extraordinary gifts as a musician and an artist; however, cultivating these talents would involve, not only achievement, but also a failure of respectability. In her own way, Junella is trying to adjust her perception of Junior, to maintain that he is a person who deserves to succeed. For her, however, this involves, not seeing his "deficits" as gifts, but seeing beyond the fat and the emotional fragility to the normative boy she feels confident is in there, somewhere.

The teachers and administrators at school police deviance and manage stigma even more dramatically. When Junior and Buddy finally show up in class, they are immediately noticed by the teacher, who is described as potentially sympathetic and humorous. Nevertheless, when Buddy asks for a science book so that he and Junior can join in the lesson (which they are capable of understanding, since they have been studying with Mr. Pool), the teacher becomes defensive about her status, feeling that "she had come too far and had worked too hard trying to teach something to let one fast-talking kid put it over on her."[14] The narrator voices a key contradiction between the teacher's having "come too far" and between her having "worked too hard trying to teach something." If her primary goal is, in fact, to teach something, she could presumably give the boys a science book or direct them to share one. Instead, she resists being bested by a school boy and sends them out of the room.

Once ejected from the classroom, they must meet with Mr. Rountree, the assistant principal, who is similarly proud of his own achievement and selectively helpful to students. The boys immediately know that Mr. Rountree is satisfied with his suit, his hair (which, Buddy notes, will not make an Afro), and his position, and they also begin to see that while Mr. Rountree has good intentions, he has no idea how to help them. Initially, when he looks at their files, he threatens them with legal action and reform school as a consequence of breaking compulsory education laws. Later, he eases off and encourages them to invest in their education, despite the fact that Buddy knows that "[h]alf the educated cats on the street couldn't remember the last time they had a lousy job."[15] Like the science teacher, Mr. Rountree believes that his job is to educate; and like her, he attempts to solve the problem of the boys' absence from class by threatening to remove them from the classroom on a more permanent basis.[16]

Furthermore, both the teacher and Mr. Rountree protect their middle-class roles as educators without either educating their more vulnerable students or working to make the school and the surrounding neighborhood places where an institutional education is worth getting. They may punish the students for not attending class, but the school remains crowded and overwhelmingly noisy, and the streets remain repositories of the educated unemployed. Jonathan Kozol describes this behavior as characteristic of some of the compromises black administrators have felt forced to make, before and after *Brown*. He quotes one principal as saying,

> The truth is that we are, to a degree, what you [white society] have made of us. The United States now has, in many black administrators of the public schools, precisely the defeated overseers it needs to justify this terrible immiseration. ... We accept some things and we forget some other things and what we can't forget we learn to shut out of our mind and we adopt the rhetoric that is required of us and we speak of "quality" or "excellence"—not justice.[17]

Kozol also notes that a popular maneuver for principals has been to raise the quality of the school by removing troublemaking students; this raises scores without addressing civil rights concerns. In a similar way, Rountree remains blissfully unaware of his successful students' fates after graduation, and he becomes more amenable to keeping the boys out of reform school (and in his own school) when he sees that their grades were high before they went on the hook.

Cathy Cohen describes this kind of pattern, in which elite members of the black community are placed in charge of managing and policing the less normative members, as "advanced marginalization"; under a regime of formal desegregation, the advances achieved by a privileged corner of the community can be celebrated, while the conditions faced by the rest of the community are overlooked.[18] Hamilton's novel highlights the failures of *Brown*'s implementation by pointing out not only how many students were excluded from its promise, but also how nominal desegregation fractured the community. The school in *The Planet of Junior Brown* is a space populated entirely by black characters, so that black teachers and administrators might be presumed to have an interest in antiracist pedagogy. In fact, however, this school is far from carrying on the pre-*Brown* Southern tradition of resistant black-led classrooms represented in the novels of the previous chapter, in which all black youths are told they can achieve and are diligently taught and encouraged so that they all do. Instead, in this Northern space of nominal opportunity, students like Buddy and Junior who are marginalized in multiple ways are allowed (even directed) to weed themselves out. In the meantime, Mr. Rountree, who does not wear an Afro, is able to achieve an administrative position and tout the benefits of a good education, while the majority of graduates remain unemployed.

In a similar way, the novel highlights the limitations of a gradual, practical approach to visionary educational reform, an approach to utopian education that has variously been termed "piecemeal engineering" and "tinkering." This approach does produce effects that accumulate over time; Buddy and Junior have a new school building, and black teachers and administrators have employment. Critics of this approach, however, point out that a sense of radical vision tends to be lost, as reforms are simply absorbed into entrenched structures of ideology and practice, rather than changing them.[19] Such absorption of radical movements toward educational justice has affected, not only the implementation of desegregation, but also the implementation of disability legislation for the classroom. Disability theorist Michael Bérubé points out how legislation has failed to alter educators' default approaches to students with disabilities, so that the basic question remains, "*Is this person sufficiently similar to the people we already value?*"[20]

The purpose of encouraging culturally sensitive teaching methods and inclusive education was always to revolutionize the mainstream normative classroom so that marginalized students would not have to be "sufficiently similar to the people we already value." Instead, the rhetoric of inclusivity and encouragement has become widespread but practice has changed very little. Thus, even caring black teachers and administrators dedicated to achievement cannot, it seems, imagine how a classroom might accommodate Buddy and Junior.

In many respects, Mr. Pool provides an antidote to this kind of entrenched resistance to reform. Yet even he must learn to value disability as well as giftedness. Mr. Pool is described as an intense, committed teacher in the mold of Sylvia's Miss Washington, who values intense interaction with students, encourages frank discussion, and believes that all students (including ones given up as hopeless by other teachers) can succeed. The narrator recalls,

> Tough, black children of city streets could lay bare their minds in his loud and open classes. But I lost heart, thought Mr. Pool. I could no longer teach in so rigid a regime. ... Only now, through his work with Buddy Clark and the example of Buddy's devotion to Junior Brown, did Mr. Pool slowly begin to believe in himself again.[21]

Mr. Pool's philosophy of teaching is clearly different from that of the science teacher's; she resents Buddy as a "fast-talking kid," whereas Mr. Pool admires and cultivates this quality so much that he clashes with the school system.

Nevertheless, while Mr. Pool can see gifts in "tough, black children of city streets," he has a harder time seeing them in Junior. He sees his primary "work" as being with Buddy, while Junior Brown is only important as an "example of Buddy's devotion." In fact, Mr. Pool has set up the basement room expressly in order to tutor Buddy, whom Mr. Pool has discovered doing advanced math in an abandoned classroom after hours. When Buddy comes for tutoring, he shows up with Junior Brown, so that Mr. Pool allows Junior's presence but has not solicited it. Having heard Junior playing the piano in the music room, Mr. Pool does recognize that Junior, too, has gifts worth cultivating; however, Junior's fatness dissuades him from taking Junior on as a protégé. Mr. Pool can recognize that the school ought to be nurturing Junior's talent; however, while he disapproves of the school's neglect, he does not seem to feel responsibility to rectify it, until Buddy brings Junior along as an appendage. This rationalizing stands in stark contrast to Mr. Pool's treatment of Buddy, another student abandoned by the school. When Mr. Pool looks at Buddy, his "heart swell[s] with pride."[22] In contrast, when he watches Junior, he wonders whether Junior sufficiently appreciates Buddy's work. Buddy is nearly always named in Mr. Pool's thoughts, whereas Junior is an unnamed "sad, fat boy," a "huge fat boy," or a "selfish black boy."[23] Buddy redeems Mr. Pool's efforts, whereas Junior is a project that exceeds what Mr. Pool feels he can do. It is not surprising, then, that when Junior begins to hallucinate, Mr. Pool wants him placed in a hospital. His reaction seems to echo Mike Rose's observations of teachers confronted with students whose needs confused or exceeded the teachers' expectations; they abdicated responsibility for remedial students by invoking the medical mystery of disability.[24] Similarly, Mr. Pool has already come to see Junior as past saving. His antiracist pedagogy, his commitment to tough cases like Buddy, cannot extend to students he sees as disabled.

The moment when Mr. Pool suggests an institution for Junior, however, also propels Buddy to reconsider his own attitude toward disability and community. Prior to this point, Buddy values strength and independence above all. As a result, he thinks of sickness as a curse that renders people incapacitated and dependent; he despises Junella for being asthmatic and needing Junior to care for her, feels grateful to his own mother for abandoning him and sparing him the sight of her suffering, and becomes afraid whenever he himself feels unwell, fearing that he will be a burden on his "planet" instead of its provider.[25] When Mr. Pool suggests sending Junior to a hospital, however, Buddy, who has been evading the gaze of state institutions since he was nine, suddenly identifies with Junior rather than with the world of the well and the independent. He connects Junior's threat of diagnosis to his other stigmatized identities, some of which Buddy shares:

> "They'll hit on how fat he is," Buddy cried, "they'll say that's it, we got to get him skinny.... They'll see how black he is," Buddy said, "and they'll say that's the problem, we got to get to the white inside."[26]

Buddy does not hallucinate and he is not fat, but he is black, and he realizes, as the others have not, that in the eyes of institutions like hospitals and schools, one stigmatized identity can take precedence over all the privileged identities a person can claim. Like Mina, one of Voigt's protagonists, Buddy decides that if he already identifies as black and poor, he may as well join forces with disability as well, since repudiating it will give no protection.

Once Buddy decides to identify with Junior as a visibly disabled person, he breaks all of the rules he has set for his own life and that of his community. Instead of absolute independence, he tells Mr. Pool about the underground system and enlists his help. Instead of telling his charges, as he does at the beginning, to completely forget the homes and families that make them vulnerable, he encourages them to take heart in the nearness of home. And instead of insisting that all his charges be as nearly self-sufficient as possible, Buddy tells them, "'We are together ... because we have to learn to live for each other."[27] Admitting Junior, who cannot enter or leave the basement without assistance, means that the philosophy of the community must be reframed for everyone. In the process, the characters not only imagine a utopian social universe into being, but also begin to work against the underlying rules and scripts that have structured their previous fantasies. In their previous model of the solar system, they add a planet of Junior Brown, but then invent a belt of invisible asteroids to balance its mass and keep the laws of physics operating as usual; it is Junior himself who observes that the gravitational pull of his enormous planet would threaten the earth's orbit and place in the solar system. Mr. Pool and Buddy acknowledge Junior's existence, and include him, unlike the school—but they continue to insist upon the fiction of natural laws that work to maintain the balance of the solar system and keep the earth spinning in its proper orbit. When the boys defy the natural protection of adult institutions and take the risk, instead, of lowering Junior Brown into Buddy's basement planet, they also implicitly suggest that the earth is no longer in balance, and should not be sheltered from the pull of Junior Brown's massive presence.

The two utopian learning communities that frame the novel—the less inclusive one at the beginning and the more inclusive one at the end—would, if presented in a policy brief, almost certainly be regarded as failed models. They are populated by dropouts—a dropout teacher who caused turnover and wasted the system's investment in training, as well as dropout students. These escaped bodies are never happily returned to the system to realize the error of their ways and be counted as successes, as they might be in many adolescent "problem novels"; Mr. Pool does not return to his middle-class salaried teaching job and the children do not turn themselves in. Nor does the system successfully reform so as to accommodate its deviant students, as it might in a revisionist school story. In effect, Buddy and Junior assign themselves to special education, in the dank, forbidding school basement, as taught by teacher-turned-custodian Mr. Pool. The situation they voluntarily choose is, in fact, exactly the kind of scenario that James Patton and Mike Rose, among others, have spent their careers desperately trying to eliminate. Thus, the novel poses a political problem; how can a text that presents this model of education as an individual "choice" be considered a critical educational utopia or a desirable example of post-*Brown* education?

Policy writers and activists, whose job it is to reform existing structures and to garner support from state agencies, are not generally free to posit education outside of state power. Like school story writers, they cannot suggest solutions that involve abandoning the measures of achievement and success recognized by the school system—graduation rates, test scores, grades, and college admissions—given that state funding, teacher assignments, and quality of instruction often depend upon such measures of success or failure and thus materially affect the conditions and opportunities of the students they represent. As Kozol points out, white suburban politicians and administrators are only too happy to frame "failures" of achievement as valid individual choices made by inner-city parents and students, so that the dominant power structure may be relieved of responsibility to provide equity. Thus, while many activists, like Kozol, Rose, and Delpit, do question how success is framed and suggest that students might have good reason to choose failure, they must also fight for these compromised forms of achievement so as not to abandon the fight for equity. Given their roles in public discourse about education, their doing otherwise would probably be irresponsible.

Young adult novelists like Virginia Hamilton, however, can sometimes say the un-sayable and think the un-thinkable, unequivocally questioning whether the school as a training ground for citizens can ever fulfill its promise of full inclusivity. As Julia Mickenberg suggests, authors for youth have historically been permitted to raise radical questions in the minds of child readers precisely because they will not be taken seriously as contributors to public education policy. Furthermore, *The Planet of Junior Brown* does not directly and openly challenge the mythology surrounding the *Brown v. Board* decision in the way that some of the novels discussed in Chapter 2 do. Despite being more radical in some ways than Mildred Pitts Walter's *Because We Are*, Hamilton's novel won the Newbery Honor, remains in print, and appears to be at least occasionally taught in the classroom (though, as I discuss in the introduction, it is not as widely recommended as her less radical novels).[28] In contrast, Walter's novel is out of print and does not even appear in the capacious Accelerated Reader program. Paradoxically, in critiquing the school and its pedagogy so radically and completely that the only solution is to exit the school altogether, the novel also evades the kinds of scripts about the school as a site of opportunity and progress that tend to constrain the genre of desegregation stories. *The Planet of Junior Brown* is not easily classifiable within recognized genres of children's literature, and thus manages to say a number of things that are un-sayable, not only in public policy discourse, but also in many young adult novels.

Despite its grim realism, the enclosed world of the novel's ending, in a new "planet," is a kind of fantasy.[29] In contrast to the school story, which fantasizes about how adults might provide a safe space for child learners, *The Planet of Junior Brown* fantasizes about how children might surpass adults in creating their own safe spaces. As Christopher Kelen and Bjorn Sundmark point out, countries ruled by children according to childhood logic (Neverland, Oz, and Narnia being notable examples) have been a staple of children's fantasy for centuries. These "nations of childhood," they argue, can not only support nation-building projects and socialize future citizens, but also lure the child temporarily to a more desirable alternative community where he or she can more freely exercise governance rights.[30] Thus, in addition to being a fantasy of youth empowerment, inclusion, and transformation, *The Planet of Junior Brown* is also a fantasy about revolution, co-opting the institutions and ideals of the nation-state and severing their connections to state power.[31] In this respect, the novel also disrupts common scripts of young adult realistic novels. Trites suggests that young adult literature commonly tells the story of a dangerously rebellious adolescent who first questions the status quo and then is contained when a sympathetic adult character simultaneously displaces the power of the adolescent narrator and teaches the adolescent reader to accept some form of societal injustice and repression.[32] In *The Planet of Junior Brown*, it is Buddy, an adolescent character, who remains the ultimate narrative authority, converting Mr. Pool to his way of thinking. The ending does not offer a resolution, and the adolescent characters do not recognize the value and necessity of dominant adult society.

Buddy, Junior, and Mr. Pool may very well begin the novel in exactly the place the school system would have placed them, and many like them—in a segregated, cramped basement with few resources and a teacher who is not "really" a teacher. Ironically, however, having found this "solution" for themselves, they are liable to legal action. Similarly, Buddy's system of "planets" may not be significantly different from the legal system of foster care, but running it places Buddy and all of his charges in danger. Thus, the novel highlights a central problem of state institutions; what matters is not the specific solution or reform that is introduced, but the fact that it is the state that controls the solution on behalf of the "problem" children under its care. Buddy and Junior embrace many of the ideals that state institutions were created to address—that schools should be places of learning, that learning is worth having, that children should be cared for and nurtured—but they imagine a society in which they are not indebted to the nation-state for fulfilling these ideals. School is supposed to make children into citizens, educated into democratic duties and privileges through the grace of national funding and compulsory education laws. When Buddy, Junior, and Mr. Pool invent their own educational solutions, they deprive state institutions of their reason for existence, and also sever the sense of duty binding them to the nation.[33] Their renegade class studies the solar system and the universe, but their focus on science lacks the patriotic Cold War subtexts and references found in desegregation stories like *Mary Jane*, *North Town*, and *The Lions of Little Rock*. Unlike the sympathetic teachers in *The Lions of Little Rock* and *With the Might of Angels*, Mr. Pool imagines that he is preparing his students for a new human race, rather than seeming to draw his inspiration from the idea that he is educating the future citizens of America.

Hamilton presents a utopia that is created not through institutional restructuring but through imagining how education might work if it remained largely the same but were separated from its originating institutions. In the process, she provides some critique of what happened to historically antiracist, inclusive black education after *Brown*; once African-American teachers and students became nominally included in the national fantasy of citizenship, they also became included in practices of advanced marginalization and in state institutions engaged as much in preserving their own internal structures as in serving the students under their care. Lennard Davis argues that the nationalist movements of the nineteenth century helped to produce disability, by positing that the fit bodies of individual citizens must contribute to the fitness of the body politic. In Hamilton's novel, a disability-inclusive learning community is incompatible with learning to be a citizen. Her protagonists embrace marginality rather than access. Similarly, in Voigt's novels, bad citizenship is often associated with disability, and it generally reflects poorly upon the citizenship models and the education offered by the school rather than upon the characters.

Cynthia Voigt's Tillerman Novels: The Mis-Education of the White and Gifted[34]

Hamilton's novel emphasizes the stigma of disability and the ethical need to embrace it. In contrast, Voigt's novels open up a disability category that allows for black students, gifted students, and diagnosable students to share a sense of identity without feeling stigmatized. In fact, like Meyer and Patton, she suggests that the students in the school system share the disability of "ain't been taught." In doing so, her novels contribute to critiques of *Brown* that object to the assumption that white education is superior. While the novelists discussed in Chapter 2 focus on the quality of Southern black schools and the racist pedagogy black students encounter in predominantly white schools, they do not address how white schools were educating white students with disabilities. While Voigt's depiction of the school system is admittedly dystopian, the community that is formed by acknowledging a common source of disability suggests a utopian vision for how to better reach the goals of integration and inclusion.

While Hamilton's novel depicts issues of inclusivity before the 1975 passage of IDEA, Voigt's series was published in the 1980s, when the law had not only been passed, but also begun to face issues in its implementation. Activists who pushed for so-called mainstreaming, or placement in the "least restrictive environment," drew a lesson from the *Brown* decision and fought for speedy compliance with the new law. Unfortunately, just as *Brown*'s intended movement toward racial justice in education was skewed upon implementation by persistent and embedded structural racism, disability activists were observing by the early 1980s that the new mainstreaming movement was resulting in the kinds of racist, able-ist, and psychologically damaging pedagogy that prevailed before 1975 and that the new law was intended to fix. According to Skrtic, as well as others like Roger Slee and policymaker Madeleine Will, the bureaucracy embedded in the system meant that mainstreamed students were still being assisted by a completely separate organizational structure (the special education apparatus) that had no influence on the school's central structure; thus, students were still pulled out of class by special education instructors, and they were not always given appropriate instruction in mainstream classes by general education teachers. Black and Latino students were increasingly diagnosed with specific disabilities that would allow for teachers and administrators to place them in segregated classrooms. Moreover, even advancements in equity made after *Brown* were disappearing, as the Reagan administration began to strip the Elementary and Secondary Assistance Act of enforcement mechanisms meant to ensure that majority-minority schools were equitably funded. Historian Phyllis Palmer also notes that by the late 1970s, "a language of color-blindness was displacing the racial power and antiracism messages of white responsibility for undoing the effects of the nation's rigorously enforced, historic racial inequality."[35] As a result, educators began to observe that teachers ceded responsibility for continuing inequities, attributing achievement gaps to slavery and Jim Crow rather than to current racist practices.[36] In response to these challenges, advocates like Will and Skrtic began to envision a new revolution, represented by the Regular Education Initiative of 1986, that would reimagine and restructure the mainstream itself to be more responsive to *all* individual students, whether diagnosed or not.[37]

Voigt's series reflects these threads of disillusionment with both desegregation and IDEA, critiquing how mainstream education fails a wide variety of students. Like Hamilton's novel, Voigt's series places narratives about race and disability in juxtaposition, rather than directly addressing re-segregation through disability diagnosis and tracking. Nevertheless, it is unusual because it does place such narratives together, and because it also highlights specific mechanisms of racist, able-ist, and gender-biased pedagogy. The Tillerman cycle follows the development of four white siblings: Dicey, James, Maybeth, and Sammy; their close friends, Jeff and Mina; and their grandmother, Gram. In the first book, the siblings are abandoned in a Connecticut parking lot by their gentle, mentally ill mother, and make their way to Crisfield, Maryland, where their bitter, eccentric grandmother lives alone. She eventually agrees to take them in, and the remainder of the series deals with how they come to terms with their family history (including a legacy of racism) and with how they navigate the challenges of school and community in Crisfield. Maybeth is never diagnosed with a disability, but she is nevertheless affected by special education debates. At one school, her teachers want to diagnose her as mentally retarded and place her in a separate school; at her next, she is mainstreamed with no accommodations and continues to struggle for the duration of her school years. The other siblings are not diagnosable, but they all struggle with the rigid mainstream: Dicey is bored and frustrated; James is intellectually curious, but fears standing out; and Sammy loves physical work but is frequently punished in school for his energy and its attendant mischief. Their friend Mina, who is black, is asked to leave a summer dance program due to racism, and later fights to include black history and current events in the social studies curriculum. One book in the series, *The Runner*, is set in the 1960s and follows the children's uncle Bullet through an unusual desegregation story that ends with the usual interracial friendship, but also with Bullet dropping out of school. In this, Voigt explicitly counters the "language of color-blindness" (and, by extension, obliviousness to disability) prevalent both in the novel's setting and in its decade of publication. Bullet responds to his white liberal classmate's assertion of color-blindness by saying, "'We aren't all the same,' ... *You've got to honor the differences, or what's similar will be useless to you*."[38] In a later interview, Voigt identified Bullet as her "spokescharacter" for a philosophy of difference.[39]

The many painful school scenes that take place in the six novels set in the 1980s effectively undercut any lessons of progress and equal opportunity that might be read into the desegregation story *The Runner*. Yet, by broadening the critiques of pedagogy to include all of the poorly served students—white and black, gifted and disabled—the perceived threat that comes from representing how gifted black students are badly taught seems to be defused; the accusation of continuing racism in schools after *Brown* is evidently much more potent than the accusation of globally poor teaching, which has been a target of children's literature for well over a century. Indeed, as with Hamilton's novel, Voigt's critiques of desegregation seem to go unnoticed and are therefore accepted into the classroom. Several books in the series won the National

Council of Teachers of English (NCTE) Teacher's Choice award, which are meant to highlight texts that lend themselves exceptionally well to student engagement and to class discussion of literary elements. *Come a Stranger*, which is the most explicitly critical of contemporary racist pedagogy, won the award in 1987.[40]

Most of the books in the Tillerman series reject a central assumption of school stories, the school system, and American society as a whole, which is that success is the sign of personal growth and societal progress, while failure is the sign of stagnation. After the advent of mainstreaming and inclusion, the education of marginalized students has often been discussed alongside the education of gifted students, with the fear that including disabled students will mean neglecting the national resource of the gifted student body. Investment in gifted education is called for because not doing so will have "potentially serious consequences for the long-term economic competitiveness of the U.S."[41] Even scholars like Henry Braddock and Robert Slavin who advocate passionately for more equitable gifted education frame their arguments in terms of national health:

> If the U.S. is to maintain its standard of living, it must develop a workforce capable of thinking, learning, and making decisions. Writing off a substantial portion of our students never made sense from a social standpoint and is rapidly becoming suicidal from an economic standpoint.[42]

Successes of various kinds are thus conflated in potentially contradictory ways. Good critical thinking and decision-making skills, as demonstrated by selective standard assessments, will naturally lead to students' making the mature critical decision to participate in the corporate economy of the United States in such a way that the nation will be advanced along with its students. An alternate future, in which the nation's gifted decide to invest their critical thinking skills in other ways, is either unimaginable or unlikely to garner funds and thus unadvertisable.

It is this alternative that Voigt forces readers to imagine. As Eliza Dresang points out, the series features a number of protagonists who might be labeled as gifted, including Maybeth.[43] Maybeth's character most closely adheres to the model of hidden giftedness prevalent in learning disability discourse; she has difficulty passing tests in school, but is consistently presented as a notable musician, abled in ways that her classroom teachers (with the exception of her music teacher) are unable to tap into or even to recognize. The other characters are talented in ways that are recognizable to the school system, yet they generally refuse to succeed according to the terms of that system. In fact, their academic successes are often framed as ethical failures.

Judith (Jack) Halberstam argues that failure has the potential to "[allow] us to escape the punishing norms that discipline behavior and manage human development."[44] Further, in a society that designates success and failure as purely individual traits of character, an appreciation of failure is necessary in order to understand and resist structural inequality. Halberstam notes that failure is an inevitable product of capitalism. According to educational philosopher David Labaree, failure is more specifically a product of the capitalist school system, which was founded in order to advance the common good but has always been treated by parents and students as an opportunity for individual competitive advantage. While the first goal requires that all students succeed, the second requires that some students fail, which means that parents and students have an interest in resisting egalitarian, redistributive reforms—including reforms like desegregation and disability inclusion.[45] Halberstam, however, suggests that this entrenched production of failure can nevertheless be a principled choice, a thing that can be done well and with style, rather than a victimizing force. Similarly, Voigt's characters frequently choose failure, and do so in a way that exposes injustice in the classroom.

The most dramatic example of artful failure is performed by Mina. When Mina enters junior high, her Social Studies teacher makes it clear that success in school demands rigid standardization and regurgitation of specific phrases. She initially deals with her feelings of helplessness by doing well on her battery of biased standardized tests, but eventually elects to wage a campaign against Mr. Bryce's curriculum and teaching methods. She asks Mr. Bryce questions about the roles of blacks and Native American tribes in the Maryland history he is teaching, even though he ignores her, and "dismisse[s] her questions, without seeming to hear them even though he was looking right at her."[46] As Mina's mother points out, Mr. Bryce feels as though he is being shown up when he is unable to answer questions about his own subject; Mina responds, however, that her questions indicate an area he ought to know better. Rather than assuming her questions are disrespectful, he might make an effort to learn more so as to answer them. Similarly, during current events, she persists in reporting about race riots in South Africa and decolonization in Rhodesia [Zimbabwe], even though Mr. Bryce tells her the events do not count as "significant news" for the assignment.[47]

As a result, she receives a 'C' in Social Studies, the only grade on her report card that is not an 'A.' Her reaction is pleased laughter:

> Mr. Bryce should have given her an A, she knew; all of her homework papers were perfect, all of her test papers were perfect. He wanted to fail her, she thought, but he didn't dare to. ... So he gave her a C and wrote a comment in the blank where teacher comments went: "Wilhemina is disruptive." The whole thing just made Mina laugh. She guessed she'd gotten through to him, all right.[48]

Mina is, in effect, being officially labeled as "disruptive" and academically sub-par precisely because she *is* using the independent critical thinking skills called for by advocates of gifted education, which in her case are evidently going to be more threatening to national mythologies than supportive of national growth. Margaret Price discusses the labels that resistant students acquire when they are being inappropriately taught and decide to push back; they have a "bad attitude" or lack the magic quality of "motivation" and thus become designated as problems who refuse to be solved, students with spoiled identities whose protests are un-hearable.[49] Price focuses on diagnosable mental disabilities, but Mina is marked as an unreliable speaker in the same way, and for the same reasons—so that her protests will not be recognizable as a critique of teaching.

Nevertheless, Mina's reaction to her unfair 'C' and unwarranted diagnosis as "disruptive" is not to renew her commitment to school success, as Emma does when she is labeled as too disruptive to succeed in the "mainstream" white school. Instead, Mina laughs, knowing that "she'd gotten through to him, all right." Her grades mean a great deal to Mina, contrary to what her shocked parents initially think; but she does not take from them the meaning, and the chastisement, that she is meant to. In Voigt's acceptance speech for the Margaret Edwards Award, entitled "Thirteen Stray Thoughts on Failure," she says,

> Failure can ... reveal false or inadequate measures of that [failed] work. I can't be the only person here who got what I call a bad A, in school, a high mark for mediocre work, or a good D, or even an exhilarating F?[50]

Mina's 'C' and poor comment are exhilarating in a way an 'A' would not have been. They are signs that her agenda of resistance is succeeding.

While this is the most obvious example of purposeful, artful failure, it is not the only one. In *Dicey's Song*, Dicey is placed in a home economics class for girls instead of the mechanical drawing class she requested, which is reserved for the boys. She is bored and resentful in class, and fails spectacularly. When she is asked to make an apron and display it, she designs the apron so as to avoid having to make buttonholes. The project requires her to use two buttons, but instead of sewing a buttoning apron as she is meant to do, she places the two big red buttons on the bib for decoration. As it happens, she has sewn them so that they sit over her nipples, a fact she does not realize until she is forced to put the apron on to display it to the class. The narrator says, "Dicey wasn't sorry she'd done as bad a job as she'd done, but she wished she didn't have to stand up so everybody else could see. ... She glared at the laughing faces, her chin high."[51] Dicey has not intended her failure to be a public one; however, the humiliating classroom fashion show turns her resistance to home economics into a stylish failure (in the literal sense) that vividly and hilariously points out the gendered inequity of the course requirement. Furthermore, like Mina, Dicey does not learn the prescribed lesson from failure; she is not sorry for doing a poor job, and she does not mend her ways, continuing to tussle with the home economics teacher.

Conversely, successes within the school system are often framed as empty and meaningless, and serve to highlight ineffective or unjust pedagogy. When Mina finally earns an 'A' in Social Studies, she knows it is merely because she has worn Mr. Bryce down and not because either her work or his views have changed. When Dicey writes a brilliant essay imagining her mother's breakdown from Liza's point of view, she is publicly accused of cheating and shamed before the class. After Mina intervenes, the teacher admits his error and promises Dicey an 'A+' for the essay and an 'A' for the year, but the grades are meaningless to Dicey, since at no point does the teacher acknowledge the significance of the work she has done. While this is not a "high mark for mediocre work," it is a different kind of "bad A." Similarly, the active and mischievous Sammy succeeds in repressing his energy in order to please his teacher; he becomes almost unrecognizable to Dicey and Gram, who have to reassure him that they value his troublesome self. Sammy's success reveals yet another form of "bad A," as the praise he garners reflects the school's hidden agenda to reward compliant behavior rather than academic inquiry. And in *The Runner*, while most of Tamer Shipp's conflicts lie outside the classroom, he notes that his newly integrated school isn't providing him with the kind of intellectual challenge he'd like, so that his grades say little about his abilities.

By focusing consistently upon the political potential of failure and the high price of success, Voigt allows for a reframing of dialogues about antiracist teaching and special education, as successful desegregation and inclusion might not neatly overlap with success at rigidly constrained or unjust academic tasks. Furthermore, questioning the framework of academic success and failure allows for a conversation about school reform that acknowledges the need for pedagogical reform without using it as an excuse for retaining segregation and tracking. Jonathan Kozol sharply criticizes the argument that schools serving white children are failing; as he rightly points out, disparaging the value of smaller class sizes, higher teacher salaries, and better-equipped facilities is only used as a way to deny equitable treatment for poorer schools, never to take these advantages away from wealthier districts.[52] Voigt's novels, however, point out serious problems with pedagogy and curriculum that do affect a variety of white students as well as minorities. She deals less with issues of funding and class size, and more with the problem of how success is defined for both white and black students. Tamer Shipp's disappointment in the historical setting of *The Runner*, juxtaposed against Mina's and Dicey's experiences a generation later, suggest that participation in the white-dominated and able-ist school system doesn't seem like much of an improvement after the Civil Rights battles of the 1960s, and the students—both black and white—deserve better.

The post-*Brown* educational world depicted in the novels also points to a lack of progress in that curricula and measures of assessment never seem to change, remaining inflexible in the face of antiracist decolonization movements like the ones Mina wants to study, protests against gender inequality like the ones Dicey raises, and—crucially—the needs of mainstreamed students like Maybeth. Presumably, other students might benefit from learning about the events Mina presents, and other female students might long for mechanical drawing instead of home economics (and vice versa for non-gender-conforming male students). Similarly, Maybeth's experience hints at shortfalls in the reading education even of students who don't struggle in the same way. For example, Maybeth's general education teacher insists that if she simply tries hard enough, she can memorize lists of sight words, and if she cannot do this, she is incapable of learning. As both Gram and Dicey realize, even tutoring provided by the school (one of the legal accommodations accorded by IDEA) is unlikely to help, as any tutor trained within the system will be using the same methods that have already failed Maybeth. Ralph Cintron, writing about learning disability education in the 1980s, describes the "magnificent circularity of schooling ... schooling historically has trained students into a fill-in-the-blanks conception of reading and then complained when students have thoroughly absorbed that training."[53] Other students may memorize the sight words more easily, but as Cintron points out, this does not mean that their training will be worthwhile.

Instead, just as Hamilton imagines a more humane alternative classroom outside the official system, Voigt imagines a method of teaching Maybeth to read that benefits both her and her gifted brother James. James is given the task of figuring out how to tutor Maybeth more effectively, which he does by researching approaches that will play to her strengths. After thinking about how Maybeth reads musical notes, James first researches phonics, and then employs Maybeth's musical sense by having her read Dr. Seuss's *Green Eggs and Ham*, thus combining phonics and whole language techniques. Crucially, however, Dicey and Gram push James to help Maybeth partly because he needs more mental stimulation than he gets at school. Gifted education advocates like Holly Hertberg-Davis cite instances of gifted students being asked to tutor struggling students as evidence that inclusion and differentiated instruction are inappropriate for advanced students, who are stalled in their individual progress and asked to stagnate intellectually in the service of others.[54] In *Dicey's Song*, the tasks of researching and thinking about pedagogy are not incompatible with intellectual growth; when Dicey finds the two of them giggling over *Green Eggs and Ham*, James lights up and says, "You had to understand everything to get the jokes. More than just the words. They said in my book that learning to read with phrasing and fluently, that was a sure sign [of reading capability]."[55] His enthusiasm seems due both to his sister's improvement and also to his own excitement about applying his reading and learning. Maybeth's success does not seem to subtract here from James's, but both suffer in the school system when inclusion is practiced with rigid pedagogy and when success is defined as the completion of individual work.

The tutoring of Maybeth, which continues throughout the series, is one example of a coalition between two kinds of learners that adults frequently assume to have opposing interests and needs. Furthermore, these opposing needs are posited as irreconcilable, due to the school's limited resources of teacher attention and money; what one side gains, the other must lose, and if both sides are given what they desire, the system will be bankrupted. James's familial rescue of Maybeth would be, for many parents and education advocates, just as fantastic and politically dangerous a solution as Buddy and Mr. Pool's illegal creation of alternative state services in poorly equipped city basements. Are all intellectually gifted students really better at pedagogy than their teachers? Would they all extend the same feelings of familial responsibility to their metaphorical brothers and sisters? And what are taxpayers paying for, if James is just going to do the teacher's job? In its own way, this extracurricular coalition provides a utopian fantasy for how the classroom might work; but such methods tend not to be implemented because they can be difficult to manage on a large, systemic scale. James and Maybeth's idealistic partnership works because it occurs outside the context of a large system where students are allotted a certain "fair share" of state resources and where reforms must be easily adapted to a mass scale. Nevertheless, in a decade of frustration with antiracist and disability-inclusive educational reforms, this moment in the novel suggests that a reform that may not transfer well to the school system may still be a valuable alternative. Furthermore, it provides an alternative space for utopian common ground between poorly served gifted and disabled students; just because that space may not be within the capitalist, competitive school system does not mean it does not exist.

The friendship between Dicey and Mina, and their respective families, is another kind of coalition, one that must work through stigmas of both disability and race. Dicey is hostile toward most of the students, assuming that most of them are either laughing at her, her slow sister, and her eccentric grandmother, or that they will if they get the chance. For her part, Mina knows that Gram's husband was openly racist, and she assumes that Dicey and her siblings are, too, especially after Dicey repeatedly snubs her. When Mina defends Dicey from accusations of cheating, then, it is not out of a sense of innocent friendship, but out of a sense of duty to herself to be "one of the minority who stood up against ... whatever was trying to press people down by lies. She was already stuck in a couple of other minorities, she thought to herself, she might as well join this one."[56] Even after this incident, when Dicey finally unbends, the two have work to do. Mina knows that Dicey's essay was about her mother's breakdown, and yet she unwittingly trips Dicey's defenses by telling Dicey that her grandmother is reputed to be mentally ill. Mina, in turn, is defensive about race, assuming that Dicey's brother is making disrespectful faces at her mother and only later realizing that Sammy was trying hard not to cry because his own mother has just died. And, in fact, the Tillermans do need to be more aware of institutional racism; when Mina eventually praises Gram because Gram hasn't asked Mina's mother if she does daily cleaning, Dicey begins to have an inkling of everything she does *not* know and can never understand about Mina. Political decisions precede and form the conditions for friendship. Mina makes the decision to join yet another minority; Dicey makes the decision to let her family's vulnerabilities be visible to "outsiders." Their mutual suspicion is too great for simple liking and attraction (which is, in fact, there from the beginning) to surmount it; they must continue to make conscious decisions to trust each other and to work through the hurts they feel at unintended slights.

In this respect, they resemble the interracial friends of desegregation stories, such as Sally and Mary Jane in Sterling's *Mary Jane*, who also must work through conflict so that their friendship can testify to the success of desegregation. For Sally and Mary Jane, however, the integrated classroom both nurtures their connection and also represents the fulfillment of their desires. For Dicey and Mina, too, the classroom facilitates their initial connection, as they notice and appreciate each other's intelligence. Unlike in desegregation stories, however, in which the school is the desired primary shelter for the interracial friendship, the hostility of the classrooms in the Tillerman series has a different kind of effect. The competitive nature of the classroom threatens to drive the girls apart; Mina is one of the crowd of girls who giggles at Dicey's public display of her failed sewing, and in turn, she risks chastisement for standing up for a fellow student in English class, so that she has little incentive to maintain solidarity. At the same time, the hostility within the school encourages interracial bonding to continue outside of it, which was ostensibly one of the goals of desegregation.

Voigt argues in an interview that Dicey and Mina are able to form a friendship across racial boundaries because they are involved in the "common endeavor" of the classroom.[57] As a former teacher herself, she expresses hope and belief in the work of teaching and learning, despite the fact that she depicts classrooms that fall short of encouraging the "common endeavor" she desires. Similarly, after winning the Newbery Medal for *Dicey's Song,* Voigt writes that "school is, for students, probably the only place where they can learn how their minds work, learn to discipline that working so that they can do more with their own abilities";[58] again, this inspiring statement is not reflected by the novel, in which all of the siblings quite pointedly are *dis*couraged in class from learning how their minds work. Nevertheless, while James and Maybeth's coalition represents the success of an unofficial, extracurricular learning space, Mina and Dicey's partnership demonstrates the possibilities for utopian citizenship education that the school setting still inspires. While the classroom pedagogy they suffer through may not afford common intellectual endeavors, it does involve them in the common endeavor of survival and resistance. Through their failures, they frequently persist in acting as though school were the utopian place Voigt describes in her interviews.

Utopian educational theorists, especially those working in the "realist utopian" tradition associated with Henry Giroux, often identify two key goals for utopian education. First, as Giroux emphasizes repeatedly, institutions of higher education need to be vital public spheres that help to "[make] visible the contradiction and tension between the reality of existing democracy and the promise of a more fully realized democracy."[59] For Giroux, this means that educators serve as public intellectuals whose responsibility is to take part in contentious and risky conversations in the public sphere. In modeling this kind of democratic participation, they can also empower students, not merely to be consumers of existing institutions, but to try to create better ones. Second, education should *both* educate students to participate in democratic government *and* also allow them to maintain identities outside of their state citizenship. As Mark Olssen notes, schools are public institutions, but they have the potential to connect marginalized communities that might not otherwise form common cause.[60] These theorists believe that state-sponsored schools should prepare students to be active citizens of a democracy, but not necessarily citizens of the existing state; rather, the very skills of deliberative democracy fostered by the schools ought to threaten the neoliberal state and the normative model of citizen as consumer.

These theorists, however, either tend to focus on higher education and other forms of adult education, as Giroux does, or to highlight the roles that adult stakeholders and community members play in elementary and secondary schools. In Voigt's Tillerman series, youth protagonists take on the roles of public intellectuals, coalition builders, and critics of the state that utopian scholars generally ascribe to adults. They often fail in these roles; and conversely, as in Hamilton's novel, their acts of resistance are sometimes expressed through failures to be conventionally good student citizens. Thus, Mina is "disruptive" because she persists in behaving as though Mr. Bryce's classroom were going to live up to her ideal of what education ought to be—a place where she can ask critical questions and challenge biased narratives of American history. She is, in fact, doing exactly what Giroux argues a public intellectual should do, and her actions are working, as he says they should, to open up the slippage between the existing state and the ideal democracy. Dicey is not a public intellectual in this way; however, she, like Mina, uses the school to figure out her values and the workings of her mind, even though the school does not seem to encourage this activity, and indeed, penalizes her for it. Additionally, she consistently works to maintain a democratic community composed of her immediate family and trusted friends, in which she is often challenged and forced to re-assess her roles and responsibilities. Yet this identity (and her considerable ability to participate in democratic governance) is held separate from her compulsory identity as a student in school, where she is a noticeably non-participatory "bad citizen." Dicey's character is valuable in thinking about utopian education and community precisely because her allegiance is so difficult to win; she will not consent to be a citizen of any community she cannot help to govern.

Parallel Utopian Education: Risks and Benefits

Classrooms in these novels are not the sites of "common endeavor" that Voigt imagines. Nor are they the sites where children can grow up learning how to participate in a racially integrated, disability-inclusive society, as scholars like Kozol and Bérubé hope. They are not places where Mina and Dicey can explore their common intellectual interests, or where James and Maybeth can work together to the benefit of both, or where Mr. Rountree or even Mr. Pool can help Junior and Buddy without further marginalizing them. Those ideal sites of common endeavor migrate outside of the school, to the Tillerman home or to the streets of Crisfield or to the abandoned basements of Manhattan. Nevertheless, in both Hamilton's and Voigt's texts, the dystopian space of the classroom contains what Mark Olssen calls a "'latent' or 'repressed' utopian ideal,"[61] a sense of the way democratic classrooms and communities *ought* to work, which the adolescent protagonists draw upon in forming the networks that help them survive their schooling. Thus, although much of the meaningful education that takes place does so outside of the classroom, the idea of the classroom provides the occasions for Dicey and Mina or James and Maybeth to form alliances, and also provides the "latent" ideals that guide them. Similarly, in Hamilton's novel, actual classrooms and state-defined identities are rejected, but the desire for what they might ideally offer—critical education and democracy—inform the creation of a new classroom "universe."

Like the counternarratives of the previous chapter, Hamilton's and Voigt's novels are published in decades when the failures and distortions of desegregation's goals were becoming apparent in various ways. These texts, however, approach the disappointments of *Brown*'s implementation in a different way, by acknowledging the persistent shadow of disability diagnosis rather than by reaching back to a history of proud academic success. In both texts, creating a site of common endeavor that can include both race and disability means that the stigmas of marginalization and potential failure must be embraced rather than repelled. In the shared history of race and disability inclusion after *Brown*, the schools have not made space for everyone to succeed, but there has been plenty of room for everyone to fail. These novels take that reality of failure and reconfigure it, finding the space within failure to create political coalitions that seem otherwise impossible.

These alternative spaces do not replace but instead parallel the school. While these texts highlight the ways that the school system limits and excludes valuable forms of citizenship, they also underscore the dangers and limitations of unofficial systems that do not have the backing of state authority. Mr. Pool, Buddy, and Junior live with the daily threat that they will be caught and with the expectation that each new haven is only temporary; Maybeth and the other Tillerman siblings must renegotiate their compromises with the classroom each year; and the interracial coalition formed between Mina's family and Dicey's never seems to extend to the rest of the town. Official recognition and institutionalization would reduce the flexibility and responsiveness that allow these learning communities to function as inclusive utopias; but without official recognition and support, they can be hard to sustain and perpetuate, not only for future generations of students, but even for the same generation from one year to the next. School story utopias are also temporary, in their own ways, as students must expect to graduate and face the world; however, in school stories, progress made tends to be progress kept. The battle with the bully, once conclusively won within school grounds, rarely needs to be re-fought. In contrast, protagonists who opt out of the school system and its scripts also continue to fight the bully, over and over again.

Nevertheless, this mode of continual struggle speaks to the continued failures of both legalized desegregation and inclusion education, and validates a way of talking about the legacy of *Brown* that is neither complacent nor cynical. In many ways, this model of a continually renegotiated educational utopia is actually quite hopeful. If improvement and success are temporary, so too is failure, and while struggle may be perpetual, it is nevertheless portrayed as being worthwhile while it lasts. The novels in the next chapter further explore the tricky relationship between unofficial, alternative forms of desegregated pedagogy and state-sponsored forms.

Notes

1 Ferri and Connor, *Reading Resistance*, 5, 25; Berube, *Life as We Know It*, 22–23.
2 One comprehensive study of Newbery winners (Medal and Honor books) from 1975–2009 found that out of 381 prized books, only 41 contained any portrayal of disability; of those, 33 were white. Furthermore, the authors note that most of the novels depict mental retardation, emotional disturbance, and orthopedic impairment (the authors use the diagnostic terms from the IDEA legislation). In contrast, only three of the characters are represented as having sensory impairments or specific learning disabilities, impairments that students are far more likely to see in schools (students with specific learning disabilities account for nearly half of the services provided under IDEA). Leininger, Dyche, Taylor, and Heath, "Newbery Award-Winning Books."
3 Lisa Delpit discusses the success of progressive education methods with white students in "Skills and Other Dilemmas," reprinted in *Other People's Children*. Lara Honos-Webb implies, rather than states, that teachers have less difficulty handling children without an ADHD diagnosis in the introduction to *The Gift of ADHD*.
4 Sterling's *Tender Warriors* and Cottle's *Busing* provide good illustrations of this hope.
5 She specifically emphasizes the Elementary and Secondary Education Act, which in its 1965 incarnation contained strict funding comparability requirements for schools that were still segregated.
6 Ogletree and Ujlaki's "The Effects of Ability Grouping" (1970) references other, similar studies, including Kenneth Clark's criticism of the practice of tracking. By 1974, Thomas Cottle was writing about the issue in the popular press ("What Tracking Did to Ollie").
7 Meyer and Patton, "Nexus of Race and Disability," 7.
8 Davis, *Enforcing Normalcy*, 3.
9 Clark, *Prejudice and Your Child*, 59.
10 Meyer and Patton, "Nexus of Race and Disability," 14.
11 Warikoo and Carter, "Cultural Explanations," 367.
12 The introduction to Kevin Gaines's *Uplifting the Race* provides a good overview of uplift politics.
13 Hamilton, *The Planet of Junior Brown*, 166, emphasis in original.
14 Ibid., 144.
15 Ibid., 154.
16 This chain of events has become notorious over the course of decades; students (often those who are marginalized due to race or disability) are removed from the classroom for an infraction and thus become visible to the juvenile justice system. More recent scholars have coined the term "school-to-prison pipeline," but the process is depicted as threatening to Buddy and Junior long before the term existed. Fenning and Rose, "Overrepresentation of African American Students," and Verdugo, "Race-Ethnicity, Social Class, and Zero-Tolerance Policies," provide useful overviews of research on the school to prison pipeline.
17 Kozol, *Savage Inequalities*, 152.
18 Cohen, *Boundaries of Blackness*, 63–64.
19 Webb, "Utopia in Contemporary Educational Theory," 748–749; Tyack and Cuban, *Tinkering Toward Utopia*, 1, 87.
20 Bérubé, *Life as We Know It*, 180, emphasis in original.
21 Hamilton, *The Planet of Junior Brown*, 13.

22 Ibid., 3.
23 Ibid., 4.
24 Rose, *Lives on the Boundary*, 120–127.
25 This dovetails with gendered critiques of the novel; see Roberta Seelinger Trites, "I Double Never Ever Lie," for a fuller critique of Buddy's masculinity.
26 Hamilton, *The Planet of Junior Brown*, 187–188.
27 Ibid., 210.
28 Kenneth Kidd, in "Prizing Children's Literature," suggests that the Newbery Honor category forms a "shadow canon" of books that are more daring and radical than the Newbery Medal winners, but also less widely known and taught.
29 Previous scholarship on Hamilton's novel has recognized this thread of fantasy. Herbert Kohl calls it "utopian" rather than "radical," highlighting imaginative alternatives rather than a reformed system (*Should We Burn Babar*, 78). Marla Harris places Hamilton's novel alongside dystopian/utopian science fiction in a new genre she calls the "urban survival novel"; she describes novels in this genre as enabling young readers to fantasize about being powerful, canny, and resilient ("Bleak Houses and Secret Cities," 64). Eric Tribunella similarly reads Buddy and Junior as child flâneurs, creative wanderers in New York City who transform hostile or indifferent urban spaces by imaginatively recreating them as "places of safety and beauty" ("Children's Literature and the Child Flâneur," 85).
30 Kelen and Sundmark, "Where Children Rule?," 263.
31 I discuss Buddy's reconfigurations of power in more depth in my article, "Solar Systems and Power Systems."
32 Trites, *Disturbing the Universe*, 74.
33 Lauren Berlant suggests that nations compel allegiance through a process of "suture[ing]"; through acts of collective fantasy, individuals imagine themselves as "the people" and local territories become "the nation." *Anatomy of a National Fantasy*, 25.
34 A version of this section was previously published under the title "Disability, Race, and Giftedness in Cynthia Voigt's Tillerman Novels" in the *Journal of Literary and Cultural Disability Studies*. It is reprinted here with permission.
35 Palmer, *Living Together*, 86.
36 Ladson-Billings, *The Dream-Keepers*, 32. Lisa Delpit also gestures to the problems of the "color-blind" approach in "Skills and Other Dilemmas," and Mildred Pitts Walter suggests in *Because We Are* that the approach produced racist pedagogy.
37 Skrtic, *An Organizational Analysis of Special Education Reform*, 3.
38 Voigt, *The Runner*, 260 (emphasis in original).
39 Jordan, *Broken Silences*, 295.
40 Recommendations for books in the series appeared in several publications for teachers, including Hylton, "Exploring the 'Academic Side' of Cynthia Voigt," for the *ALAN* review, and Eliza Dresang, "A Newbery Song for Gifted Readers," in *The School Library Journal*. In the *Journal of Reading*, Sister Regina Alfonso published a detailed teaching module on gender that specifically recommended *Dicey's Song* and *A Solitary Blue*.
41 Plucker, Burroughs, and Song, *Mind the (Other) Gap!*, 1.
42 Braddock and Slavin, "Why Ability Grouping Must End," 14.
43 Dresang, "A Newbery Song for Gifted Readers," 37.
44 Halberstam, *The Queer Art of Failure*, 3.
45 Labaree, "Public Goods, Private Goods," 42–43, 51–53.
46 Voigt, *Come a Stranger*, 133.

47 Ibid., 136.
48 Ibid.
49 Price, *Mad At School*, 67.
50 Voigt, "1995 Margaret Edwards Awards," 29.
51 Voigt, *Dicey's Song*, 54.
52 Kozol, *Savage Inequalities*, 135.
53 Cintron, *Angels' Town*, 101.
54 Hertberg-Davis, "Myth 7."
55 Voigt, *Dicey's Song*, 109.
56 Voigt, *Come a Stranger*, 199.
57 Jordan, *Broken Silences*, 254.
58 Voigt, "On Teaching," 741.
59 Giroux, "Dystopian Nightmares," 50.
60 Olssen, "Totalitarianism and the 'Repressed' Utopia of the Present," 120.
61 Ibid., 100.

4 Desegregating Literacy Skills in the Era of Accountability

Neoliberalism and the Legacy of Testing

In the last two decades, books for children have tended to address school desegregation through the genres of historical fiction, memoir, or history. A few scattered works of realistic fiction, such as Jacqueline Woodson's *Maizon at Blue Hill* (1992) and Andrea Davis Pinkney's *Hold Fast to Dreams* (1995), clearly address the ongoing challenges of tokenism and residential segregation. More often, however, recent novels dealing with race in the contemporary school setting bypass structural issues such as residential segregation and tokenism. Instead, they focus on complex scenarios of bullying or educational de-motivation in which racism (often intra-community division and colorism) is only one of the many challenges facing the protagonists.[1] This trend reflects a nuanced approach to identity politics, but it also reflects the direction of public policy and discourse regarding school desegregation. Many novels published since the 1990s that may not otherwise seem to portray issues of school desegregation actually participate in a changing discourse about what desegregation means. Overt portrayals of conflicts over school desegregation may be confined to the genre of Civil Rights-era historical fiction, but contemporary legacies of the *Brown* decision surface indirectly and subtly in many other novels. These novels address achievement gaps in knowledge rather than depicting concern with contemporary re-segregation in the classroom.

Contests over the definition and redefinition of school desegregation have been fairly continual since the original *Brown* decision, but a distinctive shift began in the 1980s when the Reagan Administration and Congress began to replace funding for comprehensive desegregation plans with funding for voluntary "choice" options such as magnet schools. Then, in the early 1990s, the Supreme Court passed a number of rulings that allowed districts to re-segregate.[2] Since that time, discourse about public schooling has largely drifted from discussion over whether *schools* are being desegregated. Instead, concern centers on whether *knowledge* is being desegregated in order to close the symbolic racial achievement gap.

Educational policy battles over standards, testing, and accountability may not seem to be connected to court-ordered school desegregation in the same kind of clear and evident way that nostalgia for segregated schooling and disability-based re-segregation are legacies of *Brown*. Indeed, the movement for testing and accountability can be attributed to multiple causes, including the rise of neoliberal approaches to government and education. Nevertheless, many observers trace the accountability movement back several decades and identify it as a conscious response to school desegregation—a response which carefully bore no traces of overt attempts to stall desegregation. R. Scott Baker, for example, observes that beginning in the 1940s, standardized test requirements were implemented in each educational setting to which black students and teachers sought access; in 1955 and 1956, a wave of standardized tests was implemented in Southern public schools. In desegregation stories, like *The Story of Ruby Bridges* and Pinkney's *With the Might of Angels*, the protagonists' performance on tests proves the unfairness of segregation. Of course, these stories tend not to focus on the students who did not perform as well. As Baker notes, the tests were meant to "rationalize restrictions that were based on race," and to legally bar as many black students as possible.[3] This mechanism of testing became a self-perpetuating phenomenon that appeared necessary for accountability of various kinds; liberal critics wished to hold desegregating schools accountable for providing an equitable education, and conservative critics held up test scores as evidence that desegregation was not working and that it had devalued the public school system.[4]

In a similar way, the ethics of neoliberalism in public education—including encouragement of consumer "choice" and reliance upon the mechanisms of the private market to solve issues of equity and justice—have helped to shape the implementation of *Brown* and the public conversation about racial equity in education. Many Southern cities, of course, stalled desegregation by allowing white students to "choose" to attend all-white private academies. Historian Philip T.K. Daniel points out that even the implementation of *Brown* was framed by many school districts as a "choice" plan, in which black students could choose to attend all-white schools (if they passed the tests) without any further attempt at large-scale integration. This framework of "choice" has allowed for the development of majority-minority charter schools and private school vouchers as more popular alternatives to desegregation plans; as long as African-American and Latino students have alternatives to problematic, highly segregated neighborhood schools, those alternatives need not involve large-scale desegregation with better-funded, majority white suburban schools.[5]

Children's books handle anxieties about accountability and racial justice in a variety of ways; however, they generally tend to reflect this emphasis upon individual choice and commitment to learn. Correspondingly, they also de-emphasize the importance of anti-racist pedagogy, or desegregation, in the school. Perhaps as a result, many texts also seem to carry the burden of amelioration, encouraging their intended audiences to "choose" literacy and providing a private alternative to school-based literacy training. This seems to be especially the case with books that feature black protagonists, across age levels and genres. For example, Sandra and Myles Pinkney's 2006 picture book *Read and Rise* features inspirational poetry about children's dreams and aspirations, paired with sets of photographs that depict black children reading books and performing, in costume, a specific career goal that the book allowed them to envision for themselves. This book was specifically sponsored by the National Urban League as part of an initiative to promote broad economic and social equality. Paul Langan's 2013 *Schooled*, written as part of the Bluford High series marketed to urban teens, echoes similar patterns. Lionel struggles in school because he is illiterate and ashamed, but eventually he is inspired by a Langston Hughes poem and a Bible story to accept help from his teachers and to regain hope in the American dream. In Vashanti Rahaman's *Read for Me, Mama* (1997), Joseph flourishes in his desegregated school, but finds that his mother cannot read to him at home; the conflict therefore centers around his mother's decision to rectify her own history of poor schooling by attending an evening vocational education class populated by other racial minority students.

Books that feature a white protagonist, or that explicitly address a mixed audience, also, in some cases, seem to provide a private alternative to school-based desegregation. For example, Kate Messner's 2015 picture book *How to Read a Story* specifies the metacognitive steps a young white boy follows as he learns to read more proficiently: finding a buddy for support, making predictions, and imagining the action. As he nears the end of his book, a multicultural cast of children and adults surrounds him to congratulate him in an armchair that is presumably located at home, not in a classroom surrounded by other students. Joyce Carol Thomas's *Linda Brown, You Are Not Alone* (2003) very explicitly narrates stories about school desegregation. Yet the introduction begins by describing a child "stealing" moments of illicit reading under Jim Crow, and ends by encouraging contemporary readers to find exciting discoveries—and racial justice—through following the example of that child and reading in extra-curricular settings.[6] Even in those texts that do feature a school setting, issues of structural desegregation and pedagogy are granted less importance than whether or not the child chooses to be receptive to and eager about reading. Crucially, this shift in focus does not necessarily represent a retreat from the goals of school desegregation. Some texts are critical of accountability rhetoric and seem to highlight extracurricular reading as part of a new strategy for racial justice, since school desegregation did not ever seem to spread out to other sectors of society.

The three novels in this chapter represent a range of approaches to accountability and choice as legacies of *Brown*—even though, in keeping with contemporary discourses, all of them accomplish their critiques without actually mentioning school desegregation. Indeed, all three novels imply some level of disconnect between the implementation of desegregation and the desired result of literacy learning, as they emphasize the literacy skills of African-American child characters while lamenting the few characters "left behind." Louis Sachar's 1998 *Holes*, published during a push for high-stakes accountability in Texas, is the most popular of the three, and also the most sympathetic to the idea that accountability can be a force for racial justice. While Sachar's novel is bitingly critical of how the state of Texas has failed to repair its historic racial injustices, it also suggests that successfully closing the literacy achievement gap (in a juvenile detention center, not in a school) will heal the nation and produce economic prosperity. In contrast, M.T. Anderson's two-volume series *The Astonishing Life of Octavian Nothing, Traitor to the Nation* is unusual in its sweeping condemnation of promises that testing and choice will produce racial justice, in the absence of a prior commitment to equality. Anderson's novels, published a few years after the implementation of the 2001 No Child Left Behind Act (NCLB) that nationalized Texas's move toward high-stakes tests, are set during the Revolutionary War. The novels evade the setting of the public school, but instead construct multiple scenes of failed education at the inception of the nation, suggesting that the nation's original sins of racial injustice stained the project of education. The third book, Sharon Flake's 2012 *Pinned*, was published two years before the NCLB deadline for all students to test proficiently, just as many educators were protesting that their schools would not meet this goal. *Pinned* reflects deep ambivalence about the rhetoric of standards and choice as a substitute for racial justice. The novel is set in a thriving contemporary charter school; on the one hand, this school "choice" fails to ensure broad economic opportunity or equality, and on the other, the protagonist's decision to become literate seems to revive the unfinished social justice projects of historical black leaders.

These novels alter the plot structure of the desegregation story in multiple ways. As the novels explore alternate settings for antiracist education besides the public school classroom, they also experiment with different genres for stories of education, and different time frames for learning other than the bounded school year. Furthermore, all three texts play with conventions of linear, transparent narrative in ways that train their implied readers in the kinds of literacy that will help them to continue the unfinished goals of *Brown*. In this way, rather than representing pedagogy as the desegregation novels of previous chapters do, they enact utopian pedagogy.

Educational philosophical debates are sometimes framed as contests between concepts of education as a publicly held common good and education as a private commodity to be acquired and used by individual consumers. In very different ways, these novels tend to collapse that distinction, suggesting that there is no real conflict between them. The protagonists of all three novels desire literacy for their own purposes and use it to redefine their own sense of citizenship roles and obligations, even as state institutions require some reckoning of their learning. The protagonists of more explicit Civil Rights-era desegregation stories are public servants in training, preparing to serve and to create a more racially just nation. In contrast, the protagonists of these tales of accountability are modeled on a different vision of citizenship, as they negotiate deals with the state for what it can offer, assess the price of learning, and imagine alternate modes of nationhood that might be constructed with their learning.

Holes: Literacy and the Rehabilitation of the Capitalist Nation

In Louis Sachar's *Holes*, the desegregation of literacy becomes the way for the United States to fulfill its utopian promise. The sharing of intellectual assets leads directly to both personal and national prosperity, enabling the state to more effectively promote unity, administer justice, and foster the material welfare of its citizens. *Holes* follows three interlocking story lines, in which two historical injustices continue to curse the land and the present-day citizens of central Texas. The first historical storyline follows the family history of the protagonist, Stanley Yelnats. His Latvian ancestor betrayed the trust of a Romani friend and drew down her curse upon him and his family, all the way up to Stanley's generation. Stanley is falsely convicted of theft and sentenced to rehabilitation at a juvenile penal institution, Camp Green Lake, which has neither greenery nor a lake, but only miles of unproductive desert. This desolation is the result of a different curse, which is explained by the other historical plot line. The Warden of Camp Green Lake is the descendant of a white landowner. The reader learns through flashbacks that 100 years earlier, this landowner had lynched a black man for becoming romantically involved with the town's white schoolteacher. After her lover was murdered, the schoolteacher, Kate Barlow, cursed the town and became a feared outlaw, robbing Stanley's ancestor and burying his fortune in the newly formed desert. Stanley, along with the other boys at Camp Green Lake, now digs holes in order to recover the fortune which the Warden regards as hers. During his time at Camp Green Lake, he meets Zero, an illiterate, orphaned black boy, who later turns out to be the descendant of Madame Zeroni, the woman who cursed his ancestor. Stanley reluctantly teaches Zero to read, and then saves his life when the two boys escape from the camp; in return, Zero uses his newly acquired literacy to read Stanley's name on the box of buried fortune found in one of the holes. The curses are broken; the boys are restored to society; the lost fortune is restored to Stanley's family; Camp Green Lake is restored to its former utopian greenery; and all of this healing is enabled because a white boy and a black boy work together to close the achievement gap.

Education in *Holes* clearly serves the public good; however, the state's role in the novel as the sponsor of education reflects historic ambivalence about who the beneficiaries of state-sponsored education ought to be. Horace Mann, one of the architects of the Massachusetts common school system, is often cited as the foundational philosopher behind the idea that a state-financed common school ought to serve the public good, by training citizens who share a body of knowledge and learn to serve their nation above their own selfish private interests.[7] Nevertheless, in speeches to raise support for his expensive proposals, Mann alternated between reasoning based on public goods and private goods. In one speech, he promotes education as a democratically owned property that can be infinitely distributed among citizens, because "[t]he same truth may enrich and ennoble all intelligences at once.... None are made poor because others are made rich."[8] In a later lecture, however, he invokes the cause of social stability, suggesting that the wealthy should be willing to subsidize common education through taxes because it is the only way to control the masses and to teach them "a sense of the inviolability of property."[9] In this appeal, the democratically shared property of literacy serves to maintain the value of deeded private property; the common good translates to the private good. Moreover, as Massachusetts Secretary of Education, Mann instituted a system of written examinations whose results could be published, so that the schools could be held accountable to taxpayers. *Holes* both reaches back nostalgically to some of these foundational ideals of democratic education, and also maintains a foundational connection between public good and accountability to private interest.

In fact, the education of Zero might have been expressly designed to demonstrate Horace Mann's philosophy. As an illiterate orphan, whose care and education is neglected both by his biological mother and by paternalistic state institutions, he walks into a homeless shelter and steals a pair of used, smelly sneakers, because he needs shoes. He reasons that if he must steal, it is better to take a used pair than a new one. The shoes are in a glass case adorned with a placard announcing that Clyde Livingston, famous baseball player, has donated his shoes for a fundraising auction. Zero, of course, cannot read the sign, and does not understand why everyone is so upset when the shoes are found missing; he tosses them off a highway underpass, where they land on Stanley's head and lead to Stanley's arrest for the theft. The next day, Zero is caught stealing a new pair of shoes from a store. Zero is thus constructed as both criminal and innocent; he *has* stolen the shoes and caused the arrest of an innocent person, but he cannot respect private property if he is unable to read a label designating whose property it is. After he learns to read, Zero is presented with a parallel test of his citizenship; he is confronted with another piece of extremely valuable property bearing a label, at which point he confirms his fitness for citizenship by *publicly* reading the label and ensuring it is restored to its proper owner.

Zero's reading performance must be public, because without this public accountability, Zero will not be recognized as a valued citizen who "counts" and the state will not be forced to address its injustices. Nevertheless, Roderick Ferguson's analysis of racial policies in American higher education suggests that the connection between accountability and antiracism is complex. Formerly racially exclusive institutions may be held accountable for becoming more diverse and inclusive, but minoritized teachers and students who enter are also held accountable for providing visible affirmation that difference has been successfully incorporated. Institutions may therefore pressure "diverse" teachers and students to support only carefully chosen forms of public citizenship that reinforce the political and capital interests of the nation-state.[10] Zero, in contrast, attempts to evade the kind of pressure that comes with being a visibly included minority. For much of the novel, Zero resembles Buddy of *The Planet of Junior Brown* in his desire to evade the gaze of the racist state. When Stanley first begins to teach Zero, he is astonished to discover how quick Zero is to learn, and how good he is at math. When Stanley presses him, Zero reluctantly admits, "'I'm not stupid. … I know everybody thinks I am. I just don't like answering their questions.'"[11] With this statement, the burden of accountability shifts to Zero, who makes choices about his assessment performance, and who therefore "owns" some responsibility for his reputation of stupidity. Thus, the resolution of the nation's curse depends not only upon Zero's learning to read, but also consenting to go on record as a success story.

The novel presents readers with a complex series of arguments for why Zero should decide to let himself become a visible symbol of racial healing in return for the rewards of literacy. As readers witness Zero being persuaded to demonstrate his literacy, they are also learning to fill in holes in the record. In addition to the literal holes that the boys dig in the desert, *Holes* is structured around a series of figurative holes, including gaps in the violent history of the Old West, achievement gaps based on race and class, and holes in cyberspace into which unwanted orphans' files can disappear. Through the course of the novel, deceptively empty spaces must be laboriously excavated; as the boys dig holes in the old lake, stories from history begin to people the barren landscape.[12] Similarly, Stanley's family curse is at first only used as a convenient source of blame when something goes wrong, but its truth must be uncovered. Madame Zeroni must be recognized not merely as the source of a curse inflicted for an historical wrong, but as the ancestor of a living human being whom Stanley continues to wrong in the present. Nevertheless, while many of the holes represent state-level failures of record-keeping or administration of services, it is child protagonists and readers who are invited to take responsibility for exposing the holes, so that the wounds of national history can begin to heal.

The task of digging up the truths that haunt those empty spaces is presented as a tiring and painful task, requiring labor on the parts of both the characters and the readers (although the readers' labor is far more entertaining than the characters'). For the boys at Camp Green Lake, this work is physical; they dig holes in the hot sun, blistering their hands and wearying their bodies. For Stanley and Zero, it is mental and emotional as well. After digging holes in the hot sun, they do the work of teaching, learning, and building rapport in a situation that engenders suspicion more often than it encourages mutual trust. Attempts to evade pain, however, only open up ugly wounds further. A central tenet in *Holes* is that literacy labor is analogous to physical labor, and that when done correctly, both build character. At the surface level, the notion of character building is ridiculed within the novel. Nevertheless, its ironic, critical depiction of the juvenile justice system resonates weirdly with the hearty school spirit and patriotism of canonical school stories.[13] In fact, both Stanley and Zero seem to get a more successful education through the juvenile penal system than they do through the school system, which has failed them both in different ways.[14] As in those school stories, the students' real education takes place outside of class hours (that is, outside of digging hours for Stanley and Zero). Their extracurricular learning, literacy and interracial friendship, is what both the school and the justice system are failing to teach them in curricular hours. As in many classic school stories, however, the seemingly pointless work of the central curriculum (whether Latin or digging) provides the conditions of discipline under which the more meaningful student-directed learning can take place.

The inane physical digging eventually uncovers racial divisions that persist between the boys. At first, Stanley adopts a sort of color-blindness, seeing all of the boys' racial diversity erased by the color of dirt from digging on the lake. When Stanley begins teaching Zero to read after hours, however, he asks Zero to pay him in labor, replicating a history of racist education when he refuses to freely share knowledge and privileges mental work over physical. Indeed, the other boys immediately begin to accuse Stanley of being a slave-master and exploiting Zero, exposing a live and present racial conflict beneath the shared color of dirt. When the racial conflict escalates into a three-way fight, camp officials are brought in to arbitrate the matter. Stanley pleads that Zero needs literacy in order to build his character, indirectly accusing the camp of neglecting its educational responsibilities; in response, the Warden and the counselor Mr. Pendanski test Zero's literacy progress and humiliate him in front of the boys when he fails to demonstrate phonics skills that Stanley has not yet taught.

Accountability, in this scene, seems to be a tool that harms the student more than it reforms the institution, so that Zero can hardly be blamed for choosing evasion. In fact, Zero's test evokes a long history of literacy tests being used by the state, not to keep schools accountable for improvement and equity, but to disenfranchise black citizens. The present-day Camp Green Lake administrators continue to have an interest in proving, and maintaining, Zero's illiteracy. As an illiterate boy, Zero rebels in a way that aids the state. When pressed by Mr. Pendanski to articulate a goal for his adult life as a citizen, he insists that he wants only to dig holes; ironically, while he understands that Mr. Pendanski wants him to embrace a goal of active ambition and upward mobility, his refusal to consent to this model of citizenship actually provides the justice system with a strong, passive body who digs for the advancement of others. As a literacy learner, however, he does what Mr. Pendanski has earlier asked him to do—he rejects the role of lifelong hole-digger. In fact, he not only rejects the idea that his future as an adult citizen is to provide labor for the State of Texas, he rejects the idea that this labor should comprise his youthful citizenship obligations, and he runs away rather than be rehabilitated for adult citizenship through this method.

Perversely, however, Zero's testing failure also causes Stanley to reassess his educational philosophy and to accept the value of physical labor in building his character, thus affirming the philosophy of Camp Green Lake. Having been responsible for the violence that drove Zero away, Stanley now digs Zero's holes as well as his own, building his strength (as it turns out) for the moment when he must carry Zero up a mountain to save his life. Ultimately, successful education is depicted as requiring both intellectual and physical skill. The two interracial pairs depicted in the historical plot lines are similar to Stanley and Zero in that literacy and physical strength are unevenly divided according to race and gender, highlighting historical achievement gaps produced by racism and sexism. The racial and physical literacy gap between the strong, illiterate Zero and the fat, bookish Stanley establishes that historical racism still lives on in the bodies and minds of youth in the present, and harms the productivity of both. Zero's illiteracy unfits him for citizenship and blocks his economic prospects, while Stanley's physical weakness more subtly leads him into immorality and signals a lack of the persistence needed for entrepreneurship. Even though other boys at Camp Green Lake can both read and perform physical labor, Zero and Stanley stand out as extreme cases who have been failed by the school system—but who must decide to be accountable to themselves, in the absence of a benevolent state institution.[15]

The two protagonists are responsible for another central task that the desegregated school system has failed to accomplish—healing the nation's troubled racial history. The novel mixes and overlaps several genres, including the fairy tale, hero's quest, Western, Bildungsroman, and mystery novel. What several of these genres have in common, both with each other and with the school story, is a plot arc in which a young protagonist is given a series of tasks to accomplish toward the achievement of some larger goal. The end goal might be to advance to a productive and successful adult role (Bildungsromans, fairy tales, and school stories) or to save the kingdom from an evil force (fairy tales, hero's quests, and mysteries). In *Holes*, which combines all of these genres, both goals are emphasized, and the mundane school tasks of sounding out words and participating in physical education are elevated to world-saving status, necessary to maintaining the interracial friendships that will save the country from its historic evil. The protagonists are posed similar educational tasks in this modern fairy tale/hero quest as they were in the classic school stories, but these are taken out of the context of the school institution. This movement acknowledges the troubled status of the school as a site of national healing, in that it becomes an unconvincing setting for a successful heroic quest to save the nation. At the same time, the reader is asked to value the same tasks that are valued within the school, and thus to view his or her own life as a student as a Manichaean heroic quest.

Despite the novel's emphasis on its protagonists' physical labor, the important work of historical excavation and healing must be done almost entirely by the reader, and purely in symbolic form. Stanley and Zero never actually learn the full story of Elya Yelnats and Madame Zeroni, nor do they learn that Kissin' Kate Barlow turned outlaw and robbed the first Stanley Yelnats because her heart was broken by racism in the town of Green Lake. It is the reader who must confront these painful histories. It is the reader alone who must be forced to remember that immigrants "innocent" of slavery brought their own racial sins across the water and that the American landscape is the site of violence as well as dreams.

Sachar suggests in an interview that *Holes* has been popular with children because "there's the whole puzzle aspect. Kids are rewarded for reading further."[16] The layering of the three plot lines does, indeed, present a rewarding puzzle to solve, but Sachar's metaphor of puzzles and rewards is crucial. The reader must do mental work to fit all of the pieces together, and in fact is told by the narrator, "You will have to fill in the holes yourself."[17] June Cummins argues that Sachar's conscious challenge to piece the text's meaning together is his way to not only teach young readers to value the hard work of literacy, but also coach them in patriotic values of "optimism, perseverance, industry, and hope."[18] In fact, due to the structure of the quest narrative, the reader is rewarded in still another way; he or she can actually feel like the hero who has lifted the historical curses upon the nation by completing the literacy task, since it is only the reader and not the characters who has the full knowledge of how the curses operate. Thus, even though *Holes* is published in era of re-segregation, when the public schools in the novel are not producing racially enlightened, well-prepared public servants like the protagonists of desegregation stories, young readers are still given a path to become a desirable citizen. This citizen is competent in both literacy and racial awareness and has earned the right to possess the intellectual wealth of national literature.[19] By emphasizing the individual reader's duty to succeed in the literary performance task, the novel subtly critiques the schools for failing to provide a proper citizenship education in literacy, national history, and ideals of civic justice (an education which the novel supplies in its place). At the same time, the remedy is taken out of the schools and placed in the realm of individual responsibility and choice.

In fact, the Texas schools are never held fully accountable for the truancy which results in Zero's illiteracy, because Zero's records disappear down a hole in cyberspace.[20] Instead, after Zero publicly proves his reading skills, the whole nation symbolically shares in the rewards of literacy and economic prosperity. True, the Warden is revealed as criminally corrupt, and the Texas Attorney General is implicated in neglect. The school system is presumably still filled with the bullies (both students and teachers) who previously tormented Stanley, and the state agencies in charge of family welfare have failed to track and to care for Zero and his mother. Nevertheless, the economic recovery of the novel's ending seems to eclipse the failures of the state, a resolution that resonates with critiques of neoliberalism. Jodi Melamed suggests that neoliberal national policies have shaped the implementation of antiracist efforts, so that cultural pluralism and diversity are valued and supported primarily under circumstances in which they can help American economic expansion into global networks.[21] This sense that national market health is an important goal of racial justice is reflected in *Holes*. Zero and Stanley share in the recovered treasure earned through historical ingenuity and present-day literacy work. Green Lake is filled with water and recovered for productive use. The nation's modernized private sector brims with successful and literate racialized representatives, such as Ms. Moreno, Stanley's feisty, private-sector Latina lawyer, and Clyde Livingston, the black baseball player who spends his childhood in a homeless shelter and his adulthood as a celebrity benefactor of homeless children. Zero's literacy puts long-lost company stocks back into circulation, and also enables Stanley's father, a failed inventor, to finally become a successful entrepreneur, reinvigorating the fabled American tradition of free-market ingenuity. The novel closes with the triumph of a nationwide commercial that uses a successful black man as the visible face of a product invented by a white one. This pluralist market, not the pathetic, racist state institutions, is where the reality of national identity and allegiance lies in the novel. The continuing divides of the nation-state—the bullying problems at Stanley's school, and the fact that the successful white man is inventing products while the successful black man is playing baseball—are allowed, in this final scene, to remain buried, covered over with the plenitude of the rewards literacy has brought.

This shift occurs in part because the meaning of literacy in *Holes* is locked down unambiguously. The official examination of literacy never produces unexpected results, and there is no question over what form literacy should take or what level of literacy should count. All demonstrations of literacy—Zero's phonics, Stanley's letter-writing, and Kate Barlow's canonical poetry reading—are collapsed into the same category and assigned the value of "good." The work of literacy can *only* produce antiracism, economic success, and national stability, and the neglect of literacy can only produce the opposite. In part, of course, these simplifications are because of the fairy-tale elements of the novel, which suggest that certain virtues must inevitably produce certain story endings, in ways similar to the school story. *The Astonishing Life of Octavian Nothing*, however, not only disturbs the correspondences between personal interest, national interest, and national virtue; it simultaneously upsets the links between literacy standards and accountability.

The Astonishing Life of Octavian Nothing: Literacy and the Treacherous Citizen

Holes, despite its critiques of a post-Civil Rights school system that apparently allows bullying, truancy, and slippage into the juvenile justice system, nevertheless reflects a certain degree of optimism that providers of education can effectively respond to transparent demands for accountability. *Octavian Nothing*, in contrast, was published in the aftermath of President George W. Bush's assertions that large-scale testing would counter "the soft bigotry of low expectations."[22] Anderson's, novels, published in 2006 and 2008, simultaneously raise the expectations of his protagonist's (and his readers') literacy to startling levels, and demonstrate that these expectations and the accountability tests that accompany them do absolutely nothing to counter bigotry. Octavian narrates his story in a credible imitation of eighteenth-century literary prose, packed with detailed references to classical philosophers and historians. While *Holes*, with its puzzle-based, inspirational challenges to young readers, has been widely adopted into curricula, *Octavian Nothing*, which is not written in a conventionally accessible style, is taught less often than other children's texts about slavery.[23]

Octavian is a slave in Revolutionary War-era Boston, held by the philosophical College of Lucidity. He is given an elite classical education from birth, and his every movement and response is observed and recorded, in order to scientifically measure whether Africans represent a separate species from Europeans. Partway through the experiment, the college falls into financial distress, and acquires funding from new investors who are slaveholders and traders, and who therefore have an interest in proving his inferiority. His education and assessment change accordingly. Octavian escapes with his sympathetic white tutor, Dr. Trefusis, and joins with the Revolutionary forces attacking Boston in the name of Liberty. The two later leave the rebels to join the British regiment of Lord Dunmore, who has promised liberty to escaped slaves willing to fight against the rebellion. In this regiment, he teaches literacy and classical mythology to some of his fellow escapees, and in return learns some of the Oyo language his mother refused to speak with him. When the Royal Ethiopian Regiment is abandoned by Lord Dunmore, Octavian and a few of his compatriots escape once more, in search of a safe harbor. Before following his friends, however, Octavian returns to the hated philosophical college in order to destroy the years of data collected about him and to replace it with his own manuscript.

Anderson maintains that this Bildungsroman about an unusually erudite eighteenth-century slave is relevant to contemporary teens. In an interview on National Public Radio, he argues,

> [Kids] know what it's like in this country to be the subject of academic experiments of some kind. I mean the series of rigorous tests and things which we now force our kids to undergo—I mean they know what it feels like to be observed and that kind of thing, even if not in as excruciating a manner as happens in this book.[24]

Anderson draws a parallel between Octavian's education and his readers' education under the No Child Left Behind Act. NCLB's statement of purpose is explicitly antiracist, specifying that it is intended to ensure that minority and nonminority students receive the same education, and that student data will be used to distribute resources.[25] Similarly, the philosophers experimenting with Octavian intend to give him an education exactly equivalent to that of a European prince.

The framework of an experiment, however, establishes that the philosophers' goal is measurement, rather than antiracist education. By using the language of experimentation, Anderson suggests that the antiracist credentials of NCLB are similarly in question; indeed, previous attempts at desegregation programs like busing were protested and eventually dismantled on the grounds that they were failed experiments, rather than commitments to justice.[26] Eventually, Octavian's data is used to "prove" his inferiority, thus implying a parallel danger for contemporary racialized students being measured under NCLB. Octavian's masters produce failure for their own political uses, and so, Anderson suggests in an interview, do contemporary politicians and administrators have uses for contemporary teens' academic struggles. In his acceptance speech for the Printz Honor Award, which he received for *The Kingdom on the Waves*, he suggests that adult readers label books inappropriate when they demand, and assume, teens' intelligence. He responds, "[I]t is unbecoming for us to be fearful of teens who love to think."[27] Teens become objects of fear for adult citizens, not when they fail to share the national wealth of knowledge or to recognize property, as Horace Mann and Louis Sachar suggest, but when they are *too* literate, independent, and curious. As a result, the Octavian novels suggest that teens of all races might be held accountable for higher achievement, were a corrupt system not invested in their failure. True, the Octavian novels take place before the abolition of slavery and even before the widespread establishment of common schools (although Boston had some common schools, they were not yet organized into a statewide system). While this setting may seem to distance the novels' critiques of data-driven education by placing the story before important historical reforms, the setting and its parallel to contemporary testing experiments also implies that the Civil Rights movement may as well not have happened, for all the difference it made to antiracist education. Instead, the original sin of racist exploitation infused all burgeoning national institutions in ways that poisoned future reforms.

From the beginning, Octavian's narration demonstrates a flaw in the idea that closing the achievement gap is a substitute for civil rights. The philosophers at the Novanglian College of Lucidity do share knowledge and literacy, but only as an exchange that ultimately benefits them. Octavian acknowledges,

> Whatever I have felt about these men, I have much to thank them for. They lavished luxuries upon me. They supported my every interest and encouraged my curiosity. They instructed me in the Christian religion. They taught me the tongues of the Greeks and the Romans and opened for me the colonnaded vistas of those long-forgotten empires, in this, the dawning of a new empire. They schooled me in music, which is my greatest delight. These are not little things.[28]

Nevertheless, before the reader (or, in fact, Octavian himself) even learns that Octavian is a slave, he tells us the price he pays for this knowledge. Not only is every morsel of his food and feces weighed and recorded, his intellectual and emotional output is also recorded and then traded for prestige. After Mr. Gitney, the College's director, poisons the food Octavian gives his beloved dog, he takes the grieving boy on his knee and inquires whether Octavian thinks the dog has gone to an afterlife, and what the nature of this afterlife might be. This paternal scene of comfort is jarred by the statement that "carefully, nodding, he transcribed my answers for study, comment, and future publication"; thus, Octavian's education provides the raw materials for Gitney's prestige and funding.[29] This scene exposes a central problem behind the assumption embedded in NCLB. Both educational experiments purposefully desegregate knowledge, aiming to provide equal access to literacy and cultural capital; and yet this sharing of cultural property does not translate to the sharing of power. In the era of No Child Left Behind, the testing of literacy has also functioned as a link between publicly funded knowledge and private wealth and power. Todd Farley and Dan DiMaggio, both long-time scorers for the reading and writing tests mandated by No Child Left Behind, write about the near-monopoly of a few testing companies who secure enormous government contracts and then hire temporary seasonal workers to score the tests for low wages and no benefits. DiMaggio notes that in 2010, Pearson received a corporate tax break under the HIRE Act because it claimed to create jobs, and both authors report that scorers are pressured to adjust the grades to comply with the desires of state officials, so that the same testing companies will continue to receive state contracts. A backdrop of greed and corruption is correspondingly exposed in the novel.

The scene when Octavian learns what his intellectual labor is being used for is a key moment in the novel. Although Octavian has observed numerous animal experiments in the various chambers of the house, one room, with his face pasted on the door, is locked and forbidden to him. After learning that he and his mother are slaves, Octavian picks the lock on the door and finds a scientific anatomical diagram of his mother's naked body and volumes containing his own records. He immediately realizes that this information is partial and selective, recording the contents of his body, but not of his memory or spirit. Nevertheless, he misinterprets the goal of the experiment, believing that it is intended to prove his equality. This belief does have a demonstrable effect on his education; he determines that he "would not fail 03–01."[30] Octavian makes the good-student choice to commit himself to learning. At the same time, in punishment for his disobedience, he is made to stand with his arms outstretched, bearing the weight of his own data as it literally as well as symbolically pushes him down. While Octavian expresses gratitude for his education, his learning is not framed as a source of personal empowerment as it is in many children's texts about the education of black students. His knowledge of Greek and Latin gives him much less power than the College's knowledge of Octavian gives them, and their knowledge feeds directly into the networks of knowledge and capital that help the expansion of the British Empire (and later the internal expansion of the new American empire). Indeed, as the novel continues, Octavian's mother learns to hide her own knowledge of her homeland, lest it be used for further empire building, and Pro Bono is punished for documenting his knowledge about the horrors of slavery. Neither learning in and of itself nor the public demonstration of learning is inherently equalizing or empowering.

When Octavian's educational experience changes, the process of data collection and assessment is more openly shown to be corrupt. After the

College falls into financial distress (in part because Octavian's mother has refused to serve as a concubine for a potential investor), the philosophers acquire new backers who are merchants and plantation owners who, Mr. Gitney admits, "'have some interest in proving the inequality of African capacities.'"[31] They therefore demand that the nature of Octavian's experimental education be changed. He is barred from reading narratives of any kind, on the grounds that they will appeal unfairly to his "hereditary savage nature," and is limited to construing decontextualized fragments of Latin and Greek "chosen for their convolution, recondite meaning, dryness, and insipidity."[32] These fragments, shorn of meaningful narrative, are intentionally much more difficult for Octavian to understand and to translate. Therefore, unsurprisingly, Octavian continues to deliver the results desired of him (although the requested results are now the opposite), and begins to fail in his studies. The new director, Mr. Sharpe, informs him in the climactic scene of *The Pox Party*, "'You have done us a wonderful service, through your failure. We have publicly noted the decline in your abilities.'"[33] Standardized literacy tests have, for several decades, been designed so as to be inexpensive to grade, and thus tend to focus on isolated skills that can be tested in a multiple choice format. In addition, poor and minority students are assumed to enter schools with deficits instead of skills, and therefore are assumed to need to be drilled on decontextualized sub-skills using insipid fragments before (or rather in place of) engaging with interesting narratives.[34] In contrast, middle-class and white students are more often assumed to possess these testable sub-skills already and are thus permitted to engage directly with narrative. Middle-class and white students then tend to perform better on tests that appear to confirm an already-presumed achievement gap. Octavian's education suggests that NCLB's goal to combat bigotry by closing the achievement gap is, in fact, producing the achievement gap in order to confirm a retreat from Civil Rights-era efforts.

This retreat from progressive goals—the goals of disinterested Enlightenment inquiry in the novels' setting and the goals of the Civil Rights era in the readers' setting—also prompts characters and readers to detach themselves from destructive concepts of nationhood. In more standard desegregation school stories, students learn citizenship and loyalty at the reformed school. Even though they have "chosen" to desegregate, they are framed as subject to the school's discipline, Cold Warriors in training. Under conditions of neoliberal school choice developed during the 1990s and 2000s (Walter's 1980s novel *Because We Are*, highlighting the "opportunity transfer," is an early example), students are instead framed as consumers who can shift loyalty, and public dollars, to the institutions that will best serve them. All of these institutions, of course, presumably prepare students to be citizens of the United States. The Octavian novels, however, problematize this issue of loyalty; the subtitle of the novels is "A Traitor to His Nation." While Octavian's readers may shop for schools that will help them close the achievement gap, Octavian himself shops for a less racist nation that might one day subsidize schools. True, due to his status as a slave, Octavian is not a consumer, but an object to be consumed. Nevertheless, he behaves as though his literacy granted him the privilege of choice.

The power to consume is not framed as a desirable mode of citizenship.[35] When Mr. Sharpe explains to the College's philosophers how their approach to knowledge must change, he voices the new educational philosophy in brutal terms: "*No institution, like no fox, may long be sustained on its own flesh. We must devour elsewhere if we are not to devour ourselves, and so perish!*"[36] At the end, when Mr. Sharpe once again describes a world vision of endless, all-encompassing consumption and competition, Dr. Trefusis poisons him, reducing his grand theory to gibberish. Nevertheless, given a system that depends upon consumption, the agency to consume his preferred literature also seems to liberate Octavian, at least temporarily, from the condition of being an object who lacks all citizenship. When Octavian is barred from browsing the Shakespeare and Pope and Virgil he has come to love, he feels

> exiled from [his] own country. By the transport of books, that which is most foreign becomes one's familiar walks and avenues; while that which is most familiar is removed to delightful strangeness; and unmoving, one travels infinite causeways; immobile and thus unfettered.[37]

Octavian's vision of his "own country," where the limitless potential for travel contrasts with his constrictions under slavery, echoes W.E.B. Du Bois's vision of reading as the temporary creation of a more utopian America. When he reads, Du Bois says,

> I sit with Shakespeare and he winces not. Across the color line I move arm in arm with Balzac and Dumas, where smiling men and welcoming women glide in gilded halls.... So, wed with Truth, I dwell above the Veil. Is this the life you grudge us, O knightly America?[38]

In selecting and reading books, Octavian and Du Bois also select another version of America, where they may travel and interact with whomever they choose.

Later, the dream of selecting a better nation is also revealed as a fraud. In the second volume, *The Kingdom on the Waves*, Octavian joins a regiment of the British army, the Royal Ethiopians, composed of escaped slaves. The Royal Ethiopians are fighting for the British Crown, but their name and uniforms also mark them as a community apart, recall a Biblical kingdom of origin, and promise a hopeful future within this reconstituted kingdom. In a move that echoes Malcolm X's rejection of the surname "Little" as a hated reminder of slave history and a symbolic internalization of the conqueror's identity, Octavian enlists in the British imperial army as "Octavian Nothing." In signing his new name to fight against his former enslavers, he says, "for the first time, I knew freedom."[39] While Octavian views his enlistment as a move toward mental decolonization and legal freedom, it is also an act of service to the British Empire and a commitment to the military violence demanded of citizens. This tension increases, as Octavian and his companions are increasingly horrified by the acts they commit in defense of their own freedom and by the despair, internal dissent, and institutional neglect that afflict the Royal Ethiopians. In the genres of school stories and desegregation stories, the violence of nation building tends to remain at a safe remove. It is implied by the analogous violence of bullying, but its full horrors and ethical implications are buffered by the setting and time frame of the enclosed childhood world of school. In Anderson's novels, the violence involved in achieving citizenship is more explicit and disturbing. Moreover, the failure of the Royal Ethiopians' endeavor haunts the entire novel, as the reader is aware from the beginning what the outcome of the Revolutionary War was.

In the Octavian novels, nationalist communities consistently fail to reward their citizens' loyalty or to foster their moral improvement. Instead of searching for the right community, Octavian and his companions begin to imagine constructing one, framing themselves as creative, collaborative citizens rather than as consumers. At the request of his friends Pomp and Slant, Octavian forms a small literacy circle, "to spread among others the gifts lavished upon me for my pains in the College of Lucidity; to loose knowledge from its corral and allow it free pasturage." This purpose stands in implied contrast to preserving private property as the newly forming United States does.[40] Initially, Octavian is clearly in the position of teacher, the others clearly in the position of students, albeit at their request. When Bono introduces him to the Oyo drummer Olakunde, however, Octavian becomes an equal participant in the exchange of knowledge. After each literacy lesson, the class swaps stories from their various cultural traditions, and instead of recording stories *about* the others, he records stories *with* them, giving the cultural inheritance of Oyo and the ghost stories and trickster tales of American-born slaves equal weight with his own retold myths of ancient Greece and Rome. This hybrid cultural heritage, he imagines, will be the foundation of the new utopian nation (though what nation, he does not specify):

> I envision the future day when this campaign is finished, and we grown older and commenced men of means—with wives of our own, and children, and farms, perhaps, laid about with barns. Olakunde shall be the Ovid of far Oyo, writing the tales of Africk metamorphoses; and Pomp recording his ghost stories for a winter night.

> I shall write sonatas *en trio*; and Slant perhaps shall be proprietor of his own plantation. Grant us, Lord, a Thanksgiving feast together in that distant day.[41]

In many ways, this combined literacy class, story exchange, and nation-building project is a Freirian endeavor, a pedagogy "forged *with*, not *for*, the oppressed ... in the incessant struggle to regain their humanity."[42] Furthermore, it is carried out in the context of organizing for freedom, as Freire argues is necessary for utopian pedagogy. Even this vision of nationhood, however, also threatens to replicate some of the problems of other established nations.

Kevin Gaines suggests that the pan-African international civil rights movement suffered as a result of the replication of gender inequality within newly decolonizing nations; and Octavian's utopian vision similarly provides no role for women, either as writers or as citizens, except as wives to be possessed alongside farms and barns.[43] While knowledge may be temporarily "loose[d] from its corral," once again, the closing of the achievement gap does not stand in for justice. The image of farms, and plantations, and non-literate wives suggests that corrals of many kinds may be re-established as part of the apparatus of financial security. This dilemma is similar to the one faced by Buddy in *The Planet of Junior Brown*. Buddy opts to sacrifice the security of his system for inclusiveness. The utopia thus created is ethical, but also temporary and haunted by anxiety. Octavian, living in a similar kind of precarious, contingent situation, longs for a pastoral utopia that promises warmth, safety, and the possibility of belonging to an establishment. The ending of the novel highlights—and does not resolve—the difficulty of choosing between the benefits of secure citizenship and the moral compromises of establishing and institutionalizing any kind of community.

After the destruction of the Royal Ethiopian regiment, Octavian returns to Mr. Gitney's house, writes his two-volume history (presumably, the volumes which the implied reader of Anderson's novels is perusing), and forces Mr. Gitney to read his account while Octavian watches. Octavian replaces Mr. Gitney's unethical, incomplete data with these volumes, which he leaves behind as a corrective before he "light[s] out for the unknown regions."[44] The last line of the novel both recalls and revises the ending of *The Adventures of Huckleberry Finn*, that canonical American novel in which the un-civilizable Huck undergoes an anti-racist transformation—and then famously proceeds to "light out for the Territory,"[45] where he will serve as a representative of the reformed American Empire, colonizing new territory on the frontier. Octavian, significantly, uses almost the exact words to end his novel that Huck does, but avoids the word "Territory" and its connotations of possession and colonization. Through the account he leaves for the nation, therefore, he in some measure seeks to correct the conception of national citizenship the implied American reader might have absorbed through other narratives about the racial and imperial history of the United States. Octavian, however, cannot claim ownership of himself except by leaving his history, his literary product, behind as a record for the nation. Even though he himself has written this record, he seems to feel it erases his identity just as Mr. Gitney's pseudo-scientific volumes did. The last section of his manuscript is entitled "Tabula Rasa," and he writes,

> There are some who believe that the mind is a blank tablet, on which experience is writ until the page be full, and the cryptic world is known; but I see rather that my own life hath been one long forgetting, the erasure of what was drawn, a terrible redaction; til all that remains is blank white and comfortless.[46]

The price of demonstrating his literacy and recording his knowledge seems to be that his identity no longer belongs to him, and he becomes a "blank white" mind emptied of nation, history, and race.

Despite the narrative's apparent skepticism regarding citizenship and literacy, Anderson places a great deal of faith in his implied readers. In fact, the degree of effort spent to re-educate American readers about their own history, and to introduce them to philosophical questions about citizenship that are generally screened from children's literature, belies the cynicism of the ending. The novels seem designed as a corrective to citizenship education because of, not despite, their lack of appeal for school curricula; if the accountability movement has corrupted schools' commitment to justice and complex literacies, then these goods must be offered elsewhere. The novels follow in a tradition of extra-curricular literature disseminated as a counterweight to state-sponsored school reading. Gargi Gangopadhyay, in discussing the development of Bengali children's literature under British rule, emphasizes that resistant Bengali nationalist texts were meant to be leisure reading, set "in opposition to the public and formal reading areas related to schools, education, and examinations … essentially situated beyond the precincts of institutional control."[47] Like Du Bois, Gangopadhyay imagines this private space of reading to be a space that can exist above or beyond national boundaries and institutionally sanctioned inequities, in an "uncontaminated space, which naturally has the sanctity of belonging to the self."[48] This framework of leisure reading implies that the student is not beholden to the school for literacy. Indeed, the data collection of the school might impede students' understanding of Anderson's dense prose, rather than allow them access. In contrast, Sharon Flake's *Pinned* represents and reaches out to those readers who threaten to damage the school's and the nation's image through their resistance to closing the achievement gap.

Pinned: Reading Beyond the Achievement Gap

Holes and *Octavian Nothing* allude to shifts in the rhetoric and implementation of school desegregation, but avoid showing re-segregation and achievement gaps within the site of the contemporary school. Flake's 2012 novel *Pinned*, the only one of the three written by a black author, takes place in a contemporary charter school in which a decade of accountability seems to have had some effect. Middle-class families seek to send their children there, the state has offered generous funding, and students of varied racial backgrounds participate in chess, honors classes, and sports. In some ways, *Pinned* incorporates contemporary rhetoric about the power of choice and consumption. The achievement gap, in this novel as in life, is not defined solely by race; many of the black characters read proficiently and thrive under the school's pedagogy. Instead, the illiterate protagonist must choose to desire to read. This reflects a trend in many other texts about struggling readers published after decades of stalled desegregation efforts, such as Langan's *Schooled* and Rahaman's *Read for Me, Mama.* With the initial choice of motivation comes the agency to choose which texts and stories will shape the characters' new literate identities. In this respect, Flake's novel represents a growing body of books for and about reluctant readers, who represent an opportunity for potential intervention into inequality. In other respects, *Pinned* exposes cracks in neoliberal rhetoric, highlighting how the original broad goals of the Civil Rights movement have been narrowed to reducing the achievement gap, a goal that has failed to produce broad-based justice or equality. Indeed, Flake's novel is unusual for texts about the achievement gap, in that it explicitly references the Civil Rights movement as an ongoing but unfinished project rather than erasing mention of the era altogether.

Concern over reluctant readers is not new. Increasingly, however, headlines about the results of international comparative tests such as the PISA have created anxiety about the literacy even of supposedly advantaged American children. Education reporter Amanda Ripley, for example, notes that if the PISA scores only of American white middle-class students were counted in the rankings, American students would still make a poor showing internationally.[49] Similarly, the authors of the Common Core standards assert that "even in high-performing states, students are graduating and passing all the required tests but still need remediation in their postsecondary work."[50] *Pinned* addresses this sense of literacy crisis in an unexpected way, suggesting that multiple literacies—reading across achievement gaps rather than erasing them—are necessary both for successful learning and for a more cohesive national citizenship.

Pinned creates an experience of tension and textual unfamiliarity, even for those readers who define themselves as highly literate. It does so by shifting between two first-person narrators who have radically different literacy skills and ways with words. One narrator is ninth grader Autumn Knight, who is a skilled wrestler and the only girl on the team. After moving from school to school as her parents pursued low-income work, she is at least three grades behind in reading and math. She loves Adonis Miller, the team's manager, who was born with no legs below the thigh, and who is one of the top students at the charter school they both attend. Adonis, the other narrator, comes from a more privileged background and cultivates a separatist disability identity. He willingly tutors and runs enrichment activities for the other students who ride the disability van, but he views non-disabled students as "lazy,"[51] and he avoids Autumn's advances, fearing to be associated with a girl who cannot read. The splits between the two narrative voices reveal fissures within the community based on class, gender, and disability status.

In order to finish the novel with any sense of satisfaction, readers must learn to appreciate the voice of whichever protagonist they have a harder time reading as well as the one they find more appealing. A glance at reader reviews of the book demonstrates that many adult readers find this task difficult. Some find Adonis's voice unsympathetic, even "agonizing [to] move through," while others objected to "the voice of the book being poor grammar" and "found the fact that Autumn's point of view was written in colloquial distracting."[52] This division points, not merely to a gap in the literacy of the two narrators, but also to an empathy gap in readers. Those readers who expected a book to avoid "poor grammar," or who were unfamiliar with "colloquial" language, found Autumn's narration a reading obstacle they had to get past or overcome. Researcher Wendy Glenn finds, in her work with pre-service teachers, that this is not an uncommon reaction. So-called "ethnic" literature is touted for introducing a majority white teaching force to the cultures of the racialized children they will teach; yet pre-service teachers need education and familiarization with a "reader's voice speaking in a tone with language that [the teacher] was not used to using."[53] Of course, this is a parallel familiarization process that students like Autumn face in confronting the language valued within the classroom. In order to not only become invested in Autumn's story, but also appreciate her evocative uses of language, readers must fight the same battle that Autumn does, and persevere through their disorientation and distraction. Conversely, other readers objected to Adonis's arrogance and rudeness to Autumn, and wished they could feel more sense of redemption at the end so that the struggles of the characters (and the readers) might be properly rewarded.[54]

By placing these contradictory narrators in parallel, Flake's novel asks readers to stretch their competence with unfamiliar narrative styles. Just as importantly, it asks readers to question the premise that closing the achievement gap will produce better-prepared citizens and a more racially just society. Instead, the novel exposes contradictions in discourses about what literacy is supposed to do for readers. Literacy theorist Sylvia Scribner suggests that national and cultural goals for literacy often center around three metaphors: "literacy as adaptation, literacy as power, and literacy as a state of grace."[55] When literacy is framed as adaptation, it is depicted as a tool for personal upward mobility. In recent discourse about inequality, access to literacy is framed as necessary for achieving racial and economic justice. This metaphor for literacy thus forms one of the rationales behind the No Child Left Behind Act. In the decades after the abandonment of busing programs, it also provides a rationale for desegregating knowledge instead of classrooms, based on the assumption that narrowing racial gaps in achievement tests will also narrow gaps in material capital. When teachers view literacy as a form of power, they credit it with conferring not only the tools but also the activist desire to challenge existing systems of cultural and material capital. When it is theorized as a state of grace, it is thought to develop students' minds and civic capacities, making them fully actualized human beings in a way that is framed as out of reach for the nonliterate. Numerous scholars question whether literacy education can actually fulfill any of these expectations. Alfred Tatum, for example, notes that college degrees have not always produced returns for black students in the form of jobs. Heather Andrea Williams and Susan Kates both note that successful literacy campaigns in black communities, both after the Civil War and during the Civil Rights movement, were pursued in the hopes of gaining civic empowerment, but that the successes of these campaigns did not result in increased respect from whites, increased community control over education, or freedom from violence and repression.[56] *Pinned* depicts a cast of characters with a variety of conflicting beliefs and goals for literacy. The novel dramatizes, not only how these goals are irreconcilable, but also how many characters fail if measured by a different metaphor. Ultimately, these conflicts also suggest that literacy cannot do the work it is being asked to do for the black community in the era of accountability and testing, without a renewed commitment to broader equality.

Both Autumn's best friend Patricia (Peaches) and Adonis are successful readers and citizens, if literacy is defined as adaptation. Both are strivers who demonstrate the benefits of access to opportunity. Peaches dreams of opening a restaurant with Autumn, becoming an illustrator, and living in France; her parents, in addition, push her to earn a scholarship for college and then attend graduate school for an MBA afterward. Adonis thinks of being a teacher and, even as a ninth grader, he plans to impress the school principal enough to ask for a college recommendation letter. At the same time, both are bitterly competitive, often treating literacy as capital to be traded for prestige, rather than as a means of imaginative escape in its own right. Adonis wishes to win respect from teachers, especially after he fears that a bullying incident has made him an object of pity. Peaches works to prove herself to her parents; her family are the poor, estranged, wrong-side-of-the-bridge branch of Adonis's wealthier family, and her parents continually exhort her to keep up with Adonis so as to prove their worthiness to be recognized by middle-class black society.

In fact, their school, Beacon Academy, highlights and encourages this kind of competition, even as it uses the two outstanding students to advertise how it is using funds to ostensibly share knowledge equitably. Both Adonis and Peaches are selected for the honor of escorting state officials on a school tour. Adonis explains,

> The state invested a lot of money into our school: built a new cafeteria, put in a pool, created culinary and horticultural programs, plus more. Beyond that, we now offer the most AP courses of any school in the district.[57]

Thus, the school is under pressure to demonstrate that the state's investment is paying off. The tour includes interdisciplinary art projects created by the Gifted and Talented program, but does not include a glance into Autumn's remedial reading class. Both Peaches and Adonis understand that they are in fact the products on show, the assets the school wishes to display as gratitude for the state funding, and they jostle for the attention of the visitors and administrators. On the face of it, the school wants many good students to shine for the state, so that the state's funding will enrich all. At the same time, the structure of the tour and selection of guides serves to convince Adonis and Peaches that such opportunities are limited, and that they must fight each other for the status of being a special asset. Horace Mann's conception of knowledge as an infinitely shareable resource seems lost on these students; instead, literacy status gained by one person devalues what is gained by another.

In their achievement of scholarly goals, their farsighted planning for their futures, and their investment in personal advancement, Adonis and Peaches might exemplify how the American Dream has successfully extended to and integrated African American students. Adonis and Peaches are both valued and involved members of the school community, without simply being tokens. The school is implied to have a majority black student body and to employ several black teachers, but is also subtly described as being multiracial, with white, Asian, and Latino students moving through the background of scenes. Nevertheless, neither the plot nor the tone of the novel endorses the success of integration or the equitable extension of the American Dream. Instead, an ethic of competition has divided the community, so that the success of some students feels meaningless to the rest, rather than a source of pride. Indeed, historian R. Scott Baker suggests that this process has been an enduring effect of the standardized tests implemented in the wake of desegregation efforts.[58] Moreover, the emphasis placed on scores as visible proof of worth encourages cheating. Numerous cheating scandals have been documented in schools trying to avoid sanctions under NCLB, and this effect is depicted in the novel through the character of Peaches.[59] Peaches is constantly under pressure from her parents to outdo Adonis, even as she shares an apartment with six cousins while he has his own room and laptop; she struggles in math, and takes to cheating, both in order to advance her own goals and in order to relieve the pressure from her parents. She even internalizes the idea that possessing grades means something even when she does not possess the attendant knowledge, telling Autumn, "If I just catch up on a few tests, she saying, I'll feel better about myself.… She telling me that without laughing at herself."[60] Peaches sits by and watches Adonis nearly drown after he is dumped into a pond by students whom he caught cheating and turned in. Adonis threatens the students' acquisition of grades and advancement, and they, in turn, attack him based on his disability, smashing his wheelchair after nearly killing him. Peaches was, in fact, one of these cheating students, and although she was not caught in the scandal, she resents Adonis for refusing to tutor her when she asked him for help. Clearly, her acquisition of literacy has not led her toward a state of self-actualized grace, nor has it prompted her to question the systems of power in which she is wholly invested.

Adonis does not cheat, but his devotion to literacy as a tool for adaptation demonstrates other flaws in the American Dream he pursues. Instead of being a cheater, Adonis is a hoarder. His main objection to cheaters is that they spoil the grading curve. While his behavior in response to cheating indicates a sense of citizenship, the reasons behind his behavior indicate a rather narrow and competitive conception of citizenship, as he is primarily worried about how cheaters interfere with classmates' chances to gain the distinction of high grades. More noticeably, Adonis is highly aware of how his own literacy possessions stack up against other students'. When Autumn first tells him of her struggles with reading, Adonis responds by counting for Autumn all the books he has already read that year, emphasizing how long each one was. Furthermore, he consistently hesitates to share his bounteous knowledge, or does so only when it will gain him prestige. While Adonis gladly gives speeches for assemblies, guest teaches for his math teacher, and even tutors struggling students before the state tests, he will not help when other students ask, as Autumn and Peaches do. He does not refuse directly, as he worries, "How can I say no, without my … teacher thinking less of me?"[61] He simply says nothing, which both Autumn and Peaches feel is even worse than saying no, because it communicates his complete indifference to their welfare.

Adonis does demonstrate a commitment to one community; he is dedicated to tutoring the other students with disabilities who ride his van. He narrates a conscious and proud disability identity, explaining that before his dunking in the pond, he never missed having legs, and that he is reluctant to work or socialize with "regulars" because "[they] are the disabled ones. They don't think logically."[62] Adonis's disdain for "regulars" who are "the disabled ones" reflects a split within the disability community. As David Mitchell and Sharon Snyder observe, physical disabilities are sometimes seen as being more easily prostheticized or integrated into able-bodied society than cognitive disabilities, creating a hierarchy within the community in which those with physical impairments have higher status than those with cognitive impairments.[63] Thus, whenever Autumn and her reading difficulties are mentioned at school, Adonis quickly dissociates himself from her. At the same time, Adonis also legitimately resents Autumn's attempts to frame herself as disabled in an attempt to gain his attention. One of Autumn's notes reads, "Disabled is me not being able to read. And you with out legs. So (u + me) = perfect. Right?"[64] In one sense, Autumn is correct; her illiteracy functions as a socially constructed disability, since it affects her life prospects more than Adonis's wheelchair does his. Nevertheless, as Josh Lukin points out, disability is often used by other oppressed groups simply as a metaphor, without recognition that disabled people carry their own historically specific identities and issues.[65] Autumn does not have a diagnosis; she simply really struggles to read. When Autumn first discusses her reading difficulties with Adonis, he asks her, "'Are you in special ed?'" Autumn assumes he is telling her that she is stupid. She does not stop to think that if she actually did ride the special ed van, Adonis would tutor her. Instead, as he disappears into the elevator, he tells her, "'I get straight As in this chair. What do you get?'"[66]; while Adonis cannot leave his chair, Autumn could mitigate her acquired, self-diagnosed disability. Even as a disability activist, however, Adonis does not use literacy as a path to empowerment, solidarity, or social critique. Both Adonis's and Peaches' success demonstrates that their integration has come at an ethical cost to both the black and the disability communities. At the same time, Autumn's experience demonstrates that a view of literacy as empowerment or state of grace may also be insufficient.

Like Adonis and Peaches, Autumn is integrated into the fabric of Beacon Academy; however, her citizenship status and identity is tied to wrestling rather than to academic performance.[67] Autumn is established from the beginning as a gifted, dedicated athlete, who fully embraces wrestling as a path to personal excellence and who demonstrates persistence and strategy on the mat. Nevertheless, her devotion to sport leads her to embody a stereotype of a dumb jock. She avoids reading so that she can feel better about herself, and pursues Adonis so aggressively that he considers quitting his volunteer work for the library to avoid her attempts to sit on his lap. Clearly, Autumn does not make the same kinds of choices about academics as she does about wrestling. The school's handling of Autumn, however, suggests a key critique of how the framework of choice actually structures her education.

At her charter school, Autumn has opportunities for extracurricular community and enrichment that protagonists in desegregation school stories did not. She gains prestige for being a female champion wrestler—she is approached for autographs and recognized in public places by her girl fans—but even as she serves as a visible representative of the school's gender equality, she also faces humiliating sexist comments on the mat. Furthermore, as her grades drop, the school keeps her trophies in the front hallway, but does not issue any consequences for her low grades. It is her parents, not the school, who step in and take her off the team when her grades do not improve. Even then, her coach tries to persuade her parents to keep her on, because she is so valuable to the team (and by extension, the school) as an athlete, if not as a scholar. It is Autumn's parents who must explain, "My mother and father sorry, they saying, to let down our team. 'But we can't keep letting her down.... Who gonna look out for her, if we don't?'"[68] Autumn's parents are placed in the position of explaining to the coach the future consequences of Autumn's illiteracy: "Dad brings up the jobs he ain't get 'cause he couldn't read the applications.... Mom's crying. 'Me. A grown woman. Asking people at work ... to read ... my paycheck.'"[69] This is the future that the state-funded school is meant to prevent its young citizens from realizing; it is, in fact, a fairly compelling argument for why so many education critics focus on literacy as a path to adaptation and economic opportunity. Yet Autumn's parents recognize that the school personnel are as worried about Autumn letting them down as they are about letting Autumn down. School-sponsored sports appear to offer an atmosphere of equality that represents progress both for racial and gender-based justice. This is why Autumn latches onto wrestling; as she explains in the beginning, sports offers her the illusion that anyone can succeed. The lure of a temporarily level playing field, the wrestling mat, however, becomes a dangerous extra-curricular distraction for her, channeling her energy away from the curricular skills the state is so lavishly funding.[70] In this respect, the illusory equality of sports parallels the equality offered by desegregation. Autumn's own parents benefitted little through the era of desegregation; they left school in tenth grade, sold blood to make money, then began a life of transience as they tried to find jobs with benefits and skipped out on rent. Despite this knowledge, Autumn feels liberated by her ability to make choices about extra-curricular sports.

In fairness, the school is not simply using Autumn for her bodily skill and then abdicating responsibility. The school is not a unified entity, and her teachers are invested in her success. Her math teacher tries to motivate his struggling students by pointing out what they do well in the world outside the classroom and asking them to pursue the same level of excellence inside it. Similarly, Miss Baker, the developmental reading teacher, tries to creatively work with her students' boredom and resistance and channel it. When a student cheekily writes "Why?" next to Miss Baker's whiteboard directive to "Read,"[71] Miss Baker opens up a metacognitive discussion about literacy, trying to acknowledge students' existing reading habits and build upon them. In this novel, the failures of desegregation goals do not seem attributable to racist pedagogy.

Instead, the structures of neoliberal education, and its substitution of a student- consumer ethic for a unified sense of Civil Rights mission, seem to inform Autumn's attitude toward her education, so that she feels empowered to choose not to learn. When Miss Baker asks the class why it is important to read, they come up with the following responses, which are funny for the reader but rather discouraging, Autumn notes, for Miss Baker:

> There's, like, only five reasons why a kid would want to read.
>
> 1 They got a text;
> 2 They on a movie star's blog;
> 3 Eating cereal. Reading the back of the box makes the cereal last longer;
> 4 Taking a dump or taking a bath is long and boring without a magazine to look at;
> 5 They got homework. Which is the worse reason of all to read.[72]

Mostly, students read in order to consume various forms of popular culture. Autumn herself asserts her right to set her own criteria for reading: "I read just fine inside my head. Maybe it ain't fast, like the teachers want.... But it's good enough for me."[73] In this way, her sense of herself as an educational consumer, attending school to meet her own needs, clashes with the school's accountability for her. Autumn's reading class opens up a key component in the sense of crisis surrounding the "reluctant reader." This is the problem of sponsorship. Deborah Brandt, in a highly influential 1997 essay, establishes the history of literacy education in the United States as a process that has always required sponsorship—financial, practical, and social backing from a person who wishes to see a subordinate gain access to literacy of some kind. Brandt does not deny that literacy sponsors may have genuine goodwill and desire to see their protégés succeed, but the concept of sponsorship implies that they expect some sort of return on their investment, "whether by direct repayment or, indirectly, by credit of association."[74] Brandt explicitly draws a comparison between literacy sponsors and commercial sponsors of athletes, who advertise for the companies that underwrite their athletic success.

The idea behind accountability is, similarly, to bestow young citizens with literacy so that they may not only give back productivity to the commonwealth, but also represent and testify to its equality of opportunity. Autumn and the reluctant readers she represents pose a threat, because they appear to reject the nation's sponsorship. Although the teachers at Autumn's school drop anxious remarks about the upcoming state testing, Autumn and her classmates in the remedial reading class evince no sense that they owe their teachers, or their state, or their nation, reading results. This rejection of sponsorship potentially reflects poorly on the nation, as its bounty and gifts are left untouched and it appears to be sponsoring poor international test scores and a low-wage service economy. As a result, Adonis reflects bitterly, everyone courts Autumn: "[I]t's unfair. A girl with her grades and habits has everyone chasing after her, begging her to be better and do better."[75] In the era of state testing, teachers vie to be accepted as Autumn's sponsor. If she does not represent the progress of integration by accepting sponsorship and demonstrating test results, the school and its teachers may pay a price for her rejection.

Teachers are not Autumn's only potential sponsors for literacy, however. The librarians in the novel provide Autumn with connections to a sense of Civil Rights-era solidarity, history, and mission that seems missing in the rest of the school. Much of the action of *Pinned* takes place in libraries; despite Autumn's belief that she is allergic to them, she volunteers to help out so that she can be near Adonis. Mrs. Carolyn, the school librarian, establishes a relaxed and welcoming environment where Autumn brings homemade cupcakes to share and where students gather, talk, and flirt. When Autumn becomes depressed after her parents take her out of wrestling, and begins cutting class to hide in the library and think, Mrs. Carolyn defends the need of all students—even failing ones—for a safe, quiet place. Despite her belief in sanctuary, however, Mrs. Carolyn is not a laissez-faire or uninvolved sponsor. When Autumn asks offhandedly about a book she picks up from the floor, Mrs. Carolyn tells her to read it and then come back to talk about it: "She hands it to me. 'I'm a librarian, Autumn. A Spelman girl, by the way. A student says she wants to read a book. I wanna know what she thinks about it.'"[76] By identifying herself as a "Spelman girl," Mrs. Carolyn gives an indication of her sense of identity as a sponsor. She has graduated from a prestigious HBCU (Historically Black College and University). These institutions were founded under conditions of segregation, to educate students barred from white institutions. According to scholars such as Marybeth Gasman and Felecia Commodore, their missions historically extended beyond this; both before and after the *Brown* decision, HBCUs also explicitly nurtured a commitment in their graduates to be politically active leaders engaged in community outreach. HBCU students and alumni were active in the Civil Rights movement. The institutions continue to reach out to students considered "at risk" and to emphasize an Afrocentric curriculum. Mrs. Carolyn seems to be following a mission as an HBCU graduate, pushing Autumn and other struggling students to improve their prospects and, in the meantime, to become involved in community life regardless of their class status or academic prestige.

Mrs. Carolyn's friend at the public library, where Autumn wanders one day to escape her house, also identifies herself as a Spelman graduate, and follows tactics similar to Mrs. Carolyn's. Upon seeing Autumn outside, she immediately pulls her in, offers to help her find *The Narrative of the Life of Frederick Douglass*, asks her to help form a teen book group, and pulls out some articles from the local newspaper she's found about Autumn's wrestling achievements. She wears African-inspired clothing, and guides patrons to books about literacy and pride like *The Color Purple*. Through their personal histories, their community-minded approach to literacy education, and their book selections, Mrs. Carolyn and the public librarian attempt to sponsor Autumn into a literacy path that will lead her to political empowerment.

It is also in libraries that Autumn, and by extension the reader, is asked to explicitly struggle with the unfinished legacy of the struggle for African-American equality and justice. The public librarian finds her in front of a statue of Frederick Douglass that stands in front of the library, which Autumn describes as being bigger and more imposing than the library itself. She offers to find his narrative for Autumn because she assumes Autumn is interested in the man behind the statue; but in fact, Autumn is uncomfortable just looking at the statue:

> Never did I like that big, gray metal statue. Those eyes. They look at you accusingly-like. In seventh grade, the librarian told us Mr. Douglass's eyes be asking people questions: "Can you do what I've done? Travel the road I walked?"[77]

Douglass fought and schemed to eke out a literacy education, and Autumn feels accused by his eyes because, with well-meaning teachers chasing her, she is not taking the one offered. With this reminder of literacy as empowerment comes a feeling that she is not merely turning down personal knowledge, but letting down her community and her history.

The Autobiography of Malcolm X shadows her narrative even more. She picks it up one day idly at the school library and asks Adonis about it. Months later, when she has decided to commit herself to improving her reading, she looks up Malcolm X online and discovers that he read all the words in the dictionary. She feels some kinship with him, since she collects words in a jar; she even contemplates reading the book, but is discouraged by its length. Later, when Adonis finally falls in love with her, he gives her a copy, signaling his newfound belief in her growth. Autumn clearly feels more comfortable with Malcolm X as a surrogate literacy sponsor than she felt with Frederick Douglass. Nevertheless, the protagonists' use of his narrative speaks to alterations, over decades, of broad Civil Rights goals. Both Frederick Douglass and Malcolm X are present for Autumn only as examples of literacy learners, not as radical activists for social justice in arenas beyond literacy. Malcolm X devoted himself to galvanizing members of the community like Autumn and her parents, who struggle against both structural economic inequality and also disdain from middle-class community members like Adonis. Yet his legacy comes to her only through his famous project to educate himself while in prison. It is especially ironic that Adonis gives her the book. Adonis has undoubtedly read it, but seems to have sloughed off Malcolm's criticisms of "misguided so-called 'middle class' Negroes—the typical status-symbol-oriented, integration-seeking type of Negroes"[78]; Adonis's narration frequently reveals his attachment to the values Malcolm criticizes, and yet he bestows the book on Autumn as a sign of approval and an aid to her further social uplift.

The ending thus offers ambivalent hope about the prospect that the goals of the Civil Rights movement may be carried on by students educated as competitive, data-conscious consumers. On the one hand, Malcolm's broad view of literacy as a path to power and resistance remains buried in the subtext, and the burden of the Civil Rights fight for justice appears to rest upon Autumn's willingness to commit to the literacy skills measured by state tests. On the other hand, her growing literacy offers hope that she may eventually read Malcolm's narrative for herself, and may formulate her own stance on the connections between personal empowerment, social justice, and literacy learning.

Similarly, Autumn's identity as a consumer seems both problematic and potentially useful for thinking about how students might pursue the goals of desegregation outside the limitations of the school. The word that inspires her to choose literacy is "intentional," and she finds it on a bus advertisement that reads, "BE INTENTIONAL ... WHEN YOU WANT TO SEND A MESSAGE, GIVE HER DIAMONDS."[79] She is more motivated by capitalist advertisements selling romance than she is by her well-meaning teachers. Nevertheless, the plot structure also implies that Autumn can repurpose the literacy messages she draws from capitalist sponsors; a word in an advertisement leads her not to diamonds and happy-ever-after romance, but to (potentially) Malcolm X and his fiery messages of social justice. As a "reluctant reader," Autumn represents a threat to the successful desegregation of knowledge, resisting the opportunity offered by the neoliberal charter school. At the same time, the reluctant reader also, increasingly, offers opportunities as a market for remedial products. For example, the American Library Association, whose Newbery award lists guarantee longevity and sales for winners, now publishes a yearly list of "Quick Picks for Reluctant Readers" as a purchasing resource for librarians, teachers, and parents. Activist organizations such as We Need Diverse Books and First Book's Stories for All seek to pressure publishers to offer more works that will represent a wide variety of children and stories, in part by framing reluctant readers as an untapped market who might read more if given the kinds of options that publishers once found too daring for the school market.[80] Autumn is, in fact, a rare semiliterate narrator who is allowed to speak for herself, in prose that makes some readers uncomfortable. She may not think of literacy education as leading her to a future of public service and community building, but her training as a consumer does not eliminate this option, either.[81]

By depending upon the narrative voice of a reluctant, left-behind reader, *Pinned* highlights how integration through the proxy of literacy cannot be accomplished without erasing the voices of the reluctant readers who are framed as the source of the gap to be eliminated. *Holes* imagines integration as convergence, as Zero and Stanley exchange and mingle their strengths and eliminate their complementary weaknesses. In contrast, by asking readers to balance between two black narrators who each have different literacies, different barriers to full inclusion in both black and white societies, and different contributions to offer their communities, *Pinned* asks the reader to imagine integration as a process of divergence and discomfort.

Learning Racial Justice Outside of School

None of these three novels constructs school desegregation as a solution for issues of racial justice. In keeping with public retreat from discussing school desegregation as a worthwhile commitment, Sachar's and Anderson's novels do not even highlight the setting of the school, and issues of large-scale residential and structural segregation seem irrelevant to Flake's school setting. Instead, the novels engage with contemporary discourses about accountability and achievement gaps that their intended young readers may recognize, but that tend to sidestep direct questions about the outcomes of *Brown* in contemporary schools. These novels go beyond highlighting the problems and inequities of *Brown*'s implementation; they cease to envision school desegregation as a viable remedy for racial injustice or a reliable source for the high-quality education desired by the architects of *Brown*.

They do not, however, cease to envision models of social justice based in education. While they suggest some of the ways that schools fail to be accountable to their students—and that students fail to account for their learning—they also imagine roles for failing students as leaders, citizens, and continuing learners outside the school setting. All three novels address, in different ways, the contemporary premise that closing the achievement gap is the route to justice; and all three suggest problems with this substitution. Nevertheless, through the ways they develop the literacy skills of their implied readers, these novels also imply that awareness of social justice is a trainable skill, like literacy, and that readers have a responsibility to learn these skills, outside of the school if not within. They work within a framework of neoliberal school choice and accountability that has its roots in the delay and dilution of racial desegregation;

but within this framework, they allow for students to shift their own commitments and loyalties, imagining alternate kinds of citizenships and community identities than the ones offered them in formal education.

Notes

1 Examples include Kekla Magoon's *CamoGirl* (2012), Sharon Flake's *The Skin I'm In* (2007), Meg Medina's *Yaqui Delgado Wants to Kick Your Ass* (2013), and Matt de la Pena's *We Were Here* (2009).
2 Saatcioglu and Carl mention the Magnet Schools Assistance Program of 1984 as a key turn toward neoliberalism in funding structures. The 1991 Supreme Court case *Board of Education of Oklahoma City vs. Dowell* allowed desegregation to be a temporary, rather than a long-term goal; the 1992 case *Freeman v. Pitts* released districts from federal desegregation requirements even if they had not yet achieved desegregation; and the 1995 case *Missouri v. Jenkins* restored the importance of local school control, even if that meant inequities in funding. Saaciolgu and Carl, "The Discursive Turn in Education," 70.
3 Baker, "Paradoxes of Desegregation," 333.
4 Kamenetz, *The Test*, 104–105; Prendergast, *Literacy and Racial Justice*, 33.
5 Daniel, "Accountability and Desegregation," 260–262.
6 Joan Bauer's *Close to Famous* also follows this pattern. Sharon Creech's *A Fine, Fine School* and M.T. Anderson's *Feed* deal less explicitly with literacy, but do criticize accountability and neoliberal education.
7 Labaree, "Public Goods, Private Goods."
8 Mann, "Means and Objects," 85.
9 Mann, "What God Does," 198.
10 Ferguson, *The Reorder of Things*, "Introduction."
11 Sachar, *Holes*, 99.
12 Kirsten Mollegard argues more specifically that the ghosts of silenced women and black men surface in the text to re-inscribe themselves into a history and regional mythology from which they are often erased. Mollegard, "Haunting and History," 139.
13 Annette Wannamaker points out that even though the task of digging holes is revealed to be the corrupt, unjust ruse of a state official, it still works as a successful character-building, masculinizing task within the construct of a male coming-of-age story. Wannamaker, "Reading in the Gaps and Lacks," 19.
14 A discussion of *Holes*'s companion novel, *Small Steps*, is outside the scope of this chapter, but that novel also emphasizes that the children released from Camp Green Lake have developed productive work habits from their time in a corrupt and unjustly managed facility.
15 In fact, Wannamaker suggests that *Holes* responds to widespread cultural anxiety about boys' disinterest in literacy and about a perceived lack of books for young male readers.
16 Trierweiler, "Louis Sachar."
17 Sachar, *Holes*, 231.
18 Cummins, "The Lessons of *The Wizard of Oz* and *Holes*."
19 In an essay published a few years earlier than *Holes*, Hazel Carby wrote critically of the trend toward replacing a public commitment to physical desegregation with symbolic desegregation through novels. Carby, "The Multicultural Wars," 192.
20 In fact, the so-called "Texas miracle" of the 1990s was found to rest upon school administrators targeting students likely to fail and holding those

students back a grade or encouraging their truancy on the day of the test. These practices, however, were not widely published until 2000, after the publication of *Holes*. Kamenetz, *The Test*, 86–88.
21 Melamed, *Represent and Destroy*, "Counterinsurgent Canon Wars."
22 Kamenetz, *The Test*, 89.
23 Schwebel, *Child-Sized History*, 88.
24 "Author M.T. Anderson on 'Octavian Nothing.'"
25 U.S. Dept. of Education, *NCLB: Title 1—Improving the Education of the Disadvantaged*, "Sec. 1001."
26 Cottle, *Busing*, 116.
27 Anderson, "On the Intelligence of Teens."
28 Anderson, *The Pox Party*, 13.
29 Ibid., 16.
30 Ibid., 52.
31 Ibid., 162.
32 Ibid., 130, 133.
33 Ibid., 337.
34 Kamenetz, *The Test*, "Ten Arguments Against Testing;" Delpit, "Lessons From Teachers;" Rose, *Lives on the Boundary*, 108–111.
35 Anderson develops this idea much further in his futuristic dystopia *Feed*, in which students go to school to learn to buy products more easily using their Internet feeds.
36 Anderson, *The Pox Party*, 124, emphasis in original.
37 Ibid., 143.
38 Du Bois, *The Souls of Black Folk*, 90.
39 Anderson, *The Kingdom on the Waves*, 132.
40 Ibid., 323.
41 Ibid., 395.
42 Freire, *Pedagogy of the Oppressed*, 48.
43 Gaines, *American Africans*, 16.
44 Anderson, *The Kingdom on the Waves*, 561.
45 Twain, *The Adventures of Huckleberry Finn*, 352.
46 Anderson, *The Kingdom on the Waves*, 561.
47 Gangopadhyay, "Our Motherland," 140.
48 Ibid., 156.
49 Ripley, *The Smartest Kids in the World*, 17.
50 National Governors Association Center for Best Practices, "Myths vs. Facts."
51 Flake, *Pinned*, 88.
52 Ms. Bernard, "Untitled Review of *Pinned*"; Briggs, "Untitled Review"; Elizabeth, "Untitled Review of *Pinned*."
53 Glenn, "To Witness and to Testify."
54 Bayla, "Untitled Review of *Pinned*."
55 Scribner, "Literacy in Three Metaphors," 73.
56 Tatum, "All Degreed Up and Nowhere to Go"; Kates, "Literacy, Voting Rights, Citizenship Schools"; Williams, *Self-Taught*, 182 and following.
57 Flake, *Pinned*, 60.
58 Baker, "Paradoxes of Desegregation," 337.
59 Kamenetz, *The Test*, 28–30.
60 Flake, *Pinned*, 155.
61 Ibid., 152.
62 Ibid., 114–115.
63 Mitchell and Snyder, *Narrative Prosthesis*, 3.

64 Flake, *Pinned*, 117.
65 Lukin, "Disability and Blackness," 311.
66 Flake, *Pinned*, 36.
67 An analysis of *Pinned* as a sports story is outside the scope of this chapter. Sports story critiques, however, are relevant to the novel's depiction of how desegregation appears to have offered opportunities, while actually limiting them. Relevant sports criticism includes Abby Ferber, "The Construction of Black Masculinity," 12, and Greg Ahrenhoerster, "Would Karl Marx Call for an Overthrow of ESPN?," 144.
68 Flake, *Pinned*, 129.
69 Ibid., 129.
70 Amanda Ripley describes in fuller detail how sports funding affects scholarship in subtle ways, including teacher hiring and parent support. Ripley, *The Smartest Kids in the World*, 84–97, 118–119.
71 Flake, *Pinned*, 66.
72 Ibid., 67.
73 Ibid., 15.
74 Brandt, *The Sponsors of Literacy*, 4.
75 Flake, *Pinned*, 154.
76 Ibid., 87.
77 Ibid., 176.
78 X and Haley, *The Autobiography of Malcolm X*, 8.
79 Flake, *Pinned*, 195.
80 First Book and We Need Diverse Books focus on providing representations of diversity for all readers; they do not target the issue of reluctant readers in particular. The We Need Diverse Books campaign did, however, solicit participation from child readers. And when First Book launched their Stories for All campaign, intended to solicit work by authors of color and to provide financial backing for children's books with significant "diverse" content, a spokesperson said,

> In a survey of more than 2,000 educators from First Book schools and programs, 90 percent of respondents agreed that the children in their programs would be more enthusiastic readers if they had access to books with characters, stories and images that reflect their lives and their neighborhoods.
>
> "The Stories for All Project"

Flake herself argues that young readers respond to marketing campaigns when they are invited to read and to share their thoughts. Omer, "Interview With Sharon Flake," 153.
81 In fact, Lizbeth Cohen argues that African Americans' identities as consumers catalyzed many key Civil Rights battles over access. Cohen, *A Consumers' Republic*, "Chapter 4: Rebellion."

Conclusion

Schooling and Resistance

On (Not) Talking About Race in the Classroom, Take Two

I began with a story of my own cowardice, when I feared to openly discuss contemporary school-related racism in the very setting where such a discussion would seem to be most relevant and necessary. Some years later, when I was offered work at a community college in the rural Southern town where I was living, I was eager for what felt like a second chance to be more courageous. Accordingly, in one assignment for a composition class, I incorporated a research topic choice on definitions of cultural identity, and I chose a few texts that addressed issues of racism in contemporary society. From my perspective, readings like Kenji Yoshino's "The Pressure to Cover" were quite gentle in speaking to a potentially hostile audience about how race- and sexuality-based employment discrimination has persisted despite the passage of laws meant to prevent such discrimination. In fact, when I had taught Yoshino's article previously, students had been eager to discuss his evidence and its ramifications. Thus, I was unprepared for the student who, even before I assigned any readings on race, sported a Confederate flag tattoo and wrote a reflection about his pride in the flag and his belief that anyone who is offended by its display is simply ignorant of United States history and Southern heritage. I was not prepared for students' responses to the Yoshino reading. Some asserted that he was racist—first, because he talked about race, which meant he was not being color-blind, and second, because he spoke of receiving angry reactions from some white audience members, which meant he was racist against white people. Others simply resisted discussing the reading, staring at me in silence.

I encountered less resistance in my course on American Literature from 1400–1865, where students certainly expected to have to confront the topic of slavery, and where issues of racial violence were safely contained before the Civil War. Even there, however, I was taken aback by one (white) student's creative project on *Uncle Tom's Cabin*, in which she managed to write an inspirational children's picture book based on the story of Little Eva without ever mentioning the word, or depicting the institution, of slavery. In her written artistic defense of the project, she explained that Little Eva was color-blind and did not recognize difference (similar, the student emphasized, to how she herself had been raised), and she wanted her book to reflect Eva's perspective rather than the dominant view of the time.

My forays into classroom discussions of race were not entire failures, however. Although they had less controversial options, several students in the composition class chose to base their final research papers on investigations of their own cultural identities, delving further into the very topics that had caused so much tension. I received papers on historical shifts in definitions of African-American religious identity, and papers on competing definitions of biracial identity, Wiccan identity, and gender identity. In the American literature class, alongside the Little Eva project that edited out slavery, I received a picture book adaptation of Frederick Douglass's "What to the Slave Is the Fourth of July?" that placed the text and pictures against a background of the present-day (not antebellum) American flag. The student began her defense by asserting that many black people in America, herself included, celebrated Juneteenth because the sentiments that Douglass expressed in the 1850s still felt relevant in 2013. Despite overt expressions of resistance, I also heard undercurrents of interest and engagement. Many students, of all backgrounds, were tense and uncomfortable when asked to speak about race in a desegregated setting; but some of the same students who would not disrupt the implied social rules of the desegregated classroom would, with more privacy, write about the continuing areas of racial segregation that they did, indeed, notice and think about.

My point in revisiting these classroom experiences is not to lament my woes as some enlightened, racially innocent Northerner forced to confront the horrifying backwardness of the rural South. On the contrary: the reason why my students' resistance surprised me more than it perhaps should have is that even many avoidant students also, by and large, demonstrated some degree of thoughtful engagement with issues that challenged their worldviews. Instead, I have offered this closing anecdote as a way to reflect upon the challenges of discussing the legacies of *Brown* in the classroom, as there is little way to assess—or even to define—the "success" of such discussions. A classroom dominated by dissent, tension, and the open airing of critical conflict (desirable in many philosophies of anti-racist teaching) did not seem to be ideal for those quiet students willing to write, but not to speak, their sympathy with more controversial readings. At the same time, more direct readings, which sparked resistance from some, seemed to offer relief for others, a sense that someone else had said what they were thinking and had spoken the previously un-speakable in a public forum. Similarly, in the world of children's literature, some texts are praised for classroom use because they seem to have the potential to circumvent resistance and provide "safe" opportunities for discussion[1]; and yet, no text, and no method of teaching a text, can really ever be "safe," because teachers do not have some kind of ultimate control over what, or how, or when students learn. A single classroom, like a single text, cannot offer multiple models of utopian education at the same time, nor can it dependably create a perfect environment by containing just the right, magical, scientifically tested components. At the same time, even encounters with less-than-successful reading options and pedagogical methods may spark change. Given the troubled history of school desegregation, we should reflect on the value of continued, persistent failure—on why continuing to fail at antiracist education, at desegregation, at educating citizens in general, is a worthwhile enterprise.

I began this book by asking what students in the post-*Brown* era are told about the racial dynamics of their own classrooms through the books aimed specifically at them. The answer is both "A great deal" and "Not much." When we mine these books for the legacies of the *Brown* decision, certain effects of the decision lie close to the surface, while others are buried deeper, and require more digging to bring to the reader's consciousness. Stories of the violence and resistance in the immediate aftermath of the decision—stories of bravery, interracial friendship, and pre-segregation foundations of black education—are relatively transparent about how, and what, they aim to teach students about their educational history. Stories of the more insidious legacies of the *Brown* decision—the disparities in disability diagnosis, the re-segregation, the unequal pressures of standardized testing—are more obliquely told, so that students and teachers may have the opportunity to think about these legacies, but are not asked to directly confront them. Furthermore, the structure and the expectations of the school system shape and constrain not only school-based social reforms, but also the ways in which these reform efforts are narrated. This process occurs in a variety of ways, from limiting the criticisms that can be published about the desegregated school for an education market, to shaping the plot lines of stories, as when academic success is used to legitimize antiracist reforms. Even when the existing school system is no longer the ideal site of reform, an alternative kind of communal learning environment is still imagined as being necessary to pursuing national racial justice.

Thus, while the focus of this project has been on what school stories tell children about desegregation, it is also useful to ask what the legacies of desegregation—and the stories that are told about it—can tell us about school. Critics of the *Brown* decision have rightly faulted it for constraining its call for change to the public school system, without making a broader statement about racial justice. Nevertheless, this means that the process of desegregation is inextricably linked with all of the other processes of change and reform that the school system undergoes, so that we cannot ask how desegregation has succeeded or failed without asking whether the school system is succeeding, or failing, as a whole—and, more importantly, without asking what we think it is meant to be succeeding or failing at doing. If desegregated schools educate a mixed-race student body equitably, but do so through stultifying or rigid methods of pedagogy, is this a success? If equitable desegregated schools educate children of all races to perpetuate global inequality and an ethos of American exceptionalism, is this a success? Child readers may not be encouraged to think too much about the school-to-prison pipeline, or about disability diagnosis, as continuing issues of racial justice that were unsolved by the sacrifices of the Little Rock Nine. Nevertheless, novels that occlude these issues reveal, even highlight, central questions about the school system that cut to the heart of how the legacies of desegregation can be conceptualized and evaluated.

Three recurring issues are central to this evaluation of the *Brown* legacy and its effect on schooling. First, the conjoined problems of control and resistance surface as potential obstacles to desired utopian education, and also as utopian desires in themselves. Next, different utopian educational schemes must account for student failure. And finally, the failed school must be considered as a potentially necessary component of a utopian democratic project.

Control, Resistance, and Incompatible Utopias

The novels discussed in this book are roughly divided according to how they depict the respective benefits of educational control and resistance. In the school stories of Chapters 1 and 2, a healthy educational setting is characterized by a sense of calm control, in which inappropriate resistance is disciplined and ultimately (hopefully) erased. This inappropriate resistance may take many forms; white students at Mary Jane's or Marlee's schools may resist desegregation, white teachers like Mr. Kooner and Dawnie Rae's science teacher may resist teaching black students, and reluctant students like Candy Castle may resist their schoolwork. These varieties of resistance share a common quality. Students and teachers in these texts have clear "jobs," whether paid or unpaid, and any behavior that interferes with those jobs is clearly inappropriate. Once desegregation becomes part of the school environment, any tasks associated with the ultimate goals of desegregation are stamped not only with legitimacy, but also with compulsion. The novels do recognize legitimate forms of resistance within the school setting, most notably when students like Dawnie Rae and Emma resist internalizing the messages of racist teaching. The legitimacy of this resistance, however, is recognizable by the restoration of order to the learning environment. In insisting that Mr. Kooner do his job, Emma and her compatriots transform the classroom from a chaotic place where there is no time for learning, to a calm place where students have the time and emotional security to do their work. When Emma triumphantly announces, "*We program the Kooners*," she is reversing the usual sequence of who programs whom, but she also supports the idea that a certain degree of programming is necessary for education to work.[2] In contrast, the novels in Chapters 3 and 4 portray programming as a suspicious form of control, regardless of who is doing it; Mr. Pool, Stanley, and Octavian all lose credibility within their narratives when they momentarily replicate dominant methods of educational control, even for worthy purposes. In these novels, successful education is characterized by the upset of established order. Educational methods of control are portrayed as being parallel to, and supportive of, methods of racist, classist, and able-ist social control.

This split between supporters of control and resistance echoes similar splits in educational theory and philosophy. Reformers such as Mike Rose, Gloria Ladson-Billings, and Lisa Delpit, whose work tends to focus on pedagogical praxis, express a continued belief in the power of good teaching and suggest that effective, *reliable* educational methods can be developed to decrease inappropriate resistance to academic and ethical lessons. Many of these theorists emphasize that the end goal of these methods is to encourage students to question dominant ideologies of inequality. Nevertheless, if teaching is successful, their feelings of resistance will be expressed outside the controlled zone of the classroom, against its proper antagonists, and not inside the classroom, against the curricular material. On the other side of the split, theorists such as Michael Apple and Henry Giroux tend to view any kind of school praxis as completely inextricable from the larger social structures to be resisted. Apple, for example, argues that changes in pedagogy cannot change the basic function of the school, which is to produce an illusion of critical democracy, a manufactured consensus that supports existing forms of oppression.[3] Both sets of thinkers optimistically hope that resistance, in some form and in some location, will indeed be directed toward the goal of social change. Other critics caution, however, that the controlled educational setting sometimes raises resistance *both* against the curricular material *and* against the goal of fighting racial injustice.[4] When antiracist teachers are unsuccessful in altering their students' desires, many students do opt for various shows of hostility toward both academic tasks and ideological change.

Utopian education is, in part, about the training of desire; the nation cannot reform and achieve its ideal potential unless its citizens are not only capable of sustaining it, but also desirous of doing so. Ostensibly, all of these desegregation novelists and antiracist theorists share the utopian desire for a racially and economically just society. They merely seem to debate whether students will be more likely to reach that common goal by adopting a stance of compliance with the classroom or a stance of resistance to it. Nevertheless, a glance at the spread of these desegregation novels indicates that while the protagonists may all want racial justice, they also want such different educational experiences that they work, effectively, toward quite different goals.

It is hard, for example, to imagine Dicey Tillerman or Buddy waving their hands around excitedly, burning to participate, as Mary Jane does when she finally feels comfortable in her science classroom; and despite Octavian's and Adonis's eagerness to please, I cannot picture them cheerfully complying with the boring, pre-determined science experiments Mr. Stiller assigns, friendly and anti-racist though his classroom may have been. Conversely, Mary Jane, Emma, and Dawnie Rae would be horrified if asked to model themselves after Mina, or Dicey, or Zero, or Octavian, even though they encounter similar problems in academic environments. Mary Jane might struggle in French, because her book teaches only phrases of friendship, rather than the phrases of hurt and anger she needs for combating bullies; Dawnie Rae may struggle in science and English, because her teachers work to sabotage her; and Emma is faced with a teacher who foments combat instead of learning; yet these characters define themselves, and their desired subjectivities, according to academic success. They would struggle to work harder, or in alternate ways, for 'A's, rather than deliberately courting a politically demonstrative 'C,' as Mina does; and even though their success might make racist teachers also look successful, they would never intentionally botch a performance, as Octavian does at one point, in order to make those teachers look bad.

If school is not merely preparation for life, but the actual "real" life of the students and teachers who spend their days there, then a racially just society, for these student-protagonists, would not be sufficient for utopia. Even were that end to be finally achieved, Dawnie Rae and Buddy (for example) would still desire fundamentally different, and incompatible, daily lives and forms of education. The divide between writers who privilege resistance and those who want an ultimate, eventual zone of safety is a very real one, which affects the kind of subjects readers are encouraged to want to be and the kind of racially just world they are supposed to create. Children's novels about *Brown* may be expected to provide some form of happy ending, but the definition of a "happy ending" is contestable, not only with respect to racial justice, but also with respect to the daily routines of education.

Academic Failure in Utopia

The legacies of desegregation are intertwined with the educational function of the school. Therefore, desegregation novels must account for the role of failing students in their utopian goals for the nation. In many, failing students represent a problem to be erased. They demonstrate the persistent evils of a racist system, and their transformation indicates the success, and the desirability, of racial justice and antiracist pedagogy.

In others, failing students are critical model subjects who expose the pedagogical and ideological flaws of the system, and who demonstrate that academic success and good citizenship are not always synonymous (and in fact are sometimes incompatible). Even in novels that grant a moral credibility to failure, failing students sometimes function as symbols, indicators of desired reforms. The implication is that in a better school system, Buddy and Junior would not need to cut school, Dicey would not need to be disengaged, and Frannie might be recognized as gifted. One might argue that these representations of failure very predictably echo the dominant representation of disability as a "problem" that should ideally be eliminated. Nevertheless, these novels also grant respect to failure, and offer important insights into questions of ideal citizenship.

Novels that strongly value resistance as a part of ideal education also tend to imagine utopias that not only accommodate, but also require failure as an integral part of their structure—not as a temporary, soluble element, but as a permanent component. Buddy's and Dicey's communities are based upon the desire for constant, restless critique of the status quo. Without some source of failure, not only would their alternative worlds be lost, but there would also be nothing to feed the critique that defines them as contributing citizens. Failed students, and failed citizens, in these ideal communities, will never lose their jobs. Such novels offer one potential model of reform for the desegregated school, reinforcing the idea that there might be other ways to measure the success of desegregation, and other goals for the school, besides the "success" of all its students. In this model, failure should not be a byproduct, but a central product of the school that should be valued and taken seriously. It provides a constant horizon of possibility, a constant source of alternative ways of thinking and doing.

Novels that frame failure as temporary, however, also offer a valuable insight into how education might be constructed as a public good to be shared rather than as a limited commodity. Currently, the failure of many students is what helps the school system to maintain the worth of education, as higher levels of education become increasingly accessible commodities. David Labaree, for example, argues that competition and failure help to elevate the value of the educational goods offered by elite institutions. Catherine Prendergast demonstrates how a commodity view of education has thwarted the goals of *Brown*, as desegregation has historically caused the perceived value of educational institutions to drop once access was opened to minority students.[5] In contrast, the desegregation novels that seek to eliminate student failure can be read as attempts to envision a utopian system in which failure does not shore up the value of education. While Horace Mann originally advanced the idea that education should be a public good, he also instituted some of the mechanisms (such as standardized testing) that enshrined failure as a measure of rigor and that held schools, and students, accountable for using taxpayer money efficiently. Novels that imagine away the need for failure do not necessarily imagine away student struggles or differences in aptitude. Rather, they conjure classrooms in which students' struggles are not framed as wasting the system's time and money—and therefore are not defined as failure.

The time frame of the school year is crucial, not only for school story plots, but also for setting the boundaries of academic success—and therefore, for establishing education as a limited commodity. The age-graded school year helps to establish "use by" dates after which the system's investment in a student is deemed to be lost. Thus, while novels such as *Because We Are*, *Fire From the Rock*, and *Feathers* tend to reinforce the perception that academic success is the primary legitimating quality for citizenship, they also imagine a system in which students who struggle to keep up with a prescribed curricular schedule are not necessarily failures. Frannie, Calvin, and Candy "succeed" in part because they are taught through effective antiracist pedagogies, but also in part because their difficulties never reach a deadline when they are conclusively labeled as "failure." In different ways, then, whether by framing failure as temporary or by enshrining it as permanent, all of these novels claim "failing" students as worthwhile investments.

Failed Schools in Utopia

Most of these novels suggest that when students fail, that failure ought to belong to the school rather than to the pupil. This revised attribution of failure is central to writers' and activists' calls for meaningful racial integration beyond body mixing. Integration (as opposed to desegregation) requires that antiracist activists should acknowledge the struggles students have experienced both academically and socially through the process of legal desegregation, without simply telling a glossy, celebratory tale of unalloyed success and progress. At the same time, re-attributing failure to institutional causes helps these writers to affirm that those same struggling students, given a different institution, are capable of making school integration work. Thus, it is unsurprising that so many desegregation novels are invested in reclaiming failing students as valuable citizens, even though (or rather, because) such failures are sometimes used as evidence that desegregation is a collapsed social experiment.

What is perhaps more surprising is that, in addition to claiming failed students as valuable citizens, desegregation novels continue to claim the failed school system as a necessary and valuable training ground for those citizens, despite the responsibility it bears for *mis*-training citizens. In part, this re-affirmation of the school may occur because desegregation novels for children are deeply embedded in the educational publishing market, which addresses readers who have a vested interest in maintaining the cultural power of the school system. Nevertheless, teachers and administrators are not a monolithic force dedicated to preserving the *status quo*, as these novels (many written by former teachers) demonstrate. Many influential adults within the school system and the publishing system also desire a different institution, and a different society, from the one in which they live and work. Therefore, I think it is important to consider some less cynical reasons for this phenomenon.

School-based utopias are attractive in part because of the element of compulsion attached to the school. Children have to go there, and most of us (adults and children alike) would prefer that that experience feel exciting and fulfilling rather than miserable. Beyond this, the school provides a compulsory identity and set of routines for children and thus seems to offer the opportunity to instill desires for utopian nationhood. Yet in school stories in general, and desegregation stories in particular, the school is not merely an engine for the transmission of desire. It is an object of desire in itself. Despite being bullied and excluded, Mary Jane, Emma, and Dawnie Rae long to feel school spirit; despite playing hooky, Buddy, Junior, and Mr. Pool want a congenial classroom; and despite his horrifying experiences with the Enlightenment, Octavian still fantasizes about a future community of philosophical exchange and inquiry. The problem of unruly desire for untenable systems haunts other antiracist activism in the United States. As Anne Anlin Cheng asks, "[C]an 'knowing better' or 'political correctness' redirect or correct, as it were, one's desires and fantasies?"[6] These protagonists (and their writers, and their readers) may "know better," yet they do not merely want the better world that a desegregated school may create. They also want a school. The work of public policy, of pedagogical reform, of utopian thinking, requires a commitment to looking for solutions. At the same time, desegregation novels provide a reminder that the problems of the school system are not necessarily obstacles to be gotten past. Utopian thinking might require a commitment to coping with critique and failure and disappointment, because the school is part of our desired utopia, not just instrumental to it.

If, as desegregation novels suggest, the experience of failure should not render students worthless for citizenship, then perhaps it should not render a social goal, or an institution, worthless either. If failure is essential to ethical learning, critique, and growth at the personal level, then it is paradoxically probably necessary to the effectiveness of institutions, too, given that institutions like schools are made up of individual teachers, administrators, community members, and support staff, who must have some leeway to fail if they are to work toward any kind of genuine utopian vision. Committing to an idea of the school system as both failing and potentially utopian would require a shift in how we think about the society we want students to desire. The United States has a long history of teaching its youth to desire a narrowly defined version of success, both for its citizens and for the state. To not only admit failure, but accept it and value what it might teach, has historically been framed as an almost unforgivable sin against American values.[7] Critics of the school system sometimes suggest that the way to make America successful is to eliminate this emblem of failure embedded within the state, whether by making it a success or by eliminating it altogether. Valuing failure as an inevitable and necessary part of learning would also require coming to accept and appreciate it as a quintessential and worthy quality of United States society and state identity. It is worthwhile to continue the work of shifting desire, not only in our students but also in ourselves, even—or especially—when this work fails.

Notes

1 Brooks and Hampton, "Safe Discussions Rather Than First Hand Encounters."
2 Walter, *Because We Are*, 171.
3 Apple, *Cultural and Economic Reproduction in Education*, 78.
4 Jennifer Trainor, for example, does an in-depth analysis of a high school English classroom taught by a consciously anti-racist, Freirian instructor. She concludes that the daily rules and rituals of the school reinforced emotional habits that reinforced racism. Specifically, students were exhorted daily to be cheerful, to view themselves as being strong and in control, and to view themselves as being equal to everyone else. Antiracist reading and pedagogy specifically challenged these habits of thinking and feeling, but it did not change them; rather, the strength of the school's reinforced routines and values undermined the antiracist teaching. Marshall Alcorn suggests that this kind of double resistance—to academic content and to social change—arises because "successful" pedagogy depends upon the manipulation of the students' desire; however, we experience changes of desire as changes in our basic sense of identity, and many subjects vehemently resist such pressure. Trainor, *Rethinking Racism*, 10, 25; Alcorn, *Changing the Subject in English Class*, 18, 59–63.
5 Labaree, "Public Goods, Private Goods," 51–54; Prendergast, *Literacy and Racial Justice*, "The Economy of Literacy."
6 Cheng, *The Melancholy of Race*, 112.
7 Ralph Waldo Emerson complains about this national intolerance for failure in "Self-Reliance"; Cynthia Voigt addresses it as a pedagogical issue in "Margaret A. Edwards Awards Acceptance Speech," and Judith (Jack) Halberstam addresses it as a component of capitalism in *The Queer Art of Failure*; but all three suggest an American tendency to place failure in opposition to nationalism.

Bibliography

Ahrenhoerster, Greg. "Would Karl Marx Call for an Overthrow of ESPN? Sports as an Opiate of the People." In *American Sports Fiction*, edited by Michael Cocchiarale and Scott D. Emmert, 131–150. Ipswich, MA: Salem Press, 2013.

Alcorn, Marshall W. *Changing the Subject in English Class: Discourse and the Constructions of Desire*. Carbondale: Southern Illinois University Press, 2002.

Alexie, Sherman. *The Absolutely True Diary of a Part-Time Indian*. Illustrated by Ellen Forney. New York: Little, Brown, and Company, 2007.

Alexie, Sherman. "Why the Best Kids' Books Are Written in Blood." *The Wall Street Journal*. 9 June 2011. Accessed 9 August 2016. http://blogs.wsj.com/speakeasy/2011/06/09/why-the-best-kids-books-are-written-in-blood/.

Alfonso, Sister Regina. "Modules for Teaching about Young People's Literature: Module 1: Gender Roles." *Journal of Reading* 30, no. 2 (1986): 160–163. Accessed August 12, 2016. http://www.jstor.org.proxygwa.wrlc.org/stable/40029710.

Alic, Margaret. "Graham, Lorenz." *Contemporary Black Biography* (2005). *Encyclopedia.com*. Accessed 4 August 2016. http://www.encyclopedia.com/doc/1G2–3431400035.html.

Anderson, M.T. *The Astonishing Life of Octavian Nothing, Traitor to the Nation. Volume #1 the Pox Party / Taken from Accounts by His Own Hand and Other Sundry Sources; Collected by M.T. Anderson of Boston*. Cambridge, MA: Candlewick Press, 2006.

Anderson, M.T. *The Astonishing Life of Octavian Nothing, Traitor to the Nation. Volume #2 the Kingdom on the Waves / Taken from Accounts by His Own Hand and Other Sundry Sources; Collected by M.T. Anderson of Boston*. Cambridge, MA: Candlewick Press, 2008.

Anderson, M.T. *Feed*. Cambridge, MA: Candlewick Press, 2002.

Anderson, M.T. "On the Intelligence of Teens." 2009. Accessed 9 August 2016. http://mt-anderson.com/blog/he-talks-talks-2/on-the-intelligence-of-teens/.

"Andrea Pinkney." *The Brown Bookshelf: United in Story*. 19 February 2009. Accessed August 9, 2016. https://thebrownbookshelf.com/2009/02/19/andrea-pinkney/.

"Andrea Pinkney Profile." *Scholastic.com*. n.d. Accessed 9 August 2016. http://www.scholastic.com/browse/article.jsp?id=3747317.

Apple, Michael W. *Cultural and Economic Reproduction in Education: Essays on Class, Ideology, and the State*. London; Boston: Routledge & Kegan Paul, 1982. Routledge Education Books.

Atkins, Laura. “What’s the Story? Reflections on White Privilege in the Publication of Children’s Books.” International Research Society for Children’s Literature Congress. *Tockla’s World of Children’s Literature.* N.p. 14 August 2009. Accessed 9 August 2016. https://sites.google.com/site/tockla/.

Atwood, Thomas M. and Wade M. Lee. “The Price of Deviance: Schoolhouse Gothic in Prep School Literature.” *Children’s Literature* 35, no. 1 (2007): 102–126. Accessed 9 August 2016. DOI: 10.1353/chl.2007.0002.

Author M.T. Anderson on Octavian Nothing. Washington, D.C.: NPR, 2007. Accessed 8 August 2016. http://www.npr.org/templates/story/story.php?storyId=7060904.

Baker, R.S. “The Paradoxes of Desegregation: Race, Class, and Education, 1935–1975.” *American Journal of Education* 109, no. 3 (2001): 320–343. Accessed 12 August 2016. http://www.jstor.org/stable/1085779.

Baldwin, James. “A Fly in Buttermilk.” 1961. In *James Baldwin: Collected Essays*, edited by Toni Morrison, 187–196. New York: The Library of America, 1998.

Baldwin, James. “The White Man’s Guilt.” 1965. In *James Baldwin: Collected Essays*, edited by Toni Morrison, 722–727. New York: The Library of America, 1998.

Banfield, Beryle and Geraldine Wilson. “Black Experience Through White Eyes—The Same Old Story Again.” In *The Black American in Books for Children: Readings in Racism*, edited by Donnarae MacCann and Gloria Woodard, 192–207. Metuchen, NJ: Scarecrow Press, 1985.

Bauer, Joan. *Close to Famous.* New York: Viking, 2011.

Bayla. Untitled review of *Pinned.* Goodreads.com. “*Pinned* by Sharon G. Flake.” 4 Dec. 2013. Accessed 9 August 2016. http://www.goodreads.com/book/show/13492511-pinned.

Beals, Melba. *Warriors Don’t Cry: The Searing Memoir of the Battle to Integrate Little Rock’s Central High.* New York: Simon Pulse, 2007.

Bell, Derrick A. *Shades of Brown: New Perspectives on School Desegregation.* New York: Teachers College, Columbia University, 1980.

Berlant, Lauren. *The Anatomy of National Fantasy: Hawthorne, Utopia, and Everyday Life.* Chicago: University of Chicago Press, 1991.

Bernstein, Robin. *Racial Innocence: Performing American Childhood from Slavery to Civil Rights.* New York: New York University Press, 2011.

Bérubé, Michael. *Life as We Know It: A Father, a Family, and an Exceptional Child.* New York: Pantheon Books, 1996.

Bowles, Samuel, and Herbert Gintis. *Schooling in Capitalist America: Educational Reform and the Contradictions of Economic Life.* New York: Basic Books, 1976.

Braddock, Jomills Henry, and Robert E. Slavin. “Why Ability Grouping Must End: Achieving Excellence and Equity in American Education.” Center for Research on Effective Schooling for Disadvantaged Students, 1992.

Brandt, Deborah, and Educational Resources Information Center. *The Sponsors of Literacy.* Report Series 7.12. Albany, NY: National Research Center on English Learning & Achievement, 1997. Accessed 9 August 2016. http://www.albany.edu/cela/reports/brandtsponsors10001.pdf.

Brasch, Walter M. *Black English and the Mass Media.* Lanham, MD: University Press of America, 1984; 1981.

Briggs, Donna. Untitled Review. *Customer Reviews: Pinned.* Amazon.com, 3 December 2014. Accessed 6 July 2015. http://www.goodreads.com/book/show/13492511-pinned.

Brooks, Wanda, and Gregory Hampton. "Safe Discussions Rather Than First Hand Encounters: Adolescents Examine Racism Through One Historical Fiction Text." *Children's Literature in Education* 36, no. 1 (2005): 83–98. Accessed 9 August 2016. DOI: 10.1007/s10583–004–2191–0.

Buck, Stuart. *Acting White: The Ironic Legacy of Desegregation.* New Haven: Yale University Press, 2010.

Bryant, Deyonne. "A Moral Compass: Dorothy Sterling's Mary Jane." In *A Narrative Compass: Stories That Guide Women's Lives*, edited by Betsy Hearne and Roberta Seelinger Trites, 102–114. Urbana: Illinois University Press, 2009.

California State Board of Education. *English-Language Arts Content Standards for California Public Schools: Kindergarten Through Grade Twelve.* Sacramento: California State Board of Education, 1997, 2009. Accessed 9 August 2016. http://www.cde.ca.gov/be/st/ss/documents/elacontentstnds.pdf.

Cameron, Ann, and Ann Strugnell. *The Stories Julian Tells.* New York: Random House, 2006; 1981.

Cameron, Ann, and Lis Toft. *Gloria Rising.* 1st ed. New York: Frances Foster Books/Farrar, Straus and Giroux, 2002.

Capshaw, Katharine. *Civil Rights Childhood: Picturing Liberation in African American Photobooks.* Minneapolis, MN: University of Minnesota Press, 2014.

Carby, Hazel. "The Multicultural Wars." In *Black Popular Culture*, edited by Gina Dent and Michele Wallace, 187–199. Seattle: Bay Press, 1992.

Carlson, Natalie Savage. *The Empty Schoolhouse.* New York: Harper & Row, 1965.

Cecelski, David S. *Along Freedom Road: Hyde County, North Carolina and the Fate of Black Schools in the South.* Chapel Hill, NC: University of North Carolina Press, 1994.

Cheng, Anne Anlin. *The Melancholy of Race.* Oxford, England; New York: Oxford University Press, 2001.

Christle, C.A., K. Jolivette, and C.M. Nelson. "Breaking the School to Prison Pipeline: Identifying School Risk and Protective Factors for Youth Delinquency." *Exceptionality* 13, no. 2 (2005): 69–88.

Cintron, Ralph. *Angels' Town: Chero Ways, Gang Life, and Rhetorics of the Everyday.* Boston, MA: Beacon Press, 1997.

Cisneros, Sandra. *The House on Mango Street.* New York: Vintage Books, 1991.

Clark, Beverly Lyon. "Cracking the Code of the School Story: Telling Tales about Telling Tales." *Bucknell Review: A Scholarly Journal of Letters, Arts and Sciences* 34, no. 2 (1990): 108–124.

Clark, Beverly Lyon. "Domesticating the School Story, Regendering a Genre: Alcott's 'Little Men.'" *New Literary History* 26, no. 2 (1995): 323–342. http://www.jstor.org.proxygwa.wrlc.org/stable/20057285.

Clark, Beverly Lyon. *Regendering the School Story: Sassy Sissies and Tattling Tomboys.* 3 Vols. New York: Garland, 1996.

Clark, Kenneth Bancroft. *Prejudice and Your Child.* Boston: Beacon Press, 1955.

Cohen, Cathy J. *The Boundaries of Blackness: AIDS and the Breakdown of Black Politics*. Chicago: University of Chicago Press, 1999.

Cohen, Lizabeth. *A Consumers' Republic: The Politics of Mass Consumption in Postwar America*. New York: Alfred A. Knopf, 2003.

Cohen, Miriam and Lillian Hoban. *First Grade Takes a Test*. New York: Greenwillow Books, 1980.

Coles, Robert and George Ford. *The Story of Ruby Bridges*. New York: Scholastic, 1995.

"Come a Stranger Social Sensitivity." Bookrags.com. n.d. Accessed 9 August 2016. http://www.bookrags.com/shortguide-come-a-stranger/socialsensitivity.html#gsc.tab=0.

Common Core State Standards Initiative. "English Language Arts and Literacy in History/Social Studies, Science, and Technical Subjects, Appendix B: Text Exemplars and Sample Performance Tasks." Common Core State Standards Initiative, 2012. Accessed 9 August 2016. http://www.corestandards.org/assets/Appendix_B.pdf.

Cooperative Children's Book Center. "Publishing Statistics on Children's Books about People of Color and First/Native Nations and by People of Color and First/Native Nations Authors and Illustrators." Last modified 5 April 2016. Accessed 22 August 2016. https://ccbc.education.wisc.edu/books/pcstats.asp.

Cottle, Thomas J. *Busing*. Boston: Beacon Press, 1976.

Cottle, Thomas J. "What Tracking Did to Ollie Taylor." *Social Policy* 5, no. 2 (1974): 21–24.

Creech, Sharon and Harry Bliss. *A Fine, Fine School*. New York: Joanna Cotler Books/HarperCollins, 2001.

Cummins, June. "The Lessons of *The Wizard of Oz* and *Holes*: A Century of American Narrative and American Values." Buffalo, NY. June 2001. Conference presentation, Children's Literature Association.

Daniel, Philip T.K. "Accountability and Desegregation: Brown and Its Legacy." *The Journal of Negro Education* 73, no. 3 (2004): 255–267. Accessed 9 August 2016. http://www.jstor.org/stable/4129610.

Darling-Hammond, Linda. *The Flat World and Education: How America's Commitment to Equity Will Determine Our Future*. New York: Teachers College Press, 2010.

Davis, Lennard J., Ed. *The Disability Studies Reader*. 4th ed. New York: Routledge, 2013.

Davis, Lennard J. *Enforcing Normalcy: Disability, Deafness, and the Body*. London; New York: Verso, 1995.

Davison, Judy C., and Donna Y. Ford. "Perceptions of Attention Deficit Hyperactivity Disorder in One African American Community." *The Journal of Negro Education* 70, no. 4 (2001): 264–274. http://www.jstor.org/stable/3211279.

"Dear America: *With the Might of Angels* by Andrea Davis Pinkney." *Kidsread.com*. Last modified 14 September 2012. Accessed 12 August 2016. https://kidsread.wordpress.com/category/dear-america-with-the-might-of-angels-lesson-plan/.

de la Peña, Matt. *We Were Here*. New York: Delacorte Press, 2009.

Deloria, Philip Joseph. *Playing Indian*. Yale Historical Publications. New Haven: Yale University Press, 1998.

Delpit, Lisa. "Lessons From Teachers." *Journal of Teacher Education* 57, no. 3 (2006): 220–231. Accessed 9 August 2016. DOI: 10.1177/0022487105285966.

Delpit, Lisa. *Other People's Children: Cultural Conflict in the Classroom*. New York: The New Press, 1995.

Dewey, John. *Democracy and Education*. 1916. Lexington: Feather Trail Press, 2009.

Dickinson, Emily. "'Hope' is the thing with feathers—(254)." 1891. *Poets.org*. Academy of American Poets, n.d. Accessed 9 August 2016. https://www.poets.org/poetsorg/poem/hope-thing-feathers-254.

DiMaggio, Dan. "The Loneliness of the Long-Distance Test Scorer." *Monthly Review* 62, no. 7 (2010): n.p. Accessed 9 August 2016. http://monthlyreview.org/2010/12/01/the-loneliness-of-the-long-distance-test-scorer/.

Douglass, Frederick. *Narrative of Frederick Douglass, an American Slave*. New York: Barnes & Noble Classics, 2005.

Douglass, Frederick. "What to the Slave is the 4th of July?" Teaching American History. Accessed 9 August 2016. http://teachingamericanhistory.org/library/document/what-to-the-slave-is-the-fourth-of-july/.

Draper, Sharon M. *Fire from the Rock*. New York: Dutton Children's Books, 2007.

Draper, Sharon M. "Homework Helper: Digging Deeper." *Welcome to the Official Site of Sharon Draper*. SharonDraper.com, 2014. Accessed 9 August 2016. http://sharondraper.com/homework-4–1.asp.

Draper, Sharon M. "Re: Fire From the Rock." Message to the author. 22 February 2013. Email.

Dresang, Eliza T. "A Newbery Song for Gifted Readers." *School Library Journal* 30, no. 3 (1983): 33.

Dubey, Madhu. *Black Women Novelists and the Nationalist Aesthetic*. Bloomington: Indiana University Press, 1994.

Du Bois, W.E.B. "Does the Negro Need Separate Schools?" *The Journal of Negro Education* 4, no. 3, The Courts and the Negro Separate School (1935): 328–335.

Du Bois, W.E.B. *The Souls of Black Folk*. 1896. New York: Penguin Books, 1996.

Dudziak, Mary. *Cold War Civil Rights*. Princeton, NJ: Princeton University Press, 2002; 2000.

Egoff, Sheila A. *Thursday's Child: Trends and Patterns in Contemporary Children's Literature*. Chicago: American Library Association, 1981.

Elizabeth. Untitled Review of *Pinned. Goodreads:* Pinned *by Sharon G. Flake*. Goodreads.com, 3 December 2013. Accessed 9 August 2016. http://www.goodreads.com/book/show/13492511-pinned.

Elliott, Zetta. "Hot Mess." *Fledgling: Zetta Elliott's Blog*. N.p. 16 June 2012. Accessed 9 August 2016. https://zettaelliott.wordpress.com/2012/06/16/hot-mess/.

Elliott, Zetta. "Something Like an Open Letter to the Children's Publishing Industry." *Fledgling: Zetta Elliott's Blog*. N.p. 5 September 2009. Accessed 9 August 2016. https://zettaelliott.wordpress.com/2009/09/05/something-like-an-open-letter-to-the-children%E2%80%99s-publishing-industry/.

Ellison, Ralph. *Invisible Man*. New York: Random House, 2002; 1952.

Emerson, Ralph Waldo. "Self-Reliance." *The Norton Anthology of American Literature*. Vol. B. 8th ed. Edited by Nina Baym and Robert S. Levine, 269–286. New York: W.W. Norton, 2012.

Eyes on the Prize—America's Civil Rights Years, 1954–1965. "Fighting Back." Directed by Judith Vecchione. 1986. Atlanta, GA: PBS Home Video, 2006.

Faderman, Lillian. *Odd Girls and Twilight Lovers: A History of Lesbian Life in Twentieth-Century America*. New York: Columbia University Press, 1991.

Fairclough, Adam. "The Costs of *Brown*: Black Teachers and School Integration." *Journal of American History* 91, no. 1 (2004): 43–55.

Farley, Todd. *Making the Grades: My Misadventures in the Standardized Testing Industry*. Sausalito, CA; LaVergne, TN: PoliPointPress, 2009.

"'Feathers' Looks to Sixth Grade for Life's Lessons." *News and Notes*. Host Farah Chideya. NPR, 23 March 2007. *NPR.org*. Accessed 9 August 2016. http://www.npr.org/templates/story/story.php?storyId=9032665.

Fenly, Leigh. "Just for Kids." *Union-Tribune* (San Diego, CA), 30 May 2004. Accessed 9 August 2016. http://www.sandiegouniontribune.com/uniontrib/20040530/news_lz1v30kids.html.

Fenning, Pamela and Jennifer Rose. "Overrepresentation of African-American Students in Exclusionary School Discipline: The Role of School Policy." *Urban Education* 42, no. 6 (2007): 536–559. Accessed 9 August 2016. DOI: 10.1177/0042085907305039.

Ferber, Abby L. "The Construction of Black Masculinity: White Supremacy Now and Then." *Journal of Sport and Social Issues* 31, no. 1 (2007): 11; 11,24; 24. Accessed 9 August 2016. DOI: 10.1177/0193723506296829.

Ferguson, Roderick A. *Aberrations in Black: Toward a Queer of Color Critique*. Minneapolis, MN: University of Minnesota Press, 2004.

Ferguson, Roderick A. *The Reorder of Things*. Minneapolis, MN: University of Minnesota Press, 2012.

Ferri, Beth and David Connor. *Reading Resistance: Discourses of Exclusion in Desegregation and Inclusion Debates*. New York: Peter Lang, 2006.

Flake, Sharon. *Pinned*. 1st ed. New York: Scholastic Press, 2012.

Flake, Sharon. *The Skin I'm In*. New York: Jump at the Sun / Hyperion Paperbacks for Children, 2007; 1999.

Fordham, Signithia and John U. Ogbu. "Black Students' School Success: Coping with the 'Burden of "Acting White."'" *The Urban Review* 18, no. 3 (1986): 176–206.

Foucault, Michel. *Discipline and Punish: The Birth of the Prison*. 2nd Vintage Books ed. New York: Vintage Books, 1995; 1977.

Francis, Betty Powers. "The Planet of Junior Brown by Virginia Hamilton." *Teaching Books.net*. Reading Right, 1999, 2005. Accessed 9 August 2016. https://www.teachingbooks.net/media/pdf/BF/PlanetofJuniorBrownBG.pdf.

Freire, Paulo. *Pedagogy of the Oppressed*. New revised 20th-Anniversary ed. New York: Continuum, 1993.

Frith, Gill, et al. "'The Time of Your Life': The Meaning of the School Story." In *Language, Gender & Childhood*, edited by Carolyn Steedman, Cathy Urwin, and Valerie Walkerdine, 113–136. London: Routledge and Kegan Paul, 1985.

Fuss, Diana. *Identification Papers*. New York: Routledge, 1995.

Gaines, Kevin. *American Africans in Ghana: Black Expatriates and the Civil Rights Era*. Chapel Hill, NC: University of North Carolina Press, 2006.

Gaines, Kevin. *Uplifting the Race: Black Leadership, Politics, and Culture in the Twentieth Century.* Chapel Hill, NC: University of North Carolina Press, 1996.

Gangopadhyay, Gargi. "'Our Motherland: Mapping an Identity in Bengali Children's Literature." In *The Nation in Children's Literature: Nations of Childhood*, edited by Christopher Kelen and Björn Sundmark, 139–160. New York; London: Routledge, 2014.

Gasman, Marybeth, and Felecia Commodore. "The State of Research on Historically Black Colleges and Universities." *Journal for Multicultural Education* 8, no. 2 (2014): 89. http://proxygw.wrlc.org/login?url=http://search.proquest.com.proxygw.wrlc.org/docview/1660759131?accountid=11243.

Giroux, Henry. "Dystopian Nightmares and Educated Hopes: The Return of the Pedagogical and the Promise of Democracy." In *Edutopias: New Utopian Thinking in Education*, edited by Michael A. Peters and John Freeman-Moir, 45–64. Rotterdam, The Netherlands: Sense Publishers, 2006.

Giroux, Henry. *Theory and Resistance in Education: A Pedagogy for the Opposition.* South Hadley, MA: Bergin & Garvey, 1983.

Glenn, Wendy J. "To Witness and to Testify: Preservice Teachers Examine Literary Aesthetics to Better Understand Diverse Literature." *English Education* 46, no. 2 (January 2014): 90–116. Accessed 17 August 2016. http://proxygw.wrlc.org/login?url=http://search.proquest.com.proxygw.wrlc.org/docview/1470801500?accountid=11243.

Glymph, Thavolia. *Out of the House of Bondage: The Transformation of the Plantation Household.* Cambridge; New York: Cambridge University Press, 2008.

Gold, Eva, Ruth Caillouet, and Tom Fick. "Teaching (W)Holes: Wordplay and Reversals in Louis Sachar's Holes." *ALAN Review* 34, no. 3 (2007): 46. Accessed 9 August 2016. https://scholar.lib.vt.edu/ejournals/ALAN/v34n3/gold.pdf.

Goldring, R., L. Gray, and A. Bitterman. "Characteristics of Public and Private Elementary and Secondary School Teachers in the United States: Results from the 2011–12 Schools and Staffing Survey (NCES 2013–314)." *U.S. Department of Education.* Washington, D.C.: National Center for Education Statistics (2013). Accessed 9 August 2016. http://nces.ed.gov/pubs2013/2013314.pdf.

Goodman, Paul. *Growing Up Absurd.* New York: New York Review Books, 2012; 1960.

Graham, Lorenz B. *North Town.* New York: Crowell, 1965.

Graham, Lorenz B. *Whose Town?.* New York: Crowell, 1969.

Graham, Patricia Albjerg. *Schooling America: How the Public Schools Meet the Nation's Changing Needs.* Oxford; New York: Oxford University Press, 2005.

Gubar, Marah. "'Where Is the Boy?' The Pleasures of Postponement in the *Anne of Green Gables* Series." *The Lion and the Unicorn* 25, no. 1 (2001): 47–69. DOI: 10.1353/uni.2001.0004.

Guinier, Lani. "From Racial Liberalism to Racial Literacy: Brown v. Board of Education and the Interest-Divergence Dilemma." *The Journal of American History* 91, no. 1 (2004): 92–118.

Halberstam, Judith. *In a Queer Time and Place: Transgender Bodies, Subcultural Lives.* New York: New York University Press, 2005.

Halberstam, Judith. *The Queer Art of Failure.* Durham, NC: Duke University Press, 2011.

Hairspray. Directed by John Waters. Los Angeles, CA: New Line Cinema, 1988.

Hairspray. Directed by Shankman, Adam, Craig Zadan, Neil Meron, et al. Los Angeles, CA: New Line Cinema Corporation, 2007.

Halperin, David M. *Saint Foucault: Towards a Gay Hagiography*. New York: Oxford University Press, 1995.

Halpin, David. "Utopian Totalism Versus Utopian Realism: A Reply to Darren Webb." *Oxford Review of Education* 35, no. 6 (2009): 761–764. DOI: 10.1080/03054980903399295.

Hamilton, Virginia. *The Planet of Junior Brown*. 1971. New York: Aladdin Paperbacks, 1999.

Hannah-Jones, Nikole. "Choosing a School for My Daughter in a Segregated City." *The New York Times Magazine*, 9 June 2016. Accessed 9 August 2016. http://www.nytimes.com/2016/06/12/magazine/choosing-a-school-for-my-daughter-in-a-segregated-city.html.

Harris, Marla. "Bleak Houses and Secret Cities: Alternative Communities in Young Adult Fiction." *Children's Literature in Education* 33, no. 1 (2002): 63–76. DOI: 10.1023/A:1014419810075.

Hartman, Andrew. *Education and the Cold War: The Battle for the American School*. 1st ed. New York: Palgrave Macmillan, 2008.

Henderson, Darwin L. and Consuelo W. Harris. "Profile: Choice, Courage, and Change Yield Character: An Interview with Mildred Pitts Walter." *Language Arts* 69, no. 7 (November 1992): 544–547. http://proxygwa.wrlc.org/login?url=http://search.proquest.com/docview/196868490?accountid=33473.

Henderson, Nia-Malika. "School Days." *The Washington Post* (Washington, D.C.), 16 May 2004: BW08. Accessed 9 August 2016. http://www.washingtonpost.com/wp-dyn/articles/A25707–2004May13.html.

Herrera, Juan Felipe. *Downtown Boy*. 1st ed. New York: Scholastic Press, 2005.

Hertberg-Davis, Holly. "Myth 7: Differentiation in the Regular Classroom is Equivalent to Gifted Programs and is Sufficient: Classroom Teachers have the Time, the Skill, and the Will to Differentiate Adequately." *Gifted Child Quarterly* 53, no. 4 (2009): 251–253. http://proxygwa.wrlc.org/login?url=http://search.proquest.com/docview/212091549?accountid=33473.

Hill Collins, Patricia. *Another Kind of Public Education: Race, Schools, the Media, and Democratic Possibilities*. Boston: Beacon Press, 2009.

Hinton-Johnson, KaaVonia. "Sharon M. Draper: Reaching Reluctant Readers." *ALAN Review* 36, no. 2 (2009): 89–93. Accessed 9 August 2016. https://scholar.lib.vt.edu/ejournals/ALAN/v36n2/johnson.html.

Honos-Webb, Lara. *The Gift of ADHD: How to Transform Your Child's Problems into Strengths*. Oakland, CA: New Harbinger Publications, 2005.

hooks, bell. "Representations of Whiteness in the Black Imagination." In *Black on White: Black Writers on What it Means to Be White*, edited by David R. Roediger, 38–53. New York: Schocken Books, 1998.

hooks, bell. *Teaching to Transgress: Education as the Practice of Freedom*. New York: Routledge, 1994.

Horn, Jim. "The LEAP for Accountability? Ideology and Practice of Testing in a Louisiana Urban Elementary School." In *Still Not Equal: Expanding Educational Opportunity in Society*, edited by Christopher M. Brown and RoSusan D. Bartee, 111–144. New York: Peter Lang, 2007.

Horsford, Sonya Douglass. *Learning in a Burning House: Educational Inequality, Ideology, and (Dis)Integration*. New York: Teachers College Press, 2011.

Howe, James. *Totally Joe*. 1st ed. New York: Atheneum Books for Young Readers, 2005.

Hubler, Angela. "Girl Power and History in the Dear America Series Books." *Children's Literature Association Quarterly* 25, no. 2 (2000): 98–106. DOI: 10.1353/chq.0.1657.

Hughes, Thomas, Andrew Sanders, and Arthur Hughes. *Tom Brown's Schooldays*. Oxford; New York: Oxford University Press, 1999; 1869.

Hylton, Jaime. "Exploring the 'Academic Side' of Cynthia Voigt." *ALAN Review* 33, no. 1 (2005): 50–55. Accessed 10 August 2016. https://scholar.lib.vt.edu/ejournals/ALAN/v33n1/hylton.pdf.

Jackson, Jesse and Doris Spiegel. *Call Me Charley*. New York: Harper & Brothers, 1945.

Jiménez, Francisco. *Breaking Through*. Boston: Houghton Mifflin, 2001.

Jiménez, Francisco. *The Circuit: Stories from the Life of a Migrant Child*. Albuquerque: University of New Mexico Press, 1997.

Jiménez, Francisco. *Reaching Out*. Boston: Houghton Mifflin Company, 2008.

Jones, Diana Wynne. *Witch Week*. 1st ed. New York: Greenwillow Books, 1982.

Jordan, Shirley Marie. *Broken Silences: Interviews with Black and White Women Writers*. New Brunswick, NJ: Rutgers University Press, 1993.

Kamenetz, Anya. *The Test: Why Our Schools Are Obsessed with Standardized Testing—But You Don't Have to Be*. 1st ed. New York: Public Affairs, 2015.

Kates, Susan. "Literacy, Voting Rights, and the Citizenship Schools in the South, 1957–1970." *College Composition and Communication* 57, no. 3 (2006): 479–502. http://proxygw.wrlc.org/login?url=http://search.proquest.com.proxygw.wrlc.org/docview/220691871?accountid=11243.

Kelen, Christopher and Björn Sundmark. "Where Children Rule." In *The Nation in Children's Literature: Nations of Childhood*, edited by Christopher Kelen and Björn Sundmark, 263–272. New York; London: Routledge, 2014.

Kidd, Kenneth. "Prizing Children's Literature: The Case of the Newbery Gold." *Children's Literature* 35 (2007): 166–190. http://proxygw.wrlc.org/login?url=http://search.proquest.com.proxygw.wrlc.org/docview/195588802?accountid=11243.

Kincaid, Jamaica. *A Small Place*. 1st ed. New York: Farrar, Straus, and Giroux, 1988.

King, Casey, Linda Barrett Osborne, and Joe Brooks. *Oh, Freedom!: Kids Talk about the Civil Rights Movement with the People Who Made It Happen*. New York: Alfred A. Knopf, 1997.

Kohl, Herbert R. *Should We Burn Babar?: Essays on Children's Literature and the Power of Stories*. New York: New Press; Distributed by Norton, 1995.

Kozol, Jonathan. *Savage Inequalities: Children in America's Schools*. New York: Harper Perennial, 1991.

Kozol, Jonathan. *The Shame of the Nation: The Restoration of Apartheid Schooling in America*. New York: Crown Publishers, 2005.

Kunjufu, Jawanza. *To Be Popular or Smart: The Black Peer Group*. 1st ed. Chicago: African American Images, 1988.

Labaree, David F. "Public Goods, Private Goods: The American Struggle Over Educational Goals." *American Educational Research Journal* 34, no. 1 (1997): 39. Accessed 10 August 2016. http://www.jstor.org/stable/1163342.

Labaree, David F. *Someone Has to Fail: The Zero-Sum Game of Public Schooling.* Cambridge, MA: Harvard University Press, 2010.

Ladson-Billings, Gloria. *The Dreamkeepers: Successful Teachers of African-American Children.* San Francisco: Jossey-Bass, 1994.

Lai, Thanhha. *Inside Out & Back Again.* 1st ed. New York: Harper, 2011.

Langan, Paul. *Schooled.* Bluford Series. West Berlin, NJ: Townsend Press, Inc., 2009.

LaNier, Carlotta Walls, and Lisa Frazier Page. *A Mighty Long Way: My Journey to Justice at Little Rock Central High School.* 1st ed. New York: One World Ballantine Books, 2009.

Larrick, Nancy. "The All-White World of Children's Books." *Journal of African Children's and Youth Literature* 3 (1991): 1–10.

Leininger, Melissa, Tina Taylor Dyches, Mary Anne Prater, and Melissa Allen Heath. "Newbery Award-Winning Books 1975–2009: How Do They Portray Disabilities?" *Education and Training in Autism and Developmental Disabilities* 45, no. 4 (2010): 583–596.

Lesko, Nancy. *Act Your Age! A Cultural Construction of Adolescence.* New York: Routledge Falmer, 2001.

Lesley, Naomi. "Disability, Giftedness, and Race in Cynthia Voigt's Tillerman Novels." *Journal of Literary and Cultural Disability Studies* 8, no. 1 (2014): 49–66. DOI: 10.3828/jlcds.2014.4.

Lesley, Naomi. "Scripting History: The Genre of Desegregation Stories." *Children's Literature in Education* (November 2014): n. pag. DOI 10.1007/s10583-014-9240-0.

Lesley, Naomi. "Solar Systems and Power Systems: Decentering the Naturalized Universe in Virginia Hamilton's the Planet of Junior Brown." *Children's Literature Association Quarterly* 36, no. 2 (2011): 124–146.

Lesson Plan: *With the Might of Angels* Discussion Guide. *Scholastic.com.* Accessed 16 August 2016. http://www.scholastic.com/teachers/lesson-plan/might-angels-discussion-guide.

Lester, Julius and George Woods. "Black and White: An Exchange." 1970. In *The Black American in Books for Children: Readings in Racism*, edited by Donnarae MacCann and Gloria Woodard, 66–72. 2nd ed. Metuchen, NJ: Scarecrow Press, 1985.

Levine, Ellen. *Freedom's Children: Young Civil Rights Activists Tell their Own Stories.* New York: Putnam, 1993.

Levine, Kristin. *The Lions of Little Rock.* New York: G.P. Putnam's Sons, 2012.

Levitas, Ruth. *The Concept of Utopia.* Oxford; New York: Peter Lang, 2010; 1990.

Lewis, Amanda E. *Race in the Schoolyard.* New Brunswick, NJ: Rutgers University Press, 2003.

Linton, Simi. *Claiming Disability.* New York: New York University Press, 1998.

Lott, Eric. *Love and Theft: Blackface Minstrelsy and the American Working Class.* New York: Oxford University Press, 1993.

Lukin, Josh. "Disability and Blackness." In *The Disability Studies Reader*, edited by Lennard J. Davis, 308–315. 4th ed. New York: Routledge, 2013.

McBride, James. *The Color of Water: A Black Man's Tribute to His White Mother*. New York: Riverhead Books, 1996.

McCaffrey, Anne. *Dragonsinger*. New York: Atheneum, 1977.

McKissack, Pat. *A Friendship for Today*. New York: Scholastic Press, 2007.

MacLeod, Anne Scott. *American Childhood: Essays on Children's Literature of the Nineteenth and Twentieth Centuries*. Athens: University of Georgia Press, 1994.

MacLeod, Anne Scott. "Writing Backward: Modern Models in Historical Fiction." *The Horn Book Magazine* 74, no. 1 (1998): 26–33. Accessed 10 August 2016. http://www.hbook.com/1998/01/creating-books/publishing/writing-backward-modern-models-in-historical-fiction/.

Magoon, Kekla. *Camo Girl*. New York: Aladdin, 2011.

Males, Mike A. *The Scapegoat Generation: America's War on Adolescents*. Monroe: Common Courage Press, 1996.

Mann, Horace. "Means and Objects of Common-School Education." In *Lectures and Annual Reports on Education*, 39–88. 1867. Charleston: Nabu Press, 2011.

Mann, Horace. "What God Does, and What He Leaves for Man to Do, in the Work of Education." In *Lectures and Annual Reports on Education*, 191–240. 1867. Charleston: Nabu Press, 2011.

Massachusetts Department of Education. *Massachusetts English Language Arts Curriculum Framework*. Malden: Massachusetts Board of Education, 2001. Accessed 10 August 2016. http://www.doe.mass.edu/frameworks/ela/0601.pdf.

Massachusetts Department of Education. *Massachusetts English Language Arts Curriculum Framework*. Malden: Massachusetts Board of Education, 2011. Accessed 10 August 2016. http://www.doe.mass.edu/frameworks/ela/0311.pdf.

Medina, Meg. *Yaqui Delgado Wants to Kick Your Ass*. Somerville, MA: Candlewick Press, 2013.

Melamed, Jodi. *Represent and Destroy: Rationalizing Violence in the New Racial Capitalism*. Minneapolis, MN: University of Minnesota Press, 2011.

Meltzer, Milton. *There Comes a Time: The Struggle for Civil Rights*. Landmark Books. New York: Random House, 2001.

Messner, Kate and Mark Siegel. *How to Read a Story*. San Francisco: Chronicle Books, 2015.

Meyer, Gwen and James M. Patton. "On the Nexus of Race, Disability, and Overrepresentation: What do we Know? Where do we Go? On Point ... Brief Discussions of Critical Issues in Urban Education." National Inst. for Urban School Improvement, 2001. Accessed 10 August 2016. http://files.eric.ed.gov/fulltext/ED462487.pdf.

Michelson, Richard and Robert Roth. *Busing Brewster*. New York: Alfred A. Knopf, 2010.

Mickenberg, Julia L. *Learning from the Left: Children's Literature, the Cold War, and Radical Politics in the United States*. New York: Oxford University Press, 2006.

Mikkelsen, Nina. "Insiders, Outsiders, And The Question Of Authenticity: Who Shall Write For African American Children?." *African American Review* 32, no. 1 (1998): 33–49. *MLA International Bibliography*. Accessed 10 August 2016. http://www.jstor.org/stable/3042266.

Miller, James A. "Black Images in Children's Literature." In *Masterworks of Children's Literature*, edited by William T. Moynihan and Mary E. Shaner, 99–118. Vol. 8. New York: Chelsea House, 1986.

Mitchell, David T., and Sharon L. Snyder. *Narrative Prosthesis: Disability and the Dependencies of Discourse.* Ann Arbor, MI: University of Michigan Press, 2001.

Møllegaard, Kirsten. "Haunting and History in Louis Sachar's *Holes.*" *Western American Literature* 45, no. 2 (2010): 138–161. Accessed 10 August 2016. http://muse.jhu.edu.proxygw.wrlc.org/journals/western_american_literature/v045/45.

Montgomery, Lucy Maud. *Anne of Green Gables.* New York: Children's Classics, 1988.

Morris, Jerome. "Research, Ideology, and the Brown Decision: Counter-Narratives to the Historical and Contemporary Representation of Black Schooling." *Teachers College Record* 110, no. 4 (2008): 713–732. Accessed 10 August 2016. http://www.tcrecord.org.proxygw.wrlc.org/libraryID.

Morrison, Toni. *Remember: The Journey to School Integration.* Boston, MA: Houghton Mifflin, 2004.

Ms. Bernards. Untitled Review of *Pinned. Goodreads*: Pinned *by Sharon G. Flake.* Goodreads.com, 4 January 2014. Accessed 9 August 2016. http://www.goodreads.com/book/show/13492511-pinned.

Muñoz, José Esteban. *Cruising Utopia: The Then and There of Queer Futurity.* New York: New York University Press, 2009.

Murrell, Peter. "Afrocentric Immersion: Academic and Personal Development of African American Males in Public Schools." In *Freedom's Plow: Teaching in the Multicultural Classroom*, edited by Theresa Perry and James W. Fraser. New York: Routledge, 1993.

National Governors Association Center for Best Practices, Council of Chief State School Officers. "Myths vs. Facts." *Common Core State Standards English Language Arts.* 2016. Accessed 18 August 2016. http://www.corestandards.org/about-the-standards/myths-vs-facts/.

Nodelman, Perry. *The Hidden Adult: Defining Children's Literature.* Baltimore: Johns Hopkins University Press, 2008.

Ogletree, Earl, and Vilma E. Ujlaki. "The Effects of Ability Grouping on Inner-City Children." *Illinois Schools Journal* 50, no. 1 (1970): 63–70.

Olssen, Mark. "Totalitarianism and the 'Repressed' Utopia of the Present: Moving Beyond Hayek, Popper and Foucault." In *Edutopias: New Utopian Thinking in Education*, edited by Michael A. Peters and John Freeman-Moir, 99–124. Rotterdam, The Netherlands: Sense Publishers, 2006.

Omer, Najat and Sharon G. Flake. "Interview with Sharon G. Flake." *Journal of Adolescent & Adult Literacy* 54, no. 2 (2010): 152–153.

Omi, Michael, and Howard Winant. *Racial Formation in the United States: From the 1960s to the 1990s.* New York: Routledge, 1994.

Palmer, Phyllis M. *Living as Equals: How Three White Communities Struggled to Make Interracial Connections during the Civil Rights Era.* Nashville: Vanderbilt University Press, 2008.

Paterson, Katherine. *The Great Gilly Hopkins.* 1st ed. New York: HarperTrophy, 1987; 1978.

Patricia. "Book Review: 'Mary Jane'—Dorothy Sterling." *The Joy of the Written Word.* Last modified 29 July 2011. https://thejoyofthewrittenword.com/2011/07/29/book-review-mary-jane-dorothy-sterling/.

Patterson, James T. *Brown v. Board of Education: A Civil Rights Milestone and Its Troubled Legacy*. Oxford; New York: Oxford University Press, 2001.

Patton, James. "The Disproportionate Representation of African Americans in Special Education: Looking Behind the Curtain for Understanding and Solutions." *The Journal of Special Education* 32, no. 1 (1998): 25–32. Accessed 10 August 2016. http://proxygw.wrlc.org/login?url=http://search.ebscohost.com/login.aspx?direct=true&db=a9h&AN=567141&site=eds-live&scope=site.

Penguin Young Readers Group. "Core Curriculum Lesson Plans for *The Lions of Little Rock* by Kristen Levine." *Teachervision.com.* Accessed 12 August 2016. https://www.teachervision.com/tv/printables/penguin/lions-of-little-rock-cc-lessons.pdf.

Perkins, Mitali. "Are Books Windows or Mirrors?" *Mitali's Fire Escape.* N.p. 14 September 2009. Accessed 10 August 2016. http://www.mitaliblog.com/2009/09/are-books-windows-or-mirrors.html. Accessed 10 August 2016.

Pinkney, Andrea Davis. *Hand in Hand: Ten Black Men Who Changed America.* New York: Disney/Jump at the Sun Books, 2012.

Pinkney, Andrea Davis. *Hold Fast to Dreams.* New York: Morrow Junior Books, 1995.

Pinkney, Andrea Davis. *With the Might of Angels: The Diary of Dawnie Rae Johnson.* 1st ed. New York: Scholastic, 2011.

Pinkney, Andrea Davis and J. Brian Pinkney. *Boycott Blues: How Rosa Parks Inspired a Nation.* New York: Greenwillow Books, 2008.

Pinkney, Sandra L. and Myles C. Pinkney. *Read and Rise.* New York: Scholastic, 2006.

Plucker, Jonathan, Nathan Burroughs, and Ruiting Song. *Mind the (Other) Gap! The Growing Excellence Gap in K-12 Education.* Center for Evaluation and Education Policy, 2010. Accessed 10 August 2016. http://www.jkcf.org/assets/1/7/ExcellenceGapBrief_-_Plucker.pdf.

Prendergast, Catherine. *Literacy and Racial Justice: The Politics of Learning after Brown v. Board of Education.* Carbondale, IL: University of Illinois Press, 2003.

Price, Margaret. *Mad at School: Rhetorics of Mental Disability and Academic Life.* Ann Arbor, MI: University of Michigan Press, 2011.

Rahaman, Vashanti. *Read For Me, Mama.* Illustrated by Lori McElrath-Eslick. Honesdale, PA: Boyds Mills Press, 1997.

Ramsey, Sonya. "'We Will Be Ready Whenever They Are': African American Teachers' Responses to the Brown Decision and Public School Integration in Nashville, Tennessee, 1954–1966." *Journal of African American History* 90, no. 1/2 (2005): 29–51. http://www.jstor.org.proxygwa.wrlc.org/stable/20063974.

Rappaport, Doreen, and Shane Evans. *Nobody Gonna Turn Me 'Round: Stories and Songs of the Civil Rights Movement.* 1st ed. Cambridge, MA: Candlewick Press, 2006.

Rappaport, Doreen. *The School Is Not White!* Illustrated by Curtis James. New York: Hyperion-Jump at the Sun, 2005.

Ravitch, Diane. *The Death and Life of the Great American School System: How Testing and Choice are Undermining Education.* New York: Basic Books, 2010.

Ravitch, Diane. *The Language Police: How Pressure Groups Restrict what Children Learn.* 1st ed. New York: Alfred A. Knopf, 2003.

Reese, William J. *America's Public Schools: From the Common School to 'No Child Left Behind'*." Baltimore, MD: The Johns Hopkins University Press, 2005.

Reese, William J. *Testing Wars in the Public Schools: A Forgotten History*. Cambridge, MA: Harvard University Press, 2013.

Reimer, Mavis. "Traditions of the School Story." In *The Cambridge Companion to Children's Literature*, edited by M.O. Grenby and Andrea Immel, 209–225. Cambridge, England: Cambridge University Press, 2009.

Review of *Lions of Little Rock*, by Kristin Levine. *Publishers Weekly* 21 November 2011. Accessed 10 August 2016. http://www.publishersweekly.com/978-0-399-25644-8.

Richardson, Judy. "Black Children's Books: An Overview." *Journal of Negro Education* 43, no. 3 (1974): 381–400. http://www.jstor.org.proxygwa.wrlc.org/stable/2966530 DOI:1.

Ripley, Amanda. *The Smartest Kids in the World: And How They Got That Way*. New York: Simon & Schuster, 2013.

Romano, Renee Christine and Leigh Raiford. *The Civil Rights Movement in American Memory*. Athens, GA: University of Georgia Press, 2006.

Rose, Mike. *Lives on the Boundary*. 1989. New York: Penguin Books, 2005.

Rottenberg, Catherine. *Performing Americanness: Race, Class, and Gender in Modern African-American and Jewish-American Literature*. Hanover, NH: Dartmouth College Press, 2008.

Rountree, Wendy. *Just Us Girls: The Contemporary African American Young Adult Novel*. New York: Peter Lang, 2008.

Rowling, J.K. *Harry Potter and the Chamber of Secrets*. Illustrated by Mary GrandPré. 1st American ed. New York: Arthur A. Levine Books, 1999.

Saatcioglu, Argun and Jim Carl. "The Discursive Turn in School Desegregation: National Patterns and a Case Analysis of Cleveland, 1973–1998." *Social Science History* 35, no. 1 (2011): 59–108. Accessed 12 August 2016. http://www.jstor.org/stable/23026432.

Sachar, Louis. *Holes*. New York: Yearling Press, 1998.

Sachar, Louis. *Small Steps*. New York: Delacorte Press, 2006.

Schulte, Emerita Schroer. "Today's Literature for Today's Children." *Elementary English* 49, no. 3 (1972): 355–363. Accessed 18 August 2016. http://www.jstor.org/stable/41387108.

Schwebel, Sara L. *Child-Sized History: Fictions of the Past in U.S. Classrooms*. Nashville, TN: Vanderbilt University Press, 2011.

Scribner, Sylvia. "Literacy in Three Metaphors." In *Perspectives on Literacy*, edited by Eugene R. Kintgen, Barry M. Kroll, and Mike Rose, 57–70. Carbondale, IL: Southern Illinois University Press, 1988.

Simon, Katherine G. *Moral Questions in the Classroom: How to Get Kids to Think Deeply about Real Life and their Schoolwork*. New Haven, CT: Yale University Press, 2001.

Simpson, Andrea Y. *The Tie that Binds: Identity and Political Attitudes in the Post-Civil Rights Generation*. New York: New York University Press, 1998.

Skrtic, Thomas M. *An Organizational Analysis of Special Education Reform*, 1987. Accessed 10 August 2016. http://files.eric.ed.gov/fulltext/ED291177.pdf.

Skrtic, Thomas M. "The Special Education Paradox: Equity as the Way to Excellence." *Harvard Educational Review* 61, no. 2 (1991): 148–206.

Sky High. Directed by Mike Mitchell, Andrew Gunn, Paul Hernandez, et al. United Burbank, CA: Buena Vista Pictures, 2005.

Slee, Roger. "Limits to and Possibilities for Educational Reform." *International Journal of Inclusive Education* 10, no. 2/3 (March–May 2006): 109–119. Accessed 10 August 2016. DOI: 10.1080/13603110600578372.

Smith, Katharine Capshaw. "Childhood, the Body, and Race Performance: Early 20th-Century Etiquette Books for Black Children." *African American Review* 40, no. 4, (2006): 795–811. Accessed 10 August 2016. http://www.jstor.org/stable/40033754.

Stepto, Robert B. *From Behind the Veil: A Study of Afro-American Narrative.* Urbana: University of Illinois Press, 1979.

Sterling, Dorothy. *Mary Jane.* New York: Scholastic Book Services, 1959.

Sterling, Dorothy. "The Soul of Learning." *The English Journal* 57, no. 2 (1968): 166–180. Accessed 10 August 2016. http://www.jstor.org/stable/811869.

Sterling, Dorothy. *Tender Warriors.* New York: Hill and Wang, 1958.

Stockton, Kathryn Bond. *The Queer Child, Or Growing Sideways in the Twentieth Century.* Durham, NC: Duke University Press, 2009.

Stowe, Harriet Beecher. *Uncle Tom's Cabin.* New York: Barnes & Noble Classics, 2005.

Tatum, Alfred W. "All 'Degreed' Up and Nowhere to Go: Black Males and Literacy Education." *Journal of Adolescent & Adult Literacy* 46, no. 8 (2003): 620–623.

Tatum, Beverly Daniel. *"Why are all the Black Kids Sitting Together in the Cafeteria?": And Other Conversations about Race.* New York: Basic Books, 2003; 1997.

Taxel, Joel. "Children's Literature at the Turn of the Century: Toward a Political Economy of the Publishing Industry." *Research in the Teaching of English* 37, no. 2 (November 2002): 145–197. Accessed 10 August 2016. http://proxygwa.wrlc.org/login?url=http://search.proquest.com/docview/215368958?accountid=33473.

Taylor, Mildred D. *Let the Circle Be Unbroken.* New York: Puffin Books, 1991; 1981.

Taylor, Mildred D. *Roll of Thunder, Hear My Cry.* 1976. New York: Puffin Books, 1991.

Thernstrom, Abigail M., and Stephan Thernstrom. *No Excuses: Closing the Racial Gap in Learning.* New York: Simon & Schuster, 2003.

"The Lions of Little Rock by Kristen Levine." *Teachingbooks.net.* Accessed 12 August 2016. https://www.teachingbooks.net/tb.cgi?tid=28490&a=1#ActivityGuides.

"The Stories for All Project." *First Book: Access to New Books for Children in Need.* First Book. 2015. Accessed 10 August 2016. https://www.firstbook.org/first-book-story/the-stories-for-all-project.

Thomas, Joyce Carol and Curtis James. *Linda Brown, You are Not Alone: The Brown v. Board of Education Decision: A Collection.* New York: Jump at the Sun/Hyperion Books for Children, 2003.

Tompkins, Kyla Wazana. *Racial Indigestion: Eating Bodies in the Nineteenth Century.* New York: New York University Press, 2012.

Tonatiuh, Duncan. *Separate Is Never Equal: Sylvia Mendez & Her Family's Fight for Desegregation.* New York: Abrams Books for Young Readers, 2014.

Trainor, Jennifer S. *Rethinking Racism: Emotion, Persuasion, and Literacy Education in an All-White High School.* Carbondale, IL: Southern Illinois University Press, 2008.

Tribunella, Eric L. "Children's Literature and the Child Flâneur." *Children's Literature* 38, no. 1 (2010): 64–91.

Trierweiler, Hannah. "Louis Sachar." *Instructor (1999)* 118, no. 4 (2009): 80. Accessed 21 April 2014. http://proxygwa.wrlc.org/login?url=http://search.proquest.com/docview/224390082?accountid=33473.

Trites, Roberta Seelinger. *Disturbing the Universe: Power and Repression in Adolescent Literature.* Iowa City: University of Iowa Press, 2000.

Trites, Roberta Seelinger. "'I Double Never Ever Never Lie to My Chil'ren': Inside People in Virginia Hamilton's Narratives." *African American Review* 32, no. 1 (1998). Accessed 10 August 2016. http://www.jstor.org.proxygwa.wrlc.org/stable/3042277.

Trites, Roberta Seelinger. *Twain, Alcott, and the Birth of the Adolescent Reform Novel.* Iowa City: University of Iowa Press, 2007.

Twain, Mark. *Adventures of Huckleberry Finn.* 1884. Garden City, NJ: Doubleday, 1954.

Tyack, David, and Larry Cuban. *Tinkering Toward Utopia: A Century of Public School Reform.* Cambridge, MA: Harvard University Press, 1995.

Ulanowicz, Anastasia. "American Adam, American Cain: Johnny Tremain, Octavian Nothing, and the Fantasy of American Exceptionalism." *The Lion and the Unicorn* 35, no. 3 (2011): 267–295. Accessed 10 August 2016. http://proquest.umi.com.proxygw.wrlc.org/pqdweb?did=0000002594752651&Fmt=3&clientId=43168&RQT=309&VName=PQD.

United States Congress. *Education for All Handicapped Children Act.* 94th Congress. Washington, D.C.: GPO, 1975. Accessed 10 August 2016. https://www.congress.gov/bill/94th-congress/senate-bill/6/text.

United States Congress. *Individuals with Disabilities Education Act.* 101st Congress. Washington, D.C.: GPO, 1990. Accessed 12 August 2016. https://www.congress.gov/bill/101st-congress/senate-bill/933/text.

United States Department of Education. Elementary and Secondary Educ. "Title 1, Sec. 1001." *The No Child Left Behind Act of 2001.* 6 Dec 2010. Accessed 12 August 2016. https://www.gpo.gov/fdsys/pkg/PLAW-107publ110/pdf/PLAW-107publ110.pdf.

Verdugo, Richard. "Race-Ethnicity, Social Class, and Zero-Tolerance Policies: The Cultural and Structural Wars." *Education and Urban Society* 35, no. 1 (2002): 50–75. Accessed 12 August 2016. DOI: 10.1177/001312402237214.

Viego, Antonio. *Dead Subjects.* Durham, NC: Duke University Press, 2007.

Vinovskis, Maris A., David L. Angus, and Jeffrey E. Mirel. "Historical Development of Age Stratification in Schooling." In *Education, Society, and Economic Opportunity: Historical Perspective on Persistent Issues*, edited by Maris A. Vinovskis, 171–193. New Haven, CT: Yale University Press, 1995.

Voigt, Cynthia. *A Solitary Blue.* New York: Simon Pulse, 1983.

Voigt, Cynthia. *Come a Stranger.* New York: Simon Pulse, 1986.

Voigt, Cynthia. *Dicey's Song.* New York: Fawcett Juniper Books, 1982.

Voigt, Cynthia. *Homecoming.* New York: Fawcett Juniper Books, 1981.

Voigt, Cynthia. "On Teaching." *Language Arts* 62, no. 7 (1985): 740–741.

Voigt, Cynthia. *The Runner.* New York: Simon Pulse, 1985.

Voigt, Cynthia. *Seventeen Against the Dealer.* New York: Fawcett Juniper Books, 1989.

Voigt, Cynthia. *Sons From Afar.* New York: Fawcett Juniper Books, 1987.

Voigt, Cynthia. "1995 Margaret A. Edwards Awards Acceptance Speech." *Journal of Youth Services in Libraries* 9 (1995): 23–30.

Walker, Vanessa Siddle. "Second-Class Integration: A Historical Perspective for a Contemporary Agenda." *Harvard Educational Review* 79, no. 2 (2009): 269–284.

Wallin, Marie. "Literacy and the Power of the Law: Louis Sachar's *Holes* and Lemony Snicket's *A Bad Beginning.*" *Angles on the English-Speaking World* 8 (2008): 101–110.

Walter, Mildred Pitts. *Because We Are.* 1st ed. New York: Lothrop, Lee & Shepard, 1983.

Walter, Mildred Pitts. *The Girl on the Outside.* New York: Lothrop, Lee & Shepard Books, 1982.

Walter, Mildred Pitts. "Response." Message to the author. 25 May 2013. Email.

Wannamaker, Annette. "Reading in the Gaps and Lacks: (De)Constructing Masculinity in Louis Sachar's *Holes.*" *Children's Literature in Education* 37, no. 1 (2006): 15–33. Accessed 12 August 2016. DOI: 10.1007/s10583-005-9452-4.

Warikoo, Natasha and Prudence Carter. "Cultural Explanations for Racial and Ethnic Stratification in Academic Achievement: A Call for a New and Improved Theory." *Review of Educational Research* 79, no. 1 (2009): 366–394. Accessed 9 August 2016. DOI: 10.3102/0034654308326162.

Watts, Jeri. *Kizzy Ann Stamps.* Somerville, MA: Candlewick Press, 2012.

Webb, Darren. "Where's the Vision? The Concept of Utopia in Contemporary Educational Theory." *Oxford Review of Education* 35, no. 6 (December 2009): 743–760. Accessed 12 August 2016. DOI: 10.1080/03054980903371179.

Wiggin, Kate Douglas. *My Garden of Memory: An Autobiography.* Boston, MA: Houghton Mifflin Company, 1923.

Wiggin, Kate Douglas. *Rebecca of Sunnybrook Farm.* 1903. New York: Puffin Books, 1994.

Williams, Heather Andrea. *Self-Taught: African American Education in Slavery and Freedom.* Chapel Hill, NC: University of North Carolina Press, 2005.

Woodson, Carter Godwin. *The Mis-Education of the Negro.* New York: AMS Press, 1977; 1933.

Woodson, Jacqueline. *Between Madison & Palmetto.* New York: Delacorte, 1993.

Woodson, Jacqueline. *Brown Girl Dreaming.* New York: Nancy Paulsen Books, 2014.

Woodson, Jacqueline. *Feathers.* New York: G.P. Putnam's Sons, 2007.

Woodson, Jacqueline. *From the Notebooks of Melanin Sun.* New York: G.P. Putnam's Sons, 2010; 1995.

Woodson, Jacqueline. *If You Come Softly.* New York: G.P. Putnam's Sons, 1998.

Woodson, Jacqueline. *I Hadn't Meant to Tell You This.* New York: G.P. Putnam's Sons, 2006; 1994.

Woodson, Jacqueline. *Maizon at Blue Hill.* GP Putnam's Sons ed. New York: Putnam, 2002; 1992.

Woodson, Jacqueline and Earl B. Lewis. *Each Kindness.* New York: Nancy Paulsen Books, 2012.

Wright, Richard. *Black Boy: A Record of Childhood and Youth.* New York: Harper & Row, 1969; 1945.

X, Malcolm, and Alex Haley. *The Autobiography of Malcolm X.* New York: Ballantine Books, 1992; 1965.

Yang, Gene Luen, and Lark Pien. *American Born Chinese.* New York: First Second, 2006.

Yenika-Agbaw, Vivian. "Disability in Africana Adolescent Literature." In *African and African American Children's and Adolescent Literature in the Classroom: A Critical Guide*, edited by Mary Napoli and Vivian S. Yenika-Agbaw. New York: Peter Lang, 2011.

Yoshino, Kenji. "The Pressure to Cover." *The New York Times.* New York Times, 16 January 2006. Accessed 12 August 2016. http://www.nytimes.com/2006/01/15/magazine/the-pressure-to-cover.html?_r=0.

Index

For Product Safety Concerns and Information please contact our EU representative GPSR@taylorandfrancis.com
Taylor & Francis Verlag GmbH, Kaufingerstraße 24, 80331 München, Germany

www.ingramcontent.com/pod-product-compliance
Lightning Source LLC
Chambersburg PA
CBHW071411100726
47908CB00004B/1141
9780367346300